920

NAOROJI

The First Asian MP

A Biography of Dadabhai Naoroji:
India's Patriot and Britain's MP

by Omar Ralph

HANSIB

First published in 1997 by Hansib Caribbean
PO Box 2773, St John's, Antigua, WI

Distributed in the United Kingdom by Readers Book Club
Tower House, 141-149 Fonthill Road, London N4 3HF
(Fax: 0171-263 9656)

Printed in the United Kingdom by Martins the Printers Ltd
Berwick Upon Tweed

British Library Cataloguing in Publication Data.
A catalogue record for this book is available from the British Library

ISBN 976-8163-05-4

DEDICATION

To my mother
Zeena Ralph (née Bharucha)

CONTENTS

Baroness Shreela Flather

The title 'The Grand Old Man of India' was given to Dadabhai Naoroji by the people of that country on account of his tireless work on their behalf. Other honours were offered to him but, as this book relates, he valued that one above any other. I believe this speaks for the sincerity of the man. Certainly, the title speaks for itself, embodying the affection in which the Indian people, of all backgrounds, held him.

I know that his story contained many twists and turns and it was never easy for him to keep on trying to win over the hearts and minds of the British public. As a Parliamentarian, and as an Indian, I have a keen interest in Naoroji and admire what he was able to achieve.

I am pleased, therefore, to be able to commend this book to the present generation, both Indian and British, so that we can learn the truth about his rich life. I hope you enjoy reading it and that it will contribute to your understanding of the special place he occupies in history

Sir David Steel MP

As a lifelong Liberal, I firmly believe that the traditions of our party are based on the desire to help realise peoples' freedom and equality. Dadabhai Naoroji, encapsulated those qualities through his life of public service. He unselfishly gave of his time to help people, whether through the individual attention paid to the many requests for help that he received, or through campaigning on the political level as a member of the Liberal Party.

I came to know more about him during the centenary year of his election and was very pleased to be able to give a talk on his life to members of the Asian community. I am pleased, therefore, to endorse the message of this book, which presents Naoroji as a sincere and honourable person. I hope it will be widely read as it has been well researched so that the reader of today might understand the abiding relevance of the actions of earlier generations to the tasks on our agenda today.

Chris Smith MP

More than one hundred years have passed since the election of Britain's first Asian MP, Dadabhai Naoroji who became MP for the Central Finsbury constituency in 1892 - which is the seat I now hold - four years after the then Prime Minister, Lord Salisbury, had claimed he was unelectable on account of his being a 'black man.' Dadabhai went on to prove Salisbury wrong, not only through being elected by a whisker but also through his work as an active and successful Liberal MP. Among those who supported his election were both Florence Nightingale and Josephine Butler. Using his influence and status as a Member of Parliament, Dadabhai campaigned both for his Central Finsbury constituents as well as for the rights of the people of India, to whom he became known as the 'Grand Old Man of India.'

Born in Western India, he was the only child of a soon-to-be-widowed mother. He was a Parsee and the members of this small religious community held their own celebrations to mark the centenary of his election.

Lord Salisbury's unkind and offensive comments were made two years after Dadabhai unsuccessfully stood for election in Holborn in 1886. He was elected to the Central Finsbury seat on July 6 1892. Although he only served in Parliament for a period of three years he had a significant input and left an abiding legacy.

A founding member of the Indian National Congress, he challenged the discriminatory policies of the Colonial authorities in terms of entry to the Indian Civil Service. He also campaigned for education for girls in India and helped to set up a Royal Commission to look at the financial exploitation of the colony that was considered the 'jewel' in Britain's imperial crown. He worked equally hard for the people of his Finsbury constituency, proposing a Bill for Lincoln's Inn Fields, and having an attendance record in the House second only to that of the Chief Whip. His election stands, even today, as a real landmark in parliamentary history. With the continuing and highly relevant struggle to ensure that Britain's parliamentary institutions reflect the make-up of our society, the publication of a fresh biography of the 'Grand Old Man of India' is indeed most timely.

FOREWORD

by Keith Vaz MP

When I think back to over one hundred years ago and consider what my predecessor Dadabhai Naoroji managed to achieve in the House of Commons, I am enormously impressed.

As I read through the manuscript of this book I found that he understood the people of his time and was neither taken in by assurances nor overawed by the prestige or status of some of his contemporaries. He was, therefore, able to retain a clear mind as to what needed to be said and to present matters to his fellow politicians, even if his message was not always to their liking. That takes courage and this quality, I believe, stemmed from the fact that he never forgot who he was speaking for, during his more than 60 years of public service. Many years have passed since Naoroji was active, but I think that the role of the politician has not changed. I found it interesting to read about the issues of his day and to see how he attempted to address them. This involved not only speaking in the House of Commons, but also constant encouragement to those around him, whether through personal correspondence or by setting up bodies in which others could participate. In these ways, he helped motivate and showed so many people the ways to move forward. His legacy, therefore, is an enduring one, more than justifying his epithet of people and society - 'Grand Old Man of India.' He helped and aided Mahatma Gandhi, and to a lesser extent Mohammed Ali Jinnah, as they guided the peoples of their respective nations, India and Pakistan to eventual independent nationhood. This book is part of the history of the Asian community in Britain as well as of the nations with which so many of us continue to identify in various ways.

I am very aware that I do not represent just one group or community of people. I was elected as a representative of all the people in my constituency. This book makes the same point about our 'Grand Old Man.' Dadabhai had a message which he delivered again and again to the British, but he had a firm belief in the British being able to respond in the right manner. So on the one hand he often had to be a spokesman for the cause of Asian people in India, South Africa or elsewhere, people who definitely needed a voice in the 'bad old days' of Colonialism. But on the other hand he also believed that justice for Asian people was in the best interests of the British. Accordingly, he can be said to have secured his place in the history of three continents.

Space does not permit me to pursue these themes any further, but I would end with the following thought. Whether you read this book because of your interest in history, or because you are concerned about the issues it covers, the society we now live in was in no small measure shaped by this man and by his contribution to the events of his time.

ACKNOWLEDGEMENTS

I wish to express my thanks to the following people, who have given me the help in those areas where I had no skills or access to contacts and therefore are part of this book in their own right.

In a rough chronological order, Zeena Ralph and Freda Moddie, my mother and aunt, who were the two dedicated typists (most of the writing was done on typewriters not wordprocessors) and who had to cope with a lot of corrections written in a handwriting style that is unique. Also my brother-in-law Mark Cuthbert-Brown and his work colleague Carol, who finally transposed the work onto a floppy disc and enabled the final changes to be made. Dr Meher Master-Moos, Principal of the Zoroastrian College, Bombay for the moral assistance she gave me from India. Brian Ralph, my father, without whose support and financial help this book may never have seen its publication. Finally my wife Ruth and the children who grew up knowing the name Dadabhai Naoroji could mean endless evenings and nights of absence, both in the preparation for this book and for the Exhibition put on in 1992.

PREFACE

Sailing through the history of time, there is a people whose forebears had ruled ancient Persia for nearly five hundred years by the birth of Jesus Christ. A thousand years after that time they had become a refugee community who had fled to the west coast of India. Nearly a thousand years after that, one of their number rose to become the 'Grand Old Man of India' and the first Asian member of the British Parliament.

That man's life is the subject of this book, which charts his story from a humble beginning in Bombay, to the time when he saw that the foundations of modern India had been laid down, with his endeavours playing no small part in that enterprise. His name was Dadabhai Naoroji. Unfortunately that name has not been remembered by many people, although he died within living memory, in 1917, and was a mentor to men such as Gandhi.

This book aims to re-live his life story, so that the work he undertook both in India and in Britain can once again be understood.

His people are the Zoroastrians or Parsees, who are now a small religious community living mainly in India. The teachings of that faith certainly had an influence on Dadabhai and this is considered in the book. He had a humble beginning to life, being a widow's son at a time when such people occupied a low position in society. The book moves through the efforts of his early life to the time when he rose to become the first Indian professor at a centre for learning.

He then saw a sea change in his life which took him to Britain and also brought him for the first time into British and Indian politics. Other books have described the multifaceted relationship between Britain and India in the days of the Raj.

This book looks at the relationship from the viewpoint of one man.

Dadabhai was a campaigner, who was never happier than when he had a bit between his teeth and was using all his resources to the full, to bring in new ways and reform old ones. He argued with the British from the highest authorities down to the local resident in British India. Yet he never lost his faith in the British love of justice, which he had from the very beginning of his adult life and despite some harrowing times, he never lost the will to see it established in reality, as well as in principle.

The reaction of both the British and the Indians given in the book, shows something of the different groups and ideas that were predominant at the time. Some of the British admired him, others detested him and his kind. The Indians saw him, in time, as a father figure. Gandhi really

11

was a disciple of his when he was campaigning in South Africa and he along with many other great Indian patriots, would refer back to the Grand Old Man with respect and gratitude.

And yet the Grand Old Man could also be remembered for some of his other achievements, which had a significant effect on the society of his day in both Britain and India. The book therefore seeks to give the reader a knowledge of these by charting them out and giving some perceptions on their context. One of these must be his election as the first ever Asian member of the British Parliament in 1892 for the Central Finsbury constituency. That achievement alone is worthy of a book and so several chapters are given to it in this book which has been written to mark the centenary of that event. That election was won through British votes and was held against the background of Lords Salisbury's infamous remarks on the "little black man."

In another field his writings and treatises on the economic strains of the trade between Britain and India marked him out as the pioneer and author on this subject, and his works were taken up by both British and Indian advocates.

Although not couched in the same terms, the themes of Race Relations, Equal Rights, the reforms in Indian society, the election of black and Asian members of Parliament, British justice and other social issues such as drugs and drink, were as common to Dadabhai in his day as they are to present day society. This book gives the reader the viewpoint on those issues as seen from those days, and makes us appreciate that history is sometimes not so removed from our own situation.

Dadabhai's latter years saw the rise of the mass movement in India's national organisations and he was the first to proclaim self rule as the aim at a national gathering. But his concern with the hardening of attitudes by both the Indians and the British tempered his desire to see this aim accomplished. His latter years were no less intensive than his early years and he was involved in the events which were taking place in both countries up to the time of the First World War.

It is hard to say if one of the things he did should be seen as more remarkable than the others. Rather the book I have written seeks to emphasize the character of the man beneath all these achievements. He set an example and that is what counts.

Omar Ralph

CHAPTER ONE

HIS ROOTS

The story of Dadabhai Naoroji began in Bombay on the coast of Western India on the 4th September 1825. It ended in the twentieth century after a significant and unique career, which saw a great many firsts and earned him the title of the 'Grand Old Man of India.' He was also a founder and mainstay of the Indian National Congress and the first to advocate Indian self rule from a public platform, when he was the President of the Congress of 1906.

What is more surprising is that when there was no conscious recognition of the issue of race equality, and when Britain was at the height of its Imperial power, a quite humble Indian made his way up the ranks to become the first Asian MP to sit in the 'Mother of Parliaments.'

But there was no hint of what was to come when Dadabhai was born. His beginnings were fairly humble, being the only child of a poor Parsee priest, Naoroji Palenji Dordi and his wife Manekbhai. His early home was the small town of Khadak, situated north of Bombay.

Being the son of a priest of the Zoroastrian religion, Dadabhai was brought up in its precepts, by his father and then on his death in 1829, by his mother. Dadabhai's family could accurately trace their own family tree through a chain of priests back to the first priest, Zarthost Mobed, who had settled in around 1200 AD in the small port of Navsari, north of Bombay. Navsari means 'New Sari', and had been given that name by the original settlers because its climate was similar to that of Sari which is a town in Iran, where they had once lived. If he had lived, Dadabhai's father would probably have insisted that his son become the ninth Mobad or Priest of the family line. To begin the story of his life it is necessary to understand some of the background of the Parsees, as that plays a role, which although not always consciously on Dadabhai's mind, had an influence that lasted throughout his life, both in terms of the religion and also in the history of the people.

In his early life an understanding would have been instilled in Dadabhai of his religion and of his community. The Zoroastrian's beliefs stem from the Gathas or sayings of the prophet Zoroaster which take the form of the 17 hymns he composed. They were more akin to inspirational pieces and were usually passed on orally in a

1 3

langage called Avestan until being finally committed to writing in a language called Pahlavi, some 1500 years later. By then other teachings and interpretations had been added to the Gathas and the writings consisted of 21 'nasks' or divisions. These were transposed into Avestan, which had to be refined to allow the original words to be rendered better, and the 'Younger Avestan' was created, which formed the basis for the Zoroastrian's beliefs. 'The Avesta' is the term for the total group of written materials and sets them out in the form of hymns, formulas, narratives and laws. It is in two principle parts, which are the Yasnas [which contains the Gathas, the Visparad and Vivedat also called the Venidad or work against the Daevas (evil beings)] and a second part made up of the Khordeh (or little) Avesta and 22 Yashts. It should be noted that many original scriptual texts were probably destroyed by Alexander the Great when he sacked the Palace city of Persepolis in 330 BC. A lot of what they contained has been lost forever.

However principle strands to a Zoroastrian's beliefs include a supreme God, an adversary who propounds 'the Lie', an individual and the final judgement and resurrection, angels and demons, heaven and a hell, salvation through works, a final saviour and other doctrines similar to Judaism and Christianity and Islam.

To be a Mobad required undergoing a very strict initiation process which includes completing the Navar ceremony and then undergoing the Martab ceremony after which the person could attend to all the ceremonies necessary to the running of the Zoroastrian Fire Temple. There are also High Priests or Dasturs who will oversee a group of priests belong to a particular temple or community and who have particular duties which only they can carry out, though they also take on some of the day to day ceremonies. The Mobads who perform more of those duties have to learn and memorize the Avesta and rituals given in Avestan, which is now a largely unknown language, and also keep themselves ritually pure by adhering to a moral and disciplined life. In particular the Zoroastrians believe that fire has pure and hence holy and God-like qualities. They do not (as is often misquoted) worship fire, but believe its representativeness is unique.

The latter parts of the Avesta and other writings appeared to have re-interpreted and hence subtly changed some of the original precepts of the Prophet Zoroaster. Misunderstandings had arisen for both the people and the Priests in Dadabhai's time and caused him to pursue some reforms in his adult life.

As there are three 'levels' of fire, it was necessary for the "Behram" or the highest level of fires to be kept in the temples which are tended to by the high priestly Dasturs. The second level of fire is the "Adaran" fire, which is kept alight in the ordinary temples and it is tended to by the Mobads. The third level of fire is called "Dadgah" fire and can be kept in a home. In India today there are eight Behram fire temples[1] and about one hundred and thirty Adaran fire temples, which gives an indication of the ratios that existed in Dadabhai's day. Currently there are plans to install at least a Dagdah in the London centre of the British Zoroastrian community and maybe even the first Atash Behram in the western world within a generation.

Because Dadabhai's father was a Priest and it is a hereditary office, Dadabhai might have spent much of his life in the direct service of his religion, including trying to reform its ideas to be more in line with the teachings of its first and only prophet.

He did go through the required Navar or initiation ceremony at 14, which qualified him for the first phase leading to the priesthood. The Navsari area was and still is a strong-hold of the Parsee priesthood many of whom call themselves 'Noshakras.' Dadabhai belonged to the Athornam group of the Dordi family. Being a Zoroastrian undoubtedly meant a lot to Dadabhai and he maintained an adherence to his faith throughout his life. He said that the tales of Persian folk heroes and readings of the Shah Nama in his early years came to mean something to him in his adulthood. He wrote and kept a copy of "The duties of the Zoroastrians" beside him during his life, and this stressed the tenets of Humata, Hukhta and Huvershta or good/pure thought, pure speech and pure deeds. However, he never came closer to a religious career than at the time of his initiation.

The Zoroastrians[2] or 'Parsees' are an ancient people, whose revealed religion goes back to around 1200 BC. Their heyday was probably the time of the Persian empire (550 BC - 331 BC) and many of the rulers of that time (Cyrus, Darius I, Xerxes I) are mentioned in a favourable way in the Bible. There is no doubt that

1. The eight temples and their dates of establishment are, Udwada (1742), Navsari (1765), two in Surat (1823) and four in Bombay (1783,1839,1845,1897). The fire had originally resided in Sanjan and well before that city was overrun by Muslim forces in 1490, it was carried to safety via Bahrot hill to the hills of Bansda and then on to Navsari in 1516. It went to Udwada in 1742 because disputes among the priests and laity of Navsari, in which both Sanjan and Surat became involved could not be resolved. Udwada is the main centre for pilgrimage in India with Navsari and to a lesser extent Sanjan as the second centres. Nowadays Bombay is the main centre for both the priests and the Parsee institutions such as the charitable trust funds, colleges and religious buildings.

2. In India Zoroastrians are normally referred to as Parsees by everyone including themselves, Parsee being similar to 'Persian' in English, and means people from Pars. Zoroaster is derived from the Latin Zoroastres, which came from the Greek Zôrastrês. In the Avesta the name is always Zarathushtra, which is the original rendition of the Prophets name.

Zoroastrian beliefs influenced Jewish beliefs (and hence indirectly the doctrines in Christianity and Islam) when the two communities lived together in the five centuries before Christ and for some time afterwards. To what extent this influence affected other doctrines is hard to gauge, but it should be recognised that sizeable portions of the Jewish people lived within three Persian Empires for over 1000 years. Maybe there was more than coincidence in mind, when the Portuguese traveller and doctor Garcia D'Orta, who was the first European to chronicle their existence in India in 1535, assumed they were the children of Israel and called them the 'Jews of the East' (or East India). Other commentators such as Aungier (1670s) and Sir William Erskine also noted a range of similarities between the two religions.

The settlement of the Zoroastrian Community in India occurred because of the rise of Islam in Persia. This came about through conquest when the Kingdom of the Sasanians, which had been the third Persian[1] Empire with Zoroastrianism as the state religion, was overrun by the forces of Islam, beginning with the invasions of the Arabs at around 637 AD and ending in 651 AD with the last Sasanian ruler's death at Merv in north-eastern Iran. From then on the adherents of the faith faced increasingly stark choices, which eventually ended with them either accepting conversion to Islam or facing increasing persecution and sometimes death.

In the earlier years of their rule the Arabs accepted that the Zoroastrians had 'a Book', like the Jews and Christians. The Qur'-an allows Muslims to treat peoples "to whom a Book (ie scripture) has been given" with greater tolerance. The followers of such religions are designated as Ahi-e-Ketab (Believers in the revealed Books) and have to pay the poll tax as a 'Zimmis', which is what Christians and Jews are still obliged to do. The Zoroastrians had been categorized as 'Zimmis' and then lost that status, and gradually saw their rights eroded by the succession of Arab, then Irani and then Mongol rulers unless they converted to Islam. It was a number of years after the overthrow of the Zoroastrian Sasanians before real pressure to convert was applied and the original Arabs were not in control of the area any more and so were not directly responsible. Depending on where one lived, the local ruler could be anything from tolerant to Zoroastrians to plain murderous. Over a period of time a clear message evolved, convert or suffer the consequences, and within a few hundred years, the community was faced with the limited choice of flight or remain and face the pressure.

1. The Empires are commonly referred to as the Persian Empire 500-331 BC (Achaemenid dynasty), the Parthian Empire 171 BC - 224 AD (Arsacid dynasty) and the Sasanian Empire 224-651 AD.

According to most sources many sought asylum in western India in the tenth century.

Even today problems still remain and there are only two major Zoroastrian districts left in Iran. Not much is definitely known about their total number, but recent contacts have established that they are able to live side by side with their Muslim neighbours. However, it is still very probable that for the remaining Zoroastrian *gabrs* (infidels) or 'crows' as the Zoroastrians are known, maintaining a low profile is a necessity of life.

There has therefore been a continuous presence for several thousand years in their land of origin and there remains a hope of better things to come. There was also a sense of identification with Persia for the Parsee community in Dadabhai's days and they had renewed their contact with their Persian counterparts in his early adulthood. This led to Dadabhai being touched by such a connection along with the other Parsees of his day.

As far as is known the Community's flight may have involved emigrations which took place over many years. But the only written records[1] tells us of only one exodus by a group of founding fathers which occurred when they congregated at Hormuz on the shores of the Persian sea. According to tradition they then sailed in seven boats, though the number is unknown, to the island of Div just off the coast of India. They stayed there for nineteen years, but then realised that they needed to make a more permanent home and sailed eastward to come to the shores of Gujerat near the town of Sanjan in 936 AD. They had not been able to bring with them the most sacred fire or Atakhsh I Varahram which is tended by the High Priests or Dasturs and also the lower priests or Mobads. In consequence they consecrated a new one, once they had landed and been able to settle.

After landfall some journeyed along the coast from Sanjan to other towns in the area. When Sanjan was taken by Islamic forces in 1490, all the remaining Parsees in the area moved along the coast to Surat or further south along the coastal region, as far as present-day Bombay. From the 1800s, Bombay became the main centre for the Parsee population as their dominance in that city probably began with the arrival of Lowji Wadia, who built the Bombay dockyard from 1736 onwards, and he is attributed as being one of the first of an entrepreneurial tradition that has lasted until the twentieth century.

It was in this area of India that many of Dadabhai's forefathers had set up their small farms or artisan concerns to support themselves. Combined with their priestly duties, this more rural style of life had carried on for hundreds of years in Dadabhai's family, with the

1. The Qissa-i-Sanjan written around 1600 AD.

priesthood being passed from father to son. They would still be there had it not been for the British. With their arrival, new ventures were opened up and trade and expansion came in, which demanded entrepreneurs and an infrastructure. Some Parsees did well at this and the Community became much more urbanised and prosperous in the nineteenth century.

But Dadabhai's family knew virtually nothing about this latest change in the community in his early years. Partly this unfamiliarity is explained by the remoteness of his home life from the current affairs of the time, which were more familiar to those who were better off and hence had more time and contacts to utilise in keeping themselves well informed. Dadabhai's earliest years would have been the same as any other child's, where a poor widow was the primary means of support. Her aim was to ensure that he went to a local school. He concentrated on his studies until he could secure a place as one of the charitable Native Education Society's pupils at their school in Bombay. His early schooling was at an indigenous school run by a Mehtaji, (master), who on sending his son to the Native education school persuaded Dadabhai's mother to send the "Exhibition boy" of his school along as well and have his fees paid for him. He had a bright mind and was a good student at both his schools, where, in order to evade abject poverty he had to use his chance for education before anything else.

Building up his academic abilities was therefore most necessary, and from his own memoirs, he showed that he undertook to do just that. He remembered how his teacher at the second school allowed his pupils to do as they wished and for a year he and his friends were able to play games all day. His story telling abilities and leadership at their games "made me a leader among the boys and I acquired a self confidence and reliance that comes with such a position". But after that year he wanted to take up the opportunity for study that had come his way, so he disciplined himself to attend to his work.. His perseverance was to be a part of his character for the rest of his life. It paid off at school as a Mrs Postans records in her book called Western India. She described him as a little boy "with an overhanging forehead and small sparking eyes". She recalled that he often took the first step forward when a question was posed and often after deep thought, gave his answer before anyone else. "The little fellow seemed wholly animated with a desire of excelling, and his mental capabilities promised him a rich reward."

Dadabhai was a 'show-boy' at his first school and took full advantage of the opportunity for free education that was made available to him. It was not available to many of his contemporaries, due to education being heavily reliant on charity. To work in a society where there was no welfare, and where even food was in short supply, would have meant little time for study, but Dadabhai found the time and was greatly helped in this by his mother. She cared for him during all those years, in a time when women were submerged and being a widow was a very lowly position in society. He summarized it all up in 1904. "There is one whom if she comes last in this narrative, has ever been first of all, my mother. Widowed when I, her only child, was an infant, she voluntarily remained a widow (for almost 50 years), wrapped up in me, her everything in the world. She worked for her child, helped by a brother. Although illiterate and although all love for me she was a wise woman. She kept a firm hand on me. She was the wise counsellor of the neighbourhood. She helped me with all her heart in my work for female education and other social reforms against prejudices of the day. She made me what I am."

As was the norm of the time, Dadabhai was betrothed to Gulbai, daughter of a local man, Sorabjee Schroff, when he was eleven and she was seven and went through the infant marriage ceremony of the time.

During Dadabhai's childhood, India was not governed by Britain, but by a trading company called the East India Company, which had been established on the last day of 1600. Since then it had found that trade had to go hand in hand with national politics. In the India Act of 1784, the British Government had given the responsibility for British involvement in the whole region to the Company, which had found that its role became a dual one. Whilst still maintaining a commercial enterprise through its monopoly, it had also begun to act with the local rulers and states and govern the lands it had acquired by the use of diplomacy or force.

The East India Company was given a new charter by the British Government in 1813, which in effect formalized its hold on India, but withdrew its monopoly of trade. This meant it was no longer still a business organization, but was both a business and the administration combined, and it governed India along both lines for at least another twenty years. In effect, whereas companies today takeover other companies through financial methods, the East India Company was taking over various states and principalities by military methods or through the use of treaties and agreements. By the 1850s it had become more of an Administration, but in Dadabhai's younger days it still aimed to run India for a profit for the shareholders back in Britain. In the previous century this had been far more exploitative, seasoned with corruption and greed. But other men had arrived at the turn of the century who were more committed to the idea of firm and fair rule.

The sheer physical size of what the company had gained was perhaps too much to comprehend at first. Now the Company was having to decide how it would continue by weighing up such ideas as governing through European staff, to building up an internal coterie of trained natives.[1] That would mean it had to spend more time and effort on investing in the country. In 1813 the Charter Act enabled £10,000 to be sanctioned for educational ends and marked the beginnings of an Indian education system maintained under British rule. These first steps in education at that time were rudimentary and even menial. The Company had mixed feelings about training the 'natives', and possibly considered that education might even make them realize that things were not being properly administered for them and give them ideas on how to get change.

Thankfully India had been given three presidencies, with a Governor-general at Calcutta, and Governors at Bombay and Madras (see Appendix 1). Being independent rulers over their areas, the men who filled these positions were able to initiate ideas themselves. One of the most famous was Macaulay, who said in 1833 that the aims for the natives was that "having become instructed in European knowledge", they "may, in some future age, demand European institutions." He went on to say, "whether such a day will ever come I know not," and "whenever it comes, it will be the proudest day in English history." The Governor of Bombay at that time was Mountstuart Elphinstone, and he was an ardent advocate of education. He helped set up and was the President of the Bombay Native Education Society, and on his retirement in 1827 many of the local people raised money for the renamed Elphinstone College to be established in gratitude for his endeavours. He had written, "It is difficult to imagine an undertaking in which our duty, our interest and our honour are more concerned." He would seek to educate the natives to a level where "it may not be too visionary to suppose a period at which they might bear to the English nearly the relation which the Chinese do to the Tartars." By this he meant that not only could they superintend a district, or be a collector or a Judge, but also that education would diffuse from the educated classes to the population in general. The Court of Directors of the Company sanctioned a scheme of his to create some professorships, but they looked no further into the future role of education than as a means of providing the articled clerks and the other personnel needed for the Company's administration. Hence when the time came for Dadabhai to change schools the Mehtaji of his native school scented the slim opportunity and that prompted him to counsel Manekbhai to send Dadabhai to the Native Education Society's school, which eventually led to him going to the Elphinstone Institute for his college schooling. Dadabhai earned a Clare scholarship to the college in 1840 and realized when he was older how

1. The term 'native' was commonly used at the time, and its use is maintained in this book because some of the connotations it carried for the leading characters of that era are better represented by this label.

20

much those early moves for native education were very timely for him.

In his own accounts of the period he stated that "had there been the fees of the present day my mother would not have been able to pay them. This incident has made me an ardent advocate of free education, and the principle that every child should have the opportunity of receiving all the education it is capable of accumulating, whether it is born poor or with a silver spoon in its mouth."

By comparison a contemporary of Dadabhai's who was only a nine year old girl in 1842, was sent to a British School by herself to receive an English education. She must have suffered from isolation and some distress, being the only Asian girl receiving such an education and also because she had to walk daily and unescorted, through the British area of Bombay, which were two matters that the Community found outrageous. All the same she went on to become a leading social reformer under her married name of Dossibai Jassawalla.

The Elphinstone College became an Institution in the same year by combining both the School and the College together, and it was to give Dadabhai his first job when he became a staff member of the Institution. Professor Orlebar at the Institution called Dadabhai, "The promise of India", and Dadabhai went on to pass with distinction in 1845. Many other Bombay residents were to become the products of the Elphinstone Institute at around the same time. A number of them rose to become the new intelligentsia like Dadabhai, while others were to succeed in new ventures in commerce. The influence of that liberal institution was apparent as many of them kept to its philosophy as opposed to adopting a more conservative approach, which was apparent in other sections of the Bombayite society.

Because Dadabhai did very well at his studies, Sir Erskine Perry, the Chief Justice of Bombay[1], suggested in 1845 that Dadabhai be sent to Britain to study as a barrister. As no-one in his family could afford this, Sir Erskine volunteered to pay half the costs himself if the Parsee community would fund the other half. But other events overshadowed the Justice's offer.

Christian missionaries had been working with the Hindu Community ever since 1813, with some success; but the much smaller and hence more tightly bound Parsee community[2] was a different matter. Based upon a belief system which is akin to monotheistic religions and being a group who had left everything already, the conversion of two youngsters in 1839, had caused a lot of chagrin and consternation.

---

1. Sir Erskine Perry was also President of the Board of Education and a leading proponent of wider education.

2. It only numbered 85,314 in 1881, and reached its nadir of 114,890 in 1941, before declining again to 71,630 in 1981.

Their conversion was seen as a threat to the integrity and the long term standing of the community and the Parsee leadership asked the Authorities to intervene in the choice made by the two youths and against the man who gave most of his attention to the Parsee community from 1829 onwards, a Dr John Wilson. The Authorities took no action and so by 1845 the Parsee Panchayat, or ruling body of the community, was against the idea of Dadabhai receiving any help which might lead to him being whisked off to England and possibility converted. The Panchayat represented the secular authority of the community as its five leading members were normally not from a priestly background. It sometimes clashed with the priests but on this occasion the Orthodox members also vetoed the offer of Sir Perry and the 'Jonglos' (a nickname for Englishmen), fearing the possible results of one of the community going to Britain. Happily better understanding developed in later years, and the work of missionaries, such as Dr John Wilson brought benefits and greater mutual co-operation, with the Parsee community giving contributions to Christian missions. But 1845 was the wrong time. For the two youngsters their early years were fraught with rejection and alienation but they were more accepted later in their lives, after they had become ministers.

One of them was named Hormasji Pestonji and the other was called Dhanjibhoy Naoroji. He lived in England and on his death in 1905, the papers caused some temporary consternation to Dadabhai's friends and family when they announced the death of one 'D. Naoroji.'

Another Parsee convert named Shapurji Edalji became the vicar of Great Wyrley in Staffordshire in the 1870s. He married a lady named Charlotte Stoneham and they had three children. Their eldest son George Edalji had to face alienation in Britain when in 1903 he was sentenced to seven years in prison for maiming horses, after having had false charges brought against him. Although he was a practising solicitor based in Birmingham, he could not get his innocence accepted in the courts. This victimization probably had its roots back in the period of 1892 to 1895 when the family was sent hoax letters and had to endure 'jokes.' All this could well tie in with Dadabhai's life at that time as he was called a 'black man" by the Prime Minister Lord Salisbury in 1888, which may have meant that such terms became more common place. The Chief Constable of Staffordshire 'thought black men were less than beasts' and had claimed that George had sent the letters to his own family.

By the turn of the century the people in Great Wyrley believed that the Reverend Edalji was making nightly sacrifices to his alien gods. They had developed a general dislike for any Asian being their vicar, and so no one really wanted to believe George was innocent. Only the lobbying of a former Chief Justice of the Bahamas, RD Yelverton, got

George Edalji released in 1906 and it was not until 11th January 1907, through a series of articles in the *Daily Telegraph* by no less a person than Arthur Conan Doyle, that the process began which led to the Home Office finally concluding that the conviction was wrong, though it never offered any compensation.

For Dadabhai the events of 1845 left him with a conflict of loyalties, which he resolved by staying in India. He had read a number of books by then and they probably influenced his thoughts on what his purpose in life should be and helped him decide on what to do next. Two books in particular may have been important to him. One was Clarkson's on the slave trade and the other was on the life of Howard the philanthropist. Hence the events of the time and Dadabhai's own self education prompted him into new directions and in the long run this situation probably worked for the better. In later years he summarized his feelings over the incident in a positive way, when he wrote, "in reality it had been the best thing that could have happened. Otherwise I would have been bound to the narrow outlook of a subordinate Government Official Servant." He said this because the first choice of a career for him had been to become a clerk in the Bombay Government services secretariat. Instead he became Head Native Assistant Master in 1845 in Mathematics and Natural Philosophy at Elphinstone. In 1850 he became the Assistant Professor and then a full Professor in 1852\3. Hence he was the first Indian or 'Native' to become a Professor, which was a major event in its own time and one he was very proud of in later life.

He was patient and gave good guidance to his pupils, often making time for extra tuition and revamping the system of tuition to make it better suited for the students. These endeavours were appreciated by the students of the time, who later gave him praise for his attention and help in those years.

Parallel to his own academic career, Dadabhai also involved himself with the Parsee Gymnasium, which was one of a number that were set up in those days, gymnasiums being popular with the Parsees. He was also a member of the Widows Marriage Association which aimed to get public acceptance for widows to remarry rather than to be excluded from remarriage. He was also a member of the Victoria and Albert Museum and of the Framjee Cowasjee Institute and the France Fund. But he was most vigorous in the social reformer's role which he commenced with the setting up of some new bodies for educational and religious reform. Under a Professor Patton he set up the "Students Literary and Scientific Society" at the Elphinstone Institute. On the 4th August 1849 one of its members named Behranji Gandhi presented a paper on the need for female education. It was a well given talk as after hearing it Professor Patton urged the students to take up the issues it raised. With Dadabhai as one of the main participants, and other leading participants such as Naoroji Furdunji, Sorabji Shapurji Bengali and Bhau Daji, they began to direct their energy towards establishing educational provision for women in the Bombay area. All of them were Elphinstonians who had acquired the liberal motivations of the Institution, and the influence that the College had on a whole strata of Indians of the day is shown up in the activities they applied themselves to. Undoubtedly Dadabhai's own initiatives in later life were greatly influenced by the liberal stance of the college, which it should be remembered had only been established because liberal minded Britons exerted enough pressure to get at least one college set up for native students.

Dadabhai had already gone around homes in the area and offered to teach the three R's to the daughters of the households, which was not always well received. The members agreed to start providing education for women at some more public venue, which was unheard of in those days. They set themselves the task of setting up and staffing these new schools, where they could provide voluntary teaching. Dadabhai was given the title of 'the father of girl's schools', though this may be unfair as other people of the time also put a lot into these early initiatives. The Society had originally involved members of all the communities who had been at Elphinstone, and although it soon split along internal communal lines, all the new groups continued to support the growth of female education.

Initially the founding members and the other participants had to provide the classes in their own home, free of charge, between 7-10am, so that money would not be a block to what was primarily a social reform of a deep seated view of a woman's place in society. Even so the early days were difficult and it took several months to get the first batch of 44 Parsee and 24 Hindu women into the schools. Dadabhai was the supervisor of what was known as the Fort School in those days. From the opening of the first 'school' in October 1849, there arose another four schools with 371 pupils up to the age of 12, who learnt Gujerati plus some geography and natural history. The financial aid of Kharshedji Nasarwanji Cama in 1850 was enough to support the continued opening of the first two girls schools, including the Fort School, as properly established centres of learning.

Later, contributions from other members of the Bombay community allowed the society to employ some teachers for two years. By this effort the first steps to what is now permanent female education were being made. However, the orthodox Parsees of the time rebuffed Sir Erskine Perry's suggestion of 1852 for a committee of women to supervise the work. These first steps taken by the 'sisoti' boys as they were known, were to mark the type of reform that Dadabhai aimed at during this life.

The Society also set up the Dhyan Prasarak Mandali in 1848 to promote general knowledge and awareness amongst the Gujerati and Marathi speaking communities at large, through holding debates on various issues.

The Rahnumai Mazdayasnan Sabha ("Society for the guidance of true believers"), was concerned with religious affairs and was begun by Dadabhai and other members of the Society, as they were Parsees who were concerned with the authenticity of what was a Zoroastrian teaching and what was not. The 'sisoti' boys had begun this very different endeavour at about the same time as their educational programme, to reform their religion which had absorbed beliefs and practices not found in Zoroastrianism. To give some perspective, it needs to be remembered that Zoroastrianism had been practised for centuries in another culture and its adherents were often rubbing shoulders with people of other religions. In consequence although many believed they knew the rights and wrongs of their faith, including many of the orthodox, any changes which had occurred had probably taken place generations ago and no one was any wiser.

It is also said that if three Parsees come together you will get four opinions and certainly in the wider Parsee community several different factions were present in its midst. At that time the Zoroastrian Priesthood was in a state of stand off to the Panchayat, because of a series of edicts it had made. The Panchayat had been losing much of its authority since 1838, which was creating a power vacuum. Therefore a reforming role was open to people like Dadabhai and Naoroji Furdunji (1817-1885), who co-founded the "Tribune of the People" on 3rd August 1851. Being outside of the debates, both the men and their supporters hoped to get closer to the truths of their faith and to remove the unfounded beliefs that were being propounded.

At the end of the day certain unauthenticated beliefs and practices were brought to light and then removed from the Zoroastrian teachings. But the in-between time was a more difficult period for both Dadabhai and Naoroji, as they had to progress the debate whilst meeting some resistance and without the blessing of the community's elders in order to enable reforms to be brought in. The Rahnumai Mazdayasnam Sabha, of which Dadabhai was Secretary for 1851 - 53, was still operating as a Religious Reform Association in its own diamond jubilee, to carry on Dadabhai's stated first aim, that is " to restore the Zarthosti religion to its pristine purity and simplicity." It is interesting to note that this is a cause which still raises a lot of concern in the Zoroastrian community today, and which brings into debate issues such as conversion. There is also a touch of irony in that if Dadabhai had become a priest he may never have been able to have begun such a far reaching reform of his religion.

CHAPTER TWO

AN EARLY ATTEMPT AT EQUAL OPPORTUNITIES

The British Empire was still a growing entity at that time and India was not yet a colony. Although it was governed, administered and run by The East India Company, it was only on paper that the Company was accountable to the government and it was not really concerned with being answerable for political issues. However, in the year 1833 when the Company's charter was renewed for the next twenty years, the Government of India Act made the Company more accountable. It also stated, "that no native of the said territories nor any natural born subject of Her Majesty resident therein shall, by reason only of his religion, place of birth, descent or any of them, be disabled from holding any place, office or employment of said Company." (or government after 1858). The Company had in effect been the administrator of India and it now became the Government of India in name too. In order to achieve this role it had to cease making trade its major pursuit and concentrate far more on administration and diplomacy. Despite the statement made in 1833, in practice it was young men from Britain, educated at Haileybury College and who then came to India who ran the territory for the Company. This was an unwritten policy which excluded the natives. In consequence no native ever held a position in the most senior levels of the administration of the country, nor did even one go to Haileybury College.

A lot of good work was brought to fruition by the Company's men and India had benefited from their efforts. But as said no Indian took a major part in the advancement of society and government and with a few exceptions the Company staff wanted it kept that way. In 1852 the people of India were very concerned that the charter would be renewed using a very similar format, which meant the company was being allowed to slowly overrun India. The Bengalee groups formed an Association and so did the Bombayites. At a meeting held on 26th August 1852 at the Elphinstone Institute, the young Bombayites, their

26

elders and some British friends formed the Bombay Association, with Naoroji Furdunji as its Secretary.

It was a period when some Indians started to think of India as a nation and it marked Dadabhai's first steps in politics. He along with others had set up what was the first Bombay based politically oriented organization. In this mixed grouping of people, there were some who were the wealthy and influential men who 4headed up the prosperous business community in Bombay. They were drawn from the city's elite and were called the Shetias representing the more traditional and pro British fraction in the city. The others were often younger men who had begun to aspire to a different kind of position, often due to the influence of the British education that they had received. They could be called the reforming class and were often men with a professional background. Both groups had a liking for the British system because the former had often built up their fortunes under British hegemony, whilst the latter had obtained their education through the Liberal minded institutions. But the latter group also wanted reform and the removal of "existing evils" and those "proposed measures which may be deemed injurious." They wanted to create an open challenge to the British authorities and this discomforted many of the Shetias.

Soon after the first meeting was held, Dadabhai made a speech, which being only his first was in consequence rather a tame affair. As he said in 1906, "In 1853, when I made my first little speech at the inauguration of the Bombay Association in perfect innocence of heart influenced by my English education into great admiration for the character, instincts and struggles for liberty of the British people, I expressed my faith and confidence in the British rulers .... such was my faith. It was the faith of the educated of the time." He was concerned along with everyone else about what the future held, without knowing how to tackle the present. He was also motivated by the liberal traditions of the Elphinstone Institute, which being a British based body, led to him and his colleagues of the time to expect such liberal views to be held by the wider British community. His words in 1906 showed how much the tuition of those earlier years had had an influence on him. He never lost a belief in those ideals and was stating this as well as outlining his naivety in 1853, when speaking in his later years. Dadabhai also put up a practical suggestion in 1853 when he proposed that the Association press for full-time staff to be appointed to tour India and bring back information on the status of the people and the land. The Shetias pressed for more work on building up an infrastructure for commercial reasons and on the running of the Justice system, which often affected them directly.

With hindsight we may see the beginnings of the Indian claiming his rights from the British, but at that time people did not see themselves as British subjects claiming British rights and justice. The British were another people and another culture, and one that did not really permeate into India. Neither did the idea of being an Indian really permeate into the hearts of the majority of its inhabitants. Their aim was to get reform within the present system of British Rule. All the same the reformers were seen as too critical by the Shetias and a number of them left in the first year. There was still going to be a lot of work for those first advocates of India both in their lifetimes and beyond, in order to get the massive support that was apparent in the twentieth century.

But Dadabhai had seen one facet of the British system, which he quite clearly felt was genuine and believed in for the rest of his life. This was that there was a desire for fairness that was embedded into the structures it employed, because of the people who ran the structures. He believed that the British people loved justice and would in consequence give a fair hearing to all-comers. Dadabhai kept this faith throughout his life. That he did, when he was quite honestly snubbed or despised by some members of that society or by representatives of its government, says more about him than about some of those people. But as the saying goes, "It takes one to know one" and Dadabhai was not a foolish person clinging to a forlorn hope, but someone who was to be remarkably fair and honest in all his future dealings. What therefore was present in his character, he was seeing as being at the centre of the British system.

His faith was put to an almost immediate test, when he met the antithesis of the just system, in the hearts and minds of the then administrators of the Company, who did not care what their fellow 'citizens' thought about the wording of the 1833 Act, or of the terms of the charter given to the Company. He carried on meeting the same contempt from other men, and from other representatives of the British Crown, whom he knew loved freedom, for the next 65 years. Significantly most of the sneering, when it did come, came from the 'Anglo-Indian' community who were the British living in India, not from the majority of those living in Britain. Yet, as he said then " ... the redress (of such wrongs), would make India a blessing to you and make England a blessing to us, which unfortunately it is not at present."

In 1906, after the moderates like him seemed to have been shown that their belief in the British had been proved wrong, by none other than the British Authorities, he would still say, "our faith and our future are in our own hands. If we live to ourselves and to our country and make all necessary sacrifices for our elevation and amelioration, I for one have not the shadow of a doubt that in dealing with such a justice loving, fair minded people as the British, we may rest fully assured that we shall not work in vain. It is this conviction which has supported me against all difficulties. I have never faltered in my faith in the British character and have always believed that the time will come when the sentiments of the British nation and our gracious sovereign, proclaimed to us in our great Charter of the Proclamation of 1858, will be realized, viz 'in their prosperity will be our strength, in their contentment our best reward" (see Appendix 1b).

Some Britons, notably Sir William Wedderburn and Mr A O Hume, along with many others, held fast to the principles of that Proclamation throughout their lives and by their efforts eventually justified the hope that there was room for faith in the British system. To do this all those people gave of their time, their efforts and their money. It is virtually impossible to make a final simple 'right' or 'wrong' judgement of the British system, but to rather show how the main participants of the period used their personal values and wills for the futures of both countries. However, it is important to realize the personal stature of a man who, no matter how agitated or brow beaten he was, would never become an anarchist, because of his belief that the system would live up to basic universal principles.

Dadabhai and others began to claim that one of the main ways to show fair dealings was for Indians to be admitted to the Indian Civil Service. Some British statesmen supported the Association's demands and the Indian Reform Society was constituted in London on the 13th March 1853. But the Government paid little heed to the proposals and kept itself in with the Company, solely following that body's perceptions and recommendations and granting its requests.

To give the reforms an independent voice, an anonymous benefactor who was later revealed to be Kharshedji Nasarwanji Cama, put up the money for a newspaper entitled 'Rast Gofter' or 'Truth Teller.' Dadabhai was one of its main editors. In its first, second and third editions most coverage had to be given to a crisis which had been precipitated by a Parsee-Moslem dispute, that had come about because of an ill-conceived article in a newspaper edited by a Parsee youth. Up until then the relations between the two communities had been cordial and business had often been conducted amicably. The upshot of the article was that local Muslims called for a 'jihad' or 'crusade' against the Parsees. Several people were beaten up and corpses were defiled[1].

Dadabhai was based in the Fort area of Bombay along with many

1. It is not exactly clear how the corpses were defiled, but in Zoroastrianism a dead body is not supposed to touch earth or fire because it is reckoned to be impure and to pass its impurity on through touch. Hence burial or cremation are not commonly allowed and the arranging of dead bodies in specifically prepared burial towers would have been the common practice in Bombay. It seems possible that the funeral arrangements were interfered with leading to pollution and prevention of the proper burial ritual for the deceased.

other members of the Parsee Community. He was an eyewitness to the disturbances and felt that the authorities were not even-handed in their dealing of the situation. What is more, the Parsee elders did not really speak out against the injustice and the people living in the Baharkote area, called on "Dadabhai master" to promote their case and so ensure some resolution was made that left them less vulnerable.

Rast Gofter spoke out, because although the editor of the other paper had offered an apology, at best only an uneasy truce was called. The threat of further violence remained partly because the police were not vigorous in their duties, and partly because the Parsee Elders were not making it clear that things had gone far enough. The apology had been humbling for the Parsees and apparently it had not been recognized nor responded to in a proper manner. This first edition on 15th November 1851 carried all these points it its article. Efforts were then made to get the Governor to bring back some public order and prevent further violence, and for the apology to be accepted. As is now known, the matter did not need to go any further, but at the time it was far more touch and go. After this active start, the paper continued in a similar vein for years. Because his knowledge and interests were wide ranging Dadabhai wrote many other articles including eighteen on Natural Philosophy and Astronomy. The paper was to be run for many years by an eight man syndicate when Dadabhai left the country. In 1874, during another communal flare-up, due to a similar set of circumstances, Rast Gofter had to make the same points again.[1]

Dadabhai's efforts of this time were commented upon in the Hindustan review of September 1915 "if today the vernacular press of Bombay is the best conducted and most successful in the country, if today female education is more advanced in Bombay than even in Calcutta, Madras or Delhi, if today there is a richer literature in Gujerati than in any other Indian vernacular (except perhaps Bengali), if today social reform and progress have made greater strides in the western presidency than in the rest of India, it is greatly due to the motivation, devotion and self sacrificing labours and youthful energies of Dadabhai Naoroji". Dadabhai was also busy in other areas and with different

1. By the late 1880s Rast Goftar had become more pro-establishment and did not wish to seek political reform but rather aimed at social reform which also meant reform of religious doctrines. The new publisher K Kabraji and Dadabhai argued over who had continued to hold to its basic principles in a series of letters published in the paper in 1902. Well before then Dadabhai had decried the political stance of the paper to Dinsha Wacha and others. The "Kaiser-i-hind" became the paper most in line with his stance and that of the Congress. K Kabraji disagreed with Dadabhai as much because of his Congress connections as anything else, both fearing the dominance of Congress by a Hindu faction at times and also wondering how Dadabhai could be so critical of Britain if he really supported it as much as he said he did. In a way Dadabhai agreed on the former issue because he wanted a secular Congress for all Indians, not one made up of clearly separate religious groups.

groups. He studied and became familiar with French, Persian, Hindustani, Gujerati and Marathi. He was a member of the Royal Asiatic Society (1851-55), the first Parsee Dramatic Society (1853) and was involved in the affairs of the Elphinstone Institute and with a charitable body.

Russia became a concern of his when it threatened to overthrow Turkey. When Russia reached the Danube it seemed likely that it could next get to the Indus river. The cold war was not only a twentieth century phenomenon, but in those days local armed conflict between super powers was not impossible in such situations, and Britain and France went to war with Russia in the Crimea (1854). A patriotic fund was started up in India and Dadabhai spoke at meetings held for the fund, because he believed justice lay with the British in this case and that the interests of both Britain and India were threatened.

Dadabhai also took an interest in the foreign affairs which effected him and his community. Reports came from the Kingdom of Persia, (modern day Iran) sent by the Zoroastrians who had remained. They spoke of the injustices they bore in daily life under their Islamic overlords. Maybe around 25000 Zoroastrians had remained in Persia after the flight into exile of their compatriots, and around the same number were living in Persia in Dadabhai's days and probably a similar number still live under constrained circumstances today. In 1478 one Parsee, Nariman Hoshang, went back to Persia to obtain information on their state of affairs. In the 19th century another Parsee, Manekji Hataria, was making longer term contacts. His letters back to India were read by Dadabhai to assemblies of Parsees and a fund called the Irani fund for their oppressed co-religionists, was raised to provide educational facilities, help for the aged and aid repairs to religious centres. Dadabhai kept his contact up for many years and was involved in leading three deputations to the Shah, when that ruler visited Britain in 1885, 1901 and 1906. His pleading for fair treatment met with some favourable response on the later occasions.

It seems true to say that Dadabhai remained faithful to his themes throughout his life, but held no lasting ties to either institutions or to the positions he was brought into. Because he had energy and vision he wanted to move on to new horizons even though he was often doing well enough in his own circumstances at any one time. For the activities he engaged in when in his late twenties he said in 1910, "the six or seven years before I eventually came to England .... were full of all sorts of reforms, social, educational, political, religious, etc. .... movements set on foot, and institutions inaugurated by a band of young men fresh from college .... Such were the first fruits of the English education given us at the Elphinstone College....". They had been busy years for him and fruitful, both in terms of experience and in the amount of change and new structures that were inaugurated, which would in some cases, carry on to bring about greater benefits to the community.

Dadabhai's life seemed to be taking shape with a career in education and in the role of a reformer. However as so often happened in his life a new venture opened up to Dadabhai and he came into another of the 'firsts' which characterized his life. Though Indians had been visiting Britain since the arrival of one Naoroji Rustam Manek of Surat in 1724, no one had sought to set up a permanent base. The first Naoroji had sought redress over the wrongful house arrest of his brothers by The East India Company. He came with a brother to appeal to the Court of Directors of the Company over both the actions of its officers and on the Rs 200 a day payment that he was forced to make for permission to feed his family. He also made known the non-payment of dues owed by the Company to his late father and owner of the family business. In both cases he was successful and restitution was made.

The next visitor to arrive came to get schooling in 1823, and thereafter a steady trickle had developed in the 1830s and 1840s. Some came to study British industrial methods and some to study at centres of learning. In 1855 two brothers, Kharshedji Rustomji and Muncherji Hormusji Cama had formed their plans to found the first Indian owned firm based in Britain. Through report backs from earlier visitors the Cama brothers had been able to surmise the potential from those first hand accounts. They set up a base in London and opened another office in Liverpool. They wanted Dadabhai to go to England with them, and invited him to help set up an export-import business in partnership with themselves. Despite the obvious change in career, it was his clear intention to join them, as he wanted to further the cause of the Indians in Britain, and felt a base in London would help in assisting students competing for places in the Indian Civil Service. He had no doubts or regrets in taking such a drastic move and for the period of his life between 1845 and 1855 he later surmised that he looked back upon it "with pride and pleasure; with satisfaction of a duty performed." He tied up his affairs and set sail on 27th June 1855, at the age of 29 to travel from Bombay docks to Aden and then through the Suez canal, picking up a boat in Alexandria to arrive at Southampton docks on 22nd August.

The style of operations amongst the new partners was to discuss almost everything and then agree on a course of action. Dadabhai's relationship to the other two members was based on past friendship and acquaintance, but of the two Kharshedji was closer to him in his opinions and moral views. Kharshedji had already worked for his relative's firm in Calcutta and then spent four years in China in the

Canton based firm of his uncle Rustomji up until 1854. Therefore he did not come into the business naively and with Muncherji being more conservative in his views and on the methods of conducting business, it was possible to say that Kharshedji and Muncherji were more ready to use the prevalent business practices and not to weigh up the ethics behind such transactions. This was not an absolute delineation of standpoints and Kharshedji did agree with Dadabhai on many occasions, leaving Muncherji to complain at times that he was left on his own when it came to discussing the conduct of business. The old saying seemed to run true that with three Parsees together you will definitely get four opinions. The partnership in the London office was no different and at times it needed to refer matters back to the Head Office in India for clarification on decisions.

It was not helpful to the business having the constant difference of opinion which was shown up in various ways. For instance it was a fairly common practice for firms to deal in any goods that were legally permissible. Many firms in those days therefore dealt in opium as under the British Empire it brought in quite a lot of revenue to the Exchequer and was a sought after commodity. For Dadabhai it posed a problem to let the old adage, "business is business", determine what he should accept. He had to think a lot on this issue and on the fact that the Camas had invited him to join them and obviously thought well of him. It took a long time for his resolution to become firmed up, but when it did Dadabhai's friendship with the Camas was outweighed by his conviction not to deal in opium, wines and spirits, and also because of the business practice of short trading. In one case Dadabhai had spent hours measuring a consignment of cotton thread, which he found contained some eighty yard reels, instead of the quoted one hundred yards. Dadabhai did not like the idea that the middleman should overlook this discrepancy and leave the buyer to sort out the problem with the original supplier, which again would have been and still is a common business practice.

It is not recorded anywhere how long or involved was the build up to this parting of the ways, but the final decision to leave the firm was his alone and he was able to part amicably with the other men in late 1858. His three years in London had therefore come to an end and he prepared to return to India. He kept up his friendship with Kharshedji, in particular through activities like Rast Goftar and Kharshedji actually left the firm shortly after Dadabhai to pursue his own interests. Although commerce had not left Dadabhai or the others any richer, he had gained experience he would use later on and had kept himself busy in other ways.

Hearing Gladstone or Cobden or Bright, leading statesmen of their day, expound the new spirit of Liberalism, was something he would never have experienced if he had stayed back in India. Having been to Britain, he was now better informed on how to understand and develop a relationship with the British when he returned to the fray. In some ways it was a quick three years, as he spent more time learning and absorbing the new ways, rather than making his own way. The company itself maintained its trading base after his departure, and also kept a generally good relationship with Dadabhai for many years to come.

Subtle changes occur when a visitor arrives to set up shop and for Dadabhai this was partly shown by the change in his dress and home life. Shortly after the three men arrived in 1855, and had set up offices in London and Liverpool, one of the members, being a fairly conservative Zoroastrian (presumably Muncherji) arranged for a Parsee cook and waiter to come over so that all the proper Zoroastrian rites were observed. In those days Dadabhai went around in the Parsee style of dress. By the time of his return to India, he had adopted the British style of clothing. Some of his younger contemporaries noted his and they in turn adopted British fashions prior to their arrival in the country, following on from this pioneer's example. During the stay in Britain Dadabhai was nominated Professor of Gujerati at University College, London. He held this position from 1856 to 1866.

On his return to India in 1858 he took on many tasks and two are noted in the 'Parsee Prakash' of the time. Firstly he began writing articles for a colleague's journal named 'Stri Gnyan Mala', which was published for women readers, to enrich their knowledge of public events, education and general affairs.

Secondly he suggested that a proposition be made for a site to be made available to erect a memorial to mark the loyalty of Bombay citizens to Queen Victoria. This was soon after the Indian mutiny of 1857 and it must be assumed that this proposal was a direct consequence of all that was happening in Indian and British affairs. Dadabhai had not shown any active interest in this major event, though being in Britain at the time he did not have much contact in the day to day sense, but developed a pessimistic mood as the news came in. The Indian mutiny was also called the Sepoy War, as it began amongst the two hundred and fifty seven thousand sepoys of the three standing armies based in India. There were thirty four thousand European troops and although the figures sound disproportionate, many sepoys did not join in. It began because the new Enfield rifle used greased cartridges and both cows grease and pigs grease were used. Many Hindu and Muslim soldiers felt this was done in order to defile them and then force Christianity into the ranks. The order to use bees wax or vegetable grease came through quickly enough in January 1857, but by then the distrust was too great. A young soldier called Mangal Pande found it too much at one parade and shot his sergeant-major and then wounded the adjutant. A General named Hearsey arrived literally on the spot, and Pande fired at him, but was wounded by his own gun. He was hung shortly afterwards.

Within weeks the third light cavalry mutinied en bloc, killed all the Europeans, then fled to escape the expected reprisals. None came and they next cajoled the old titular King of Delhi to be their leader. The mutiny had a leader but no plan. Even so by June 1857 the British had lost control in many provinces. The Indian princes by and large remained aloof. By 1859 India was back in British hands, and the savagery of one side was now repeated by the other, with the British public demanding blood. The new Governor-general tried to restore order, but got called "clemency Canning" in contempt for not going all out for retribution. However, the mutiny did bring about a change in the rule of India because the Crown assumed the responsibility of rule over India and the East India Company was not to be of real consequence to India's future history. It was at this time that Queen Victoria was to make her proclamation (1858) which promised equality of treatment for her Indian subjects. It also gave the following ground rules for relationships with the native rulers, namely that "equality among all Her Majesty's subjects and honesty with the Princes of India, be enjoyed by the Government" and "we shall respect the rights and dignity and honour of native Princes as our own" (see Appendix 1b). These pronouncements brought cheer to Dadabhai and he often quoted them in later years, because their wording and tenor were of the same ilk as Dadabhai's own aims for the Indians.

In constitutional terms the administration of the East India Company, and principally its Board of Control and the Court of Directors, was dissolved. But much of the Administration was in practice simply transferred over to the Governor-general who added the honorific of Viceroy to his title. He was given powers unknown in any other part of the Empire and was appointed for five years. The fact that he had real control in his hands is shown up by the fact that in 1896 and 1897 Westminster had no reason to pass legislation dealing with India. There were seven provinces, broken down into two hundred and thirty districts. A Collector or Magistrate often presided over them on his own. The Viceroy governed with a remodelled Legislative Council under him, which contained up to twelve members who were not on the Executive Council (see Appendix 1a). Half of this twelve were to be non-official and came from aristocratic India, or were other men of substance. It was a very small token, and one which could be used to reward those who had not mutinied. And yet it also had the significance of being the thin edge of the wedge, as Indians were included in the governing bodies of the land for the first time. A second change was to guarantee the lands or domains of the gentry and Princes of India and in such a way that they now became part of the system.

What the British did was to leave five hundred and sixty five Indian states able to govern their subjects as before, but with the ultimate responsibility on each ruler no longer being to his " praja" or people but to the British. Many of these States already had treaties with Britain, and these were in effect all codified into a single treaty. They were given a guarantee of their independence and in that regard it could be said that many gained in terms of their future being assured. However the assurance now depended on the British and so each state also became a dependency on the British guarantor. Also no longer could any ruler be called a King of Mogul and they could not call the "gadis" or cushion that they sat on, a throne. Their titles became Maharaja or Maharao and they were also ascribed a fixed gun salute. Amongst the one hundred and eighteen first division states, only five were given a twenty-one gun salute. Anyone called Maha (Maha Raja or 'great' Raja) had over thirteen guns in their salute. Below them came one hundred states where no salute was given and the three hundred and twenty seven estates who did not have criminal or civil jurisdictions. The smallest states had a petty ruler called a "Thakar". Then there were Zamindars or non-hereditary rulers who were given land, but were not recognised as being pukka Princes. What they all received was some direct aid, and the change meant something for the immediate futures of those who were affected. At the same time no Prince has ever truly been independent, both then nor ever since.

Dadabhai was therefore to deal both with and within the British Parliament in the years to come, and not with the representatives of a large company. In a way this was preferable as a government administers a country, whereas a company only seeks to make it a profitable enterprise. However, although it transpired that the East India Company was the worse of the two systems, it is also true that a government could be just as rapacious in its dealings, when it came to revenues and expenditure; and this was to be one of the major themes for Dadabhai, in his future work. The India office was based at the old East India Company's headquarters in Leadenhall Street, London.

Dadabhai's intention to return was soon realized when he set out on a second journey to Britain on 9th January 1859. This time he took a nephew and two younger members of the Cama family and moved into 63 Oxford Street, Liverpool. Dadabhai Naoroji & Co became the headquarters of a small concern set up in march 1859 which dealt in commerce, but using its own succinct ethics in accordance with Dadabhai's personal views. The younger Camas dealt with the firm but were not partners in it. In these days it would be a welcome example for propounders of ethical investments, who could show that profitability and honest dealing can be combined together. The practices included never short trading, nor accepting payments from both buyers and sellers at the same time. That can be interpreted as a form of bribery if viewed as being a seller sweetening the way for the middleman to either pick him over and above another tenderer, or electing to work for the sellers interests as much as the buyers, as he could get paid by either. Dadabhai showed that he did not agree with this procedure when he had put out a tender for the building of four ships for an Indian client. Lastly the firm had no dealings in the opium trade. Hence the present day ethical investor can note that the business did grow, but more particularly perhaps, non-ethical businesses should note this fact too!

During this stay in Britain, and on top of running the firm, Dadabhai became a director of the Queen Insurance Co. He gave money to public bodies such as the Zoroastrian fund for Europe and to a group giving English education for Parsee girls. The number of societies this busy businessman joined or was asked to join is quite surprising. He gave a speech entitled "The Parsee Religion" on the 18th March 1861 at the Liverpool Literary and Philosophical Society, in which he explained the religious practices of the religion and at the end noted his surprise at the similarities it had to the parts of the Old Testament that he had been reading. He was also connected to the Philomathic Society, the Council of the Liverpool Athenaeum, the Royal Institute of London, the Royal Asiatic Society of Great Britain and Ireland, the Anthropological Society, The Society of Arts, the National Indian Association and a Masonic Lodge, the 'Marquess of Dalhousie.' He also became a member of the Manchester Cotton Supply Association.

Dadabhai had not forgotten the first reason for his coming to Britain in 1855 and believed it was time for the British to begin to become acquainted with their fellow subjects in India. Dadabhai continued giving presentations on his own community, namely the Parsees in India, both from the stand point of the reformers which were current at that time and also from the viewpoint of the more conservative elements. He was very fair in his talks, and gave a balanced view, despite being firmly of the Reform camp. From that he very quickly broadened his range of subjects and gave talks on the lifestyles of Indians and on the needs for reform in British rule.

At this time one Samuel Smith, a leading cotton merchant, met Dadabhai through business and the two men began what was to be a lifelong dialogue. Samuel Smith was very much a temperance man active in campaigns in Britain which sought to at least control the access to cheap alcohol. It was a cause that Dadabhai felt was needed and later sought to provide in the different climate of India's society, where the problem was of a different order of magnitude.

Now Dadabhai's role began to take shape and form. For through all these activities he began to become India's unofficial ambassador to Britain. So when the first Indian student, Mr Rustomji Hiribhai Wadia, came to Britain to take the 'open' Indian Civil Service Competition at the age of 23, he sought out Dadabhai after being informed that the upper age limit had been reduced from 23 to 22. Mr Wadia was not trying to join the lower ranks of the Service, but was seeking an appointment at the higher, covenanted levels. The covenanted Service was usually around a thousand strong and consisted of those officers who had 'covenanted' with the Secretary of State to accept the codes and discipline of the Service. The Indian Civil Service Act 1861 had reserved all the higher graded posts for this branch of the organization. Because the exams to enter the Service had to be taken in Britain, both the costs of travel for Indians and crossing the 'black water' which would entail breaking a religious observance for some people, were factors which acted as barriers to most Indians ever trying to enter the Service.[1] Dadabhai also pointed out the injustice of natives only being found in the uncovenanted service, because they would always be paid less until the time they entered the Covenanted Service. As his paper read by the East India Association on the 17th April 1868 said, "there are about 1700 Europeans in the Covenanted Service of India at a cost of about 3 million per annum, at a salary of from 240L to 25000L per annum. There are 849 Europeans and Anglo Indians in the uncovenanted Service, at salaries of 300L and upwards; while of natives there are only about 600 at a salary above 240L a year, of whom about 350 are between 240L to 260L per annum .... very few - only about a dozen natives are at salaries at and above 840L per year." In Rustomji Wadia's case Dadabhai immediately wrote to Lord Stanley, the Secretary of State, saying this decision should have been decided in advance and not left to such a discriminating moment. Bureaucracies move slowly except when speedy decisions are considered 'essential.' He also asked Sir Erskine Perry and an interested MP, John Bright, to assist with Mr Wadia's case for the right to sit the exam. Mr Bright had the matter tabled for discussion in the House, but the American Civil War broke out and it never had time to be debated. By that time Dadabhai had

1. Twenty one different papers were offered, covering subjects such as advanced mathematics (900 points), or Roman history (400 points). After getting through the tests by achieving a sufficient total of points a years probation at an English or Scottish University awaited the candidate. Then a second set of compulsory papers had to be sat, which included the Indian penal code, a principal Indian language, a code of civil procedure on Hindu or Mohammedan law, other languages and the "ability to perform journeys on horseback". This last one could be passed in India, but no salary rise was allowed until it was.

achieved some success in the case when a letter from the Secretary of State for India, said that such arbitrary decisions would not be allowed to pass through so casually in the future. Dadabhai still had to make further representations to get Mr Wadia to be finally admitted to the Service, where he later rose to a senior position.

Later on in 1869, three other Indians who were to become some of Indian's leading men, took and passed the exams in London, at the age of 23. They were Ramesh Chandar Butt, Behan Lal Gupta and Surendranath Banerjea. For them their timing proved to be more providential because the age bar had been raised once again. This was to the good for the Indians because their education was progressed at a slower rate in comparison to the education of English applicants, and 22 was too early an age for Indian-educated applicants to complete their studies. Surendranath Banerjea was expelled from the Indian Civil Service after a few years through some fairly improper methods being brought to bear. As his expressed opinions were in line with those who wanted reform in the governing of India his seniors were unhappy with his presence in the service and no doubt were instrumental to his expulsion. He was to become an active and prominent member of the Indian National Congress when that body had formed, and despite the setback he suffered in his earlier life he carried on to play a full role in his later years.

In 1874, when the number of Indians who were applying to join the Service had risen to twelve per year, the age limit was lowered once again by the conservative government of Lord Salisbury to 19. It was raised by the Liberals to between 21-23 in 1893 and from 22-24 in 1906. Hence the age limit became an other important way to bar Indian students from applying because as has been said their schooling was completed at a later age than their British counterparts in the public school system, and they also still had to travel a long way to sit the exams. Dadabhai did persist with his arguments over entry to the Civil Service for the rest of that century, and he unknowingly faced the racial prejudice of men such as Lord Lytton, who was Viceroy from 1876-1880. Dadabhai found the general tone of Lord Lytton's Viceroyalty was heavy handed on Indians, but was never to know the depth of his prejudice, as he never made too blatant a statement to allow for outright criticism to be possible. He found this period was to be one of his more depressing times, when officialdom seemed to obliquely sideline any efforts made by the Indians for themselves.

With hindsight it is now clear that Lytton's idea was to form two types of Civil Service, and make sure Indians were excluded from one of them, namely the Covenanted Service, and that they would then be 'plainly and publicly warned that natives must never aspire' to it. By a despatch sent on 2nd May 1878 he effectively killed off any hopes for Indians entering the Covenanted Service. Other officials at this time wrote letters between March 1877 to April 1878 concurring with Lytton and these included Sir John Strachey, Sir Ashley Eden and Sir George Cowper, who were also members of Council and who held the most Senior posts. Lytton did not have everything go his own way but he succeeded in rallying those who wanted India to be governed over the heads of the Indian rather than by seeking to use the common sense and intelligence held in the heads of the Indians. Real change did not come until well into the next century, and Dadabhai saw the age limits become more appropriate in that time. By 1903 the annual intake of Indians through all channels into the higher levels of the Service was ninety two out of one thousand three hundred and seventy, compared to only two appointments by 1867, or sixteen out of eight hundred and ninety covenanted members in 1887.

The calls on Dadabhai for assistance with entry to the official bodies did not only cover the Indian Civil Service and he was requested to help another entrant two years after Mr Wadia's case. This was due to the Indian medical service making some other out-of-the-blue type conditions that barred Indian students from applying to the service. The corny ploy used that time was to say that the hopeful student, a Mr Mancherji Colah, would probably suffer from the change of climates he would experience as he was moved from post to post and that Her Majesty's government was concerned for the well being of Indian youths. Eventually, through his further remonstrations, Dadabhai was able to get Mr Colah admitted for the post of Assistant Surgeon. Mr Colah did well and later on he rose to a senior position. Quite clearly the climate of mid-nineteenth century India was not assumed to be a bar to the European youths despite the death rate amongst the Europeans based there. It was the attitude of the British authorities which could be most inclement for Indian subjects.

Dadabhai became aware of a small but increasing number of Indian arrivals to Britain at around that time, especially in London. He therefore co-formed a London Zoroastrian Association in 1861 alongside Mancherjee Hormasjee Cama under the name of the 'Religious Funds (or Society) of Zarathushtrians in Europe'. This Association was to act as a common reference point for all new arrivals, and provided support for these visitors. He remained on as its President from 1862 until 1908 and this body still actively works for the community from its base in North London. Its first and major act was the acquisition of a lease on a burial ground on December 11th 1863. The ground was based in the Brookwood Cemetery in Surrey and is still in use to this day.

Although Dadabhai had maintained regular correspondence with his family in India, his absence allowed problems to percolate on the domestic side. Dadabhai had married Gulbai and set up home in India with her before his second prolonged residence in Britain. Their first son, Ardeshir or 'Adi', was born in 1859 and she had been left to care for their child while he was away, which was no simple task. But there were other domestic troubles too for the newly married couple, as Gulbai was not and never would be of a similar persuasion with Dadabhai, either in public matters or in terms of their respective thinking patterns. She never properly learnt to read and write, nor did she seem to want to try and improve herself academically. Dadabhai did go out and about with her, but the couple were obviously very different and Gulbai was never comfortable in public settings. They had a second child in 1861, a daughter whom they named Shirin.

It was Dadabhai's mother who now regretted the early marriage arrangement and this view was clearly transmitted as the two women lived in the same house as an extended family. Manekbhai was trying to make another match for Dadabhai, on top of his still fairly new marriage and presumably wanted someone quite different this time. Zoroastrianism does not approve of bigamy, but some Parsees had entered into it, since their arrival on the shores of India. The Parsee Panchayat had allowed it, which being the recognized ruling body in the earlier years, had meant the practice began to creep in as an acceptable custom. Dadabhai and others had campaigned for the Parsee Matrimonial Law to be bought in so as to outlaw bigamy in the community as well as seeking to allow widows to remarry. This religious and legal reform was passed in 1865 and was a current issue at the time of Dadabhai's domestic upheavals.

The consequence was to put Dadabhai in conflict with his mother. Domestic civil war could be seen to be setting in and the wear on both sides was obvious, given the strength of the mother-son relationship in the early years. Gulbai in a sense had no say in the matter as the mother-in-law and other senior members of the family would be making the arrangements for another choice of wife. This wife would be emphasizing to Gulbai how she had failed her husband. The husband himself being so far away was neither a support to Gulbai nor a counter balance to his mother's views.

At that time the residence facing Dadabhai's home in Britain was inhabited by a Dr Archer who had three daughters. It was not long before the rumours crossed back to India that Dadabhai was to convert to Christianity and so marry an Englishwoman. Dadabhai became extremely concerned when he got some inkling of these rumours and dropped everything. He booked a passage back to India and arrived on

9th September 1863. He arrived at the family home at night and awoke the major-domo, who thought the man at the door was an imposter. Manekbhai and Gulbai were both living under the same roof and were asleep at the time. Eventually the entire household had to be aroused and when Dadabhai was finally recognized for himself, he was allowed in to greet them. The outcome of the visit was a proper resolution of the whole matter for husband and wife, mother and son and mother-in-law and daughter-in-law. In time the issue of another wife was dropped and the reason for so much discord could be put behind by the members of the family. Politics never seemed so poignant and dramatic.

Dadabhai stayed in India for some time after his hurried visit and consequently was to become involved in another incident, this time regarding himself, two friends, a donkey, a British Captain and a horse.

Dadabhai and his friends were walking one evening, one of them being seated on the donkey. It was normal at the time for travellers to request those in front of them to clear a way, and this was done by saying 'poice.' The Captain on a horse, when asked for 'poice', took umbrage, turned around and struck the donkey on the head. The donkey bolted and the officer then entered the gateway of a nearby bungalow. No one was badly hurt, but to incite matters more the Captain gave vent to a tirade against the three men and only stopped when he obtained one of their names. He refused to give his own, though they did learn that he was the commandant of the military post of Parandhar.

One of the men was a Ardeseer Cama, and he returned home and wrote to the Commandant whose name was Captain Morgan, to seek an apology. Nothing happened and the correspondence became acrimonious and the three men were then expelled from the cantonment. Mr Cama then filed a suit for damages. The case went before a sessions judge who decided against their complaint and approved that the costs be met by the three men. Mr Cama then appealed to the High Court, where he was awarded nominal damages and received positive feedback on his conduct from the bench. Who says the law is an ass?

Dadabhai used this time in India to challenge and begin the dismemberment of another social norm that was separating the sexes. At this time it was not considered the right thing for ladies to dine with the men. A Society of Parsees set themselves up to bring in mixed dining, under the leadership of a social reformer named Manockji Cursetji and Dadabhai. The Orthodox faction decried it, but Dadabhai's experiences in London were one factor for the groups persistence at promoting new habits. The new Society had in fact made an oath not to eat without ladies at the same table, which was not a lightly taken action. Eventually everyone got their just desserts, as the practice of separating the men and women became less prevalent.

42

The society was based at the home of Manockj Cursetji who lived at Villa Byculla in Pavel Road, Bombay. Apart from tackling the customs around eating arrangements the group was also teaching English to Indian girls, in conjunction with the women students of the Literary and Scientific Society's schools in Bombay.

As the Governor of Bombay was present for the prize giving held by the schools in 1863, it seems possible to assume that progress was being made and that the establishment of the new ideas were taking root, which was a compliment for the reformers of a decade before.

CHAPTER THREE

MAKING NEW ASSOCIATIONS

The next major move for Dadabhai was to come back to Britain with his family, his wife, son Ardeshir or Adi and their daughter Shirin, and his mother. The household established themselves in a rented house at 'Parsee Lodge' in Hornsey, North London. Dadabhai's business had maintained its momentum and because the American Civil War had stopped cotton being supplied from America to Lancashire, a boom time for India's suppliers had opened up. The family also became more acquainted with British society and Adi went to a primary school, acquiring a more western education than was the norm. An insight into the family's life is given at this time in the memoirs of a Miss Cursetji who was the daughter of Manockji Cursetji and a live-in companion accompanying the family in Britain. She wrote, "It was a sight at once charming and delightful to see him when off work, unbend himself, squatted on the drawing room carpet, playing with his little boy and girl. His conversation was always interesting, informative and instructive, decked out with anecdotes and stories, and flashes of friendly fun and ready wit. His voice had a singular charm."

Dadabhai's business was able to grow and prosper with this expansion, but others who were more heavily involved in speculation to make an even bigger buck, were to end up going bust. Dadabhai was sometimes left with their debts unpaid, but he also stood in good stead for one or two friends who had been silly and had almost been made insolvent. By standing in one friend's stead, Dadabhai paid off all his debts and almost bankrupted himself. Another friend called Karsandas Madharji asked him to honour his debts of almost £60,000 (nearer £1.5 million by 1990s values), which he then had to do, and that cost him the proverbial arm and a leg.

Dadabhai's attitude is either magnificent benevolence or naivety, but perhaps the former, because he placed all his accounts before the English creditors when he faced bankruptcy because of his efforts for his friends. The creditors were so impressed by his integrity that they released him from his liabilities and then engaged him to handle his own liquidation proceedings, and then they and Indian friends offered fresh loans to set up his own business again. One writer for the 'Investors Review' of 1917 (17th July) wrote, "Many years after, when his character and attitude happened to come up in the Bank of England's discount office, its Chief, while as a Conservative pooh-poohing and sneering at Mr Naoroji's utterances, told us he knew him to be a man of strict integrity in business and as proof added, 'he met all his engagements in 1866, a thing comparatively few in the East were able to do'." Good thoughts, good words and good deeds are meaningful when given a good recommendation. Another story relates that the Governor of the Bank of England at the time called on Dadabhai at his office. The visit was not made because of his scrupulous behaviour but because he had fought the refusal of some banks to accept the bonafides of Cama and co. He had eventually won his argument and the Governor had been impressed by his "spirited resistance and the justness of his contention".

However, in terms of the priorities in his life, Dadabhai found the firm was taking up too much time and his bailing out of friends in debt created incredible problems for Dadabhai which led to pressures on him and at home. These can be guessed at by the entries in Miss Cursetji's diary. On June 26th 1866 she wrote, "Poor Dadabhai has truly a deal of patience and his troubles he bears marvellously. I learnt from Papa that his affairs will have to be wound up in a day or two, this will be done more through the misconduct of his creditors, many of whom have behaved shabbily, very shamefully towards him, but I feel sure God will reward him for his righteousness."

By Friday 29th June, it was all over and she wrote, "None could think from the unshaken calmness and patience that reigned on Dadabhai's face as well as action, that his affairs were in such a dreadfully painful condition. As usual he took his breakfast - but poor Dadabhai's mother was sad and kept crying for the whole day and speaking in more harsh terms to poor Mrs Dadabhai. All this was very painful." Dadabhai's business life was not to end that year, and he was back again in the commercial field shortly after this event.

Dadabhai was now able to allow time for those other pursuits. Gulbai, Manekbhai and the children stayed for a year before they returned to India, where Gulbai had a second daughter on 10th October 1868. She was named Manekbai or 'Maki,'

Dadabhai's main area of work was to seek reform and for many years this would involve looking at and analysing the economic and political well being of India, to enable him to present rational arguments for his reforms. Because he knew many of the British officials in India were likely to express contempt for the ideas of the natives and to have an arrogant assurance of their own position, he entrusted the arguments he developed to the British public in their home country. It should be stressed that his efforts in India were not always badly treated, and some residents gave enormous support for his ideals or formulated their own proposals for reform whether based in India or back in the British Isles. It was just that whenever he propounded an idea then his main detractors were invariably based in the Anglo-Indian community, and that led both Dadabhai and other leading campaigners to the view that they would never get a proper hearing or see reforms from that quarter.

It seems very likely that Dadabhai's ideas on reform must have owed a lot to three men, and two of them were Anglo-Indian. The first one was John Dickinson (1815-1876), who was the son of a wealthy paper manufacturer. His uncle was a retired officer of the Bombay Engineers and held shares in the East India Company. He was therefore a member of the Court of Proprietors and John Dickinson also had another connection with India through a cousin who was a barrister in Bombay. Through them he learned of and became involved in Indian affairs. Dickinson soon joined a group who were able to prevent the annexation of the Rajput state of Kerowlee. He also published a book 'The government of India under a bureaucracy' which spoke up for allowing succession in Hindu states to be carried through by adoption. He warned against any further British annexations and also said that the discontent that arose from such measures may breed a conspiracy, "of which ..... we have not even a suspicion until the Native regiments open their fire on our barracks."

Such a thing happened only five years later in 1857.

He was also a founder of the Indian Reform Society set up on 13th March 1853 which was made up of members of a group who called themselves the "friends of India". There is a strong likelihood that the Bombay Association's petition of the year before on admission of Indians to the Indian Civil Service was a significant factor behind the Indian Reform Society being established. Dickinson was its Secretary from 1856 to 1861. Dadabhai must have met him after 1866, but as the London India Reform Society and the Bombay Association were in regular contact with each other it may be that they also met during his first stays in Britain. Dickinson published a pamphlet on "The famine in the North-West Provinces of India", where he argues for more British investment in the area. Dadabhai began working on such economic problems from around this time, and worked exclusively on them from 1867. Dickinson also advocated greater employment of the Natives in the Indian Civil Service, and believed that the proper end was to enable them to develop their skills and experience for self rule. He felt around five percent of higher offices could be transferred from Europeans to Indians each year, for twenty years.

46

In this area Dadabhai was probably more directly influenced by Major Evans Bell, the second Anglo-Indian who pressed for reforms. Bell had written about the need for simultaneous examinations in his book, "The Empire in India, 1864", written in that year. Dadabhai first mentions the idea in 1867 in a paper entitled 'England's duties to India'. Evans Bell (1825-1887) had come to India in 1841 in the East India Company's military service. After an interrupted career, because of his support for Indians, he retired in 1863 and wrote a number of books including 'The Mysore Reversion' in 1865 and 'Retrospect and Prospect of Indian Policy: The Great Parliament Bore' in 1869. In the latter book he wrote, "I do not think that any Indian question can be viewed in a true light unless the Hindus and Mahomedans of India are regarded as British subjects, with all the rights, immunities, and privileges of the European fellows at home and abroad." He also wrote in support of the Native states keeping their autonomy and his own time in Mysore was an example of how this could be done to the benefit of both sides.

The third man to influence Dadabhai was John Bright MP (1811-1889). He had made speeches in India on the renewing of the East India Company's Charter in 1853 and Dadabhai must have heard him at one of those talks. In a speech on 3rd June he criticized the policy which left Indians without the wherewithal to build up an infrastructure in their country. His speech also contained a passage Dadabhai was fond of quoting, when he said, "It is my belief, that if a country is found possessing a most fertile soil, and capable of bearing every variety of productivity and that, notwithstanding, the people are in a state of extreme destitution and suffering, the chances are that there is some fundamental error in the government of that country." In another speech of June 24th 1858 in the House of Commons on the Bill for the transfer of the government of India from the Company to the Crown, Bright pointed out that, "the population of India are in a condition of great impoverishment, of great dejection, of great suffering" and that "The taxes of India are more onerous and oppressive than the taxes of any other country in the world." Bright was Chairman of the India Reform Society from 1856-1861 and brought many of its views to Parliament's attention and built up a core of interested MPs, just as Dadabhai was to do thirty plus years later.

These three men had quite different backgrounds, but the similarity in their basic arguments on the impoverishment of India had a combined effect on Dadabhai which, along with exams for the Indian Civil Service and to a limited degree, the independence of Native States, were the major issues in Dadabhai's long campaigning life. They also viewed official impedances as the main reason to these issues being unresolved, as did Dadabhai when he appeared before the Welby Commission a third of a century later, and said, "the way of the Indian Authorities is first to ignore any Act or resolution of Parliament or report of any Committee or Commission in favour of Indian interests. If that is not enough then to delay replies. If that does not answer, then openly resist; and by their persistence carry their own point, unless a strong Secretary of State prevents it". He had found that even with regard to the terms of reference used for that Commission, the original proposal passed in Parliament was considerably altered by the members of the Commission, to give a much more restrictive field of investigation. He also went on to say that the Secretaries of State changed too often and they often listened to the Anglo-Indian community alone. He continued by saying that whereas "the principles of 1833 were 'Be just and fear not', the principles of the present statesmen appear to be 'fear and be unjust.' Let India know which of the two is her fate."

Lord Lytton took the path of delaying and frustrating the efforts of the Indians and listened far more to the Anglo-Indian community. On the other hand a strong Viceroy, in the person of Lord Curzon, who headed the Indian administration at the turn of the century, ruled with a forcefulness that represented the other extreme of British rule. So much so that for Dadabhai the views that he had expressed a few years earlier to the Welby Commission that no Indian representation and heavy handed rule would lead to rebellion, seemed to hold a lot of truth in them, and left no room for hoping in fair treatment by the British authorities.

He expressed his own negative feeling for fair rule ever coming in when in 1906, he was asked if he still had a hope in just British rule, and replied, " .... and now owing to the non fulfilment of solemn pledges, what a change has taken place in the mind of the educated. Since my early efforts I must say that I have felt so many disappointments as would be sufficient to break my heart, and lead me to despair and even, I am afraid, to rebel. My disappointments have not been of an ordinary kind, but for worse and keener I fought and won on several occasions, but the Executive did not let us have the fruit of those victories." He therefore continued to see the Anglo-Indian administration as the main bulwark to reform, as well as still believing in the British desire for fair rule. He also went on in that year to keep on asking Indians to hold out for change from the British themselves, in the belief that fair play would count at the end of the day.

Dadabhai's basic view of the positive side of British society meant he first decided he had to educate them to the real conditions in India as a preliminary to awakening their call for reform. The establishment of the London Indian Society in 1865 with members of both countries, was one building block he jointly established with Womesh Chandra

Bonnerjee to further those aims. As its first meeting on 24th March 1865 in University Hall, Gordon Square in London, it was unanimously decided that the Society needed to be led by the Indians with Bonnerjee as Secretary and Dadabhai as President. This may have caused a problem as over the years a good number of the British public who were behind the call for change, had joined societies like the London Society but would find their role there liable to being marginalized.

Although not confirmable a broader based Association was formed on 1st October 1866 to perhaps allow more general participation. The membership of what was called the East India Association was up to 594 in 1868, of whom 324 were Indians, many of whom did not live in Britain. But Dadabhai, along with other founder members of the East India Association, had seen the need for a more campaigning type of organization to being Indians' needs to the attention of the British public. This was more likely to have been the main reason for forming the East India Association over the London Indian Society. As Dadabhai put it in May 1867, the Association had to make political issues its testing and training ground, 'for that great end, a Parliament of Parliaments in India.' It began by publishing a quarterly journal from its base at 55 Parliament street in London.

In 1872 the London Society was re-established with a primarily student membership. Dadabhai was its President until 1901 and it aimed "to bring into closer union the Indians residing in England, and to furnish an opportunity for the interchange of thought and feeling on all matters concerned with India." Hence in a different form, this society carried on an active programme for around fifty years, though with Dadabhai at the helm it became more like the Association, as well as maintaining a strong support role for the students.

The East India Associations's first move at the time was not one of education, but of counter attack. The President of the Ethnological Society of London was a Mr John Crawford in 1866. In a paper he presented in February that year he said that the European races were superior to the Asiatic races, both morally and intellectually. He was not alone in this supposition of racial superiority, which was being propounded by groups across most of Europe, with a lot of scientific backing being given to support their claims. Dadabhai was probably already aware of these theories through his membership of the Ethnological and of the Anthropological societies. His reply in March sought to disprove and then quash the theory and the supposed moral superiority that flowed from it, that any white person was a better human being than one of another race. His rejoinder covered the academic attainments of Indian students at 18 compared to that of British students, who were better taught. Dadabhai brought out how the education systems were the cause of the difference and went on to look at the literary accomplishments of Asians, their progress in the fields of astronomy, medicine and metaphysics and in other subjects. He then looked at the "immoral haunts in London" to point out that there is enough in any nation that can be used to besmirch its character. At the end of the day it was not really the thinking of his contemporaries that Dadabhai had to address but their pride and he did that by drawing out the hypocrisy of their theories. This was one example of the numerous times Dadabhai had to defend character rather than debate issues, and shows how opponents would seek to use untrue assertions of lower capability to win their arguments. The London Indian Society was not broad based enough to respond to slurs of this nature, but Dadabhai was able to respond with the help of the members of the East India Association and this included Lord Lyvedon as its first President. Many British statesmen, ex-governors and ex-officials were also willing to help in publicly countering the assertions of John Crawford and joined forces with the Association.

The Association recognized that just countering such blasts of bigotry was not the best way to continue, if it was to look to the longer term welfare of India. Sir Erskine Perry had sent Dadabhai information at around that time, about the India Office's suggestion for a joint exam for the Indian Civil Service in both India and London. One of the Society's members, Sir Herbert Edwards, suggested as a parallel proposal that scholarships be set up to allow Indian students to come to England to sit the exams. As the proposals were not viewed as more then tentative suggestions, which could easily flounder, another member of the Association, Sir Stafford Northcote, wanted to try and support both sets of proposed actions. Dadabhai was able to communicate with Henry Fawcett MP to formulate an appropriate motion which would have a chance in the House of Commons. Unfortunately it was not put to the House and was eventually withdrawn. Nevertheless the first moves were now being made, by both Dadabhai and Britons, to secure reform in the rules used by the Administration in India.

As the founder member, Dadabhai had set the tone for the Association with a paper entitled "England's duties to India." He now wanted to encourage a similar type of body in India and travelled to India for a lecture tour in 1868. He concentrated on the cities of Bombay, Calcutta and Madras, where new associations were formed. In a paper published in 1868 Dadabhai pointed out the need for such associations arising because, "a large proportion of Indians are not as yet sufficiently well prepared to understand and discuss political matters ... this states of affairs creates the first duty of the Local Indian Associations, viz. That of educating the people in their political duties and rights .... next to educating the people in the duties of the Local Associations is to watch and discuss every measure that is brought before the Local Legislative Councils and Governor General's Legislative Council .... The third duty is with regard to their relation with the Association and Authorities (in Britain)."

Having Indian branches meant that Indians could become actively involved in the reform movement and also enabled information to be passed first hand back to the British branch. Members of the old and largely defunct Bombay Association became part of the Bombay branch of the East Indian Association largely due to Dadabhai's influence. He also wanted a change in the make-up of the membership, as he put it, "We have hitherto been in the habit of depending and throwing the whole burden upon the rich. The rich of Bombay have at times done their part nobly, as we all know. Let us, the middle Class, do our share also - let us bear our share of the burden." Hence gradually the make-up of the Associations Dadabhai helped set up, became more reforming in their nature, although the Shetias continued to play a part. This move from the merchant princes to the newer educated reformers was happening in other places too.

The Bombay Association did carry on for a number of years into the mid 1870s, under the leading Shetias. They set up the ancillary Ratepayers Committee in 1870 and their main target soon became the reform of the Municipality. Although a franchise reform of 1872 gave a few more votes to non-Shetia members, the real campaigning effort of the Association dropped off quite quickly. By the mid 1870s it had become the Shetia's instrument for maintaining an influence on matters of commercial as well as municipal concern and it was evident that they wanted it that way. One of their number, the second Sir Jamsetjee Jejeebhoy, wrote to Lord Northbrook in 1876 that he, ".... had no sympathy with men like Naoroji Furdunji and Dadabhai Naoroji, whom I look upon as mere political agitators, who pretend to have at the heart the interest of their countrymen, but whose aims and purposes are purely selfish ...." Yet despite these obvious differences all sides met and continued to work together within the Associations and in particular over certain issues, they would speak as one. By 1888 the Reform Act brought many more members of the Association into the voting and political arena and also brought them together to act in a unified way to achieve this end.

CHAPTER FOUR

TRYING TO FIGURE IT OUT

Shortly after this Dadabhai re-embarked for Britain, where he could begin to delve further into issues such as the transport system of India, the adulteration of cotton and India's finances. Many members of the Association gave proofs of the impoverishment of India by the Imperial government. The Association had started to undertake a serious reckoning of both the finances and famines in India, following up on a lengthy dissertation Dadabhai had left with the members in 1866 prior to his departure back to India. The Association challenged the wisdom of the government on spending £100 million on railways from the 1840s onwards, when there were no plans for large scale irrigation in a country facing widespread famines.

To be fair, the Administration had used that large sum of money to a beneficial effect as it laid down a complete rail system from 1853-1900. That system could then have been used to speed commerce along its way, but in reality its effect for the average Indian was negligible. It did not help him develop his country because he was not given the wherewithal to produce the goods in the first place. Regarding the irrigation projects both sides could argue their case, as a lot was done and a yet a lot was also left undone. A seperate but related issue was the point that although capital works could bring benefit, no Indian was ever properly consulted on how they would affect their lives. In particular as these were large scale capital projects, a lot of borrowing had to be countenanced and most of that debt was charged against India. In effect the British signed the contracts for the Indians to pay the builders and those builders were always British not Indian. The work was beneficial but the cost of the loan repayments was crippling.

Dadabhai's views on the benefits of capital projects changed over the years from support in the early years to a questioning and more negative attitude in his later years. In 1880 Dadabhai wrote from 32 Great St Helens in London that "to every other country English capitalists lend and there is an end of their connection with the matter. The people of the country use and enjoy the benefits of the Capital in every way and pay to the capitalists their interest or dividend .... But with India the case is different. English capitalists do not merely lend, but with their capital, they themselves invade the country. The people themselves of the country do not derive the same benefit."

Dadabhai got the Association to complain about the methods used for raising the financial backing needed for the building of such projects. The projects were often administered by people who approached the awarding of the contracts from the angle of finding anyone who can give a loan, no matter what terms were written into the contract. They rarely sought out those enterprises who could give concessions. Nor did they make the awarding of contracts more competitive. Even if they had got tenders from various enterprises it would not have helped as those who won the contracts and those who invested their money got guaranteed payments if extra costs were incurred on materials and salaries or on interest on their loan stock. By giving companies a guarantee, the government in effect said that all the losses arising from waste or over runs on the contract always fell upon the State, while the profit went mainly to the companies engaged to do the work and hence out of the country and back to Britain.

This very uncompetitive system of awarding contracts impoverished India to a large degree, as the State taxed the Indians to fund the payment of the loans. Then rather then penalize the contractor when problems arose they raised further taxes to pay for their losses and any extra interest payments.

At the same time, the Association was seeking reform in other fields and Henry Fawcett MP, who was dubbed 'the Member for India', began what became an annual resolution in the House of Commons for 'simultaneous examinations' for the Indian Civil Service. Henry Fawcett continued to support Indian's needs throughout his long parliamentary career, which began in 1865 and carried through for many years even though he had to overcome the loss of his sight a few years previously in 1858.

The Association began to give members regular information for them to use and a library was set up to meet this end. Dadabhai was a mainstay in researching the information required, working in all the areas that could be of concern, as well as answering letters for the Association and still making sure that all the letters he personally received got a written reply from him. He combined the research for the Association with his own which he was using as background material for published articles, or when giving speeches or undertaking more in-depth types of study. He also returned to India for a while to tour Kathiawar and Rajputana to raise fresh funds for the Association in 1871 and again in 1875.

It was the growing poverty of India that was becoming the real challenge for the Association and other contemporary reformers. As time went on it had become clearer to the Association that it had to concentrate its efforts in Britain because the greatest hope for changing the poverty in India was seen to lie with the actions and policies executed by the British Government. But it was the British Government who often set up the rules that took away more than was given. The Association produced four papers on economic policy between 16th June and 28th July 1870. There was "Indian Finance" by I T Pritchard, "Public Works in India" by Sir Bartle Frere, "Wants and means of India" by Dadabhai and the "Finance of India" by Sir Charles Trevelyan. Sir Trevelyan chaired the meeting of the 27th July when Dadabhai outlined four basic 'wants'. These were sufficient food, clothing and shelter, then sufficient 'to provide for all social wants', followed by sufficient saving by each individual to meet any unforeseen calamity' and lastly 'means of improvements of public works' and 'means to pay for the high price of foreign rule.' He pointed out that if Britain would guarantee the national debt of India then the interest payments that British capitalists wanted to set to make sure they received good returns would also be guaranteed. The Indian would not always have to pay more taxes to meet some hefty interest payment if the person making the loan knew that the British Government undertook to guarantee he would get his money and interest back. Dadabhai felt that investors and government should see loans as a means to building India up, not as a method of making a quick fortune. He expressed this as "what the anxiety of the Finance Minister or any (Anglo) Indian Statesman should be, is not so much to discover new sources or revenue as new sources of production or prosperity .... Blood cannot be got out of a stone. When prosperity is fairly served, revenue will take care of itself."

Of course these papers did not establish the facts straight away and Dadabhai had really just begun to set up his 'Drain theory', while conducting his researches in the early 1870s. The 'Drain theory' and Dadabhai's work on the impoverishment of India, place him as the leading proponent of the criticism made of the financial culling of India and his work was still being reviewed and utilized ninety years later. He was a self taught economist and analyst and had no one school or thought behind his methods, which gave his ideas some ingenuity without losing their clarity. His work on this subject was regarded as the authoritative source of the time.

What was known was that India bore the costliest administration in the world and yet it was not a rich country. No one kept comprehensive accounts of incomes and expenditure, the closest being the figures kept in the governments's 'Blue Books' which were compiled yearly. There was also one journal in existence, the "Indian Economist", which tried to keep information on a few sectors of the economy. Even the Chancellor of India had two sets of accounts, one for the local government and one for the government back in the United Kingdom, but could not tell which were the real figures overall! No other material existed, and for most of the proceeding years the budgets of the entire country seemed to have been kept by a company who had a profit motive. In 1868 or soon after, Lord Mayo (the Viceroy), had himself expressed his dismay at not knowing the state of the deficit borne by India.

Because little information was available, Dadabhai began to build up a picture of the Indian economy. This may sound a daunting task for one man, who in effect had to both audit the accounts of a country and also produce some new ones from raw figures, because no accounts were being kept properly.

He worked out that from 1835 to 1882 India had imported goods valued at £943 million and had made £1.5 billion on exports. Seemingly a healthy trade balance. But then Dadabhai went on to research the interest (called an 'export'), that had to be paid on the debt enforced on India through loans it had to take out and work out the extra cost of the interest payments. He also pointed out that money earned in India also went out of the country through European pay packets. Lastly India had to make hefty payments to the British, whether for the Administration or for any military campaign. India was actually making payments which Britain should have met, which was a further burden that it had to bear and left it in perpetual debt.

In one way his efforts were rewarded early on, as the administration had to start researching its own figures and keep better accounts so that it could answer the questions and challenges of Dadabhai. They also came to dislike Dadabhai's attempts and, as late as 1881, refused Dadabhai access to a note prepared by Sir David Barbour, upon which the Finance Minister (Lord Cromer) based a statement on the poverty of the people.

Dadabhai began by looking at the produce of the country, its capital, layout and industry. He came to a conclusion in his paper of 1878, called "Wants and Means of India" that the yearly income of the people averaged out at 40 shillings or 20 rupees and yet they needed 34 rupees a year to be able to live. In this task he was especially helped by two members of the Association, Naoroji Furdunji and Sir Charles Trevelyan, who was a past Finance Minister in India. Dadabhai became more angered over the years at the way the country was bled and his phrases moved from "Material and moral drain" to "Deprivation of resources" to the "Bleeding drain" when writing on the subject.

The last phrase was meant literally and in fact in all his writings and speeches Dadabhai was never seen to use profane language no matter how worn down he was made to feel. He had this resolve from childhood when hearing his classmates swear, he would say to them that their improper language "would return unto them." He had cause enough to use such language, when he saw in later years the connection between the economic drain and the famines and disease that caused so much death.

Some examples of the poor financial administration came to light. As has been said public works were commenced without any real regard for possible bankruptcies or overruns. Presumably it was expected that if a project was in danger of going bust, then extra revenues could be raised from the population by their masters, to enable the project to continue. Military expenditure accounted for a third of the gross revenue, and was more then Britain spent on the rest of the world. One man based at the Admiralty, named Colonel Irvine, was greatly distressed by the excesses that went unchallenged. He died after using his best efforts to get financial controls introduced. If an insider could not get any reform in the system, the question was, who could?

Dadabhai conceived of the 'Drain Theory' as an external drain built into the internal economy with a bias whereby the ruling power was always able to extort resources out of a colonial economy. If any surplus existed it was drawn out by the process of the profit on exports almost always going to the colonial rulers, who would say they were taking the profit from the 'external trade' earned by India as being something owed to them. Hence India was never to receive the full share of her export earnings, because in effect she did not own herself.

Dadabhai pointed out that as India was a colonial economy, it was almost run by a remote control from Britain. It did not attract capital or labour as did other white colonies. It had an expensive administration and military to support, and was a strategic centre for the burden of Empire building. All these functions were for the Empire first and then India. Hence the principal income earners were either transitory or did not spend their money within the country to a large extent (most of the administration's well paid staff were white), and so little private expenditure was coming the way of India's home traders. He estimated that India lost around £30-40 million annually at that time through all sources of wealth and tried to draw the links between such trade imbalances and poverty, hunger and misery.

For resolutions to the problem Dadabhai pointed out first that the population's size and growth rate did not destroy a real chance for economic growth which was the point made by some analysts, but to quote John Stuart Mill, "industry is limited by capital." He was saying that the British government had not created the laws and methods for capital formulation in India and had certainly not spread the capital out fairly. Without capital investment there was no stimulus for economic development and so no ability to improve the situation. Conversely proper capital investment in India would change the scenario, if only the government would pass the necessary laws or promote such practices. To quote, "If English capital is encouraged, in a reasonable manner, to open up new sources of production, what great benefit may be the consequences to England and India."

The Association asked for a select committee of both Houses to enquire into the problem. It was set up shortly afterwards in 1873 by the Liberal government and included Henry Fawcett MP. It was an opportunity for members of the government to listen to Dadabhai's meticulous figure-work but the Committee was unfortunately dissolved in 1874. This was because the Liberals were defeated on the issue of higher education in Ireland and so that government went back to the polls in 1874, and lost to the Conservatives. The effect of their premature dissolving of the Select Committee was that no conclusions could be published on what many MPs considered to be a defunct issue of minor consideration. This attitude was partly corroborated by Dadabhai at a meeting held in 1885 on a proposal to set up a memorial to Henry Fawcett. Dadabhai explained to his audience that both he and Naoroji Furdunji had made presentations to the Committee. In his case he had written beforehand to Professor Fawcett to outline the content of his material and Mr Ayrton, the Chairman, had not liked that move. He had made his presentation difficult and called it unconnected to the Committee's business. Henry Fawcett had given the right kind of questions on the second day of the presentation, but it was not enough to change most peoples minds. Dadabhai had stated by then that out of a revenue of £50m, around £12m were taken out of India for England alone, and that Indian's useful capital was drastically reduced.

Lord Mayo was to introduce certain changes in India at that time which did have an alleviating effect on the financial drain. In general terms his main aim was to split the Administration in India onto a more provincial basis. But although they had a beneficial effect on the financial drain as a consequence, that was not one of the principal reasons behind the changes. What was needed was a purely financial solution and that was not being sought at that time. The Association continued to try and get its aims addressed in Parliament and was ever available to prompt and advise Members of Parliament. Hence Mr Chamberlain, John Bright, the Earl of Derby and General Jacob were amongst those who presented Parliament with the views of the Association. Sir David Wedderburn, who was the elder brother of William Wedderburn, is recorded as having advocated "representation of India in the House of Commons" in an address made on 15th March 1877.

CHAPTER FIVE

A BRIBE, A BRIBE, MY KINGDOM FOR A BRIBE

At this juncture, a request came to Dadabhai which was to cause him to follow a different path for a while and give him much trouble while it lasted. Mulharrao Gaekwar had inherited a corrupt state on 25th November 1870.[1] The new ruler was allowed to establish himself without any interference from the British resident or the Bombay government who felt it was best to leave him to conduct his affairs. This was done despite the fact that the problems of that Native state had been a cause for concern for several years and warranted a close watch being kept on its internal affairs.

The arms length approach was maintained between both sides until a particular matter of protocol came to a head when a ceremonial Durbar was arranged, and a disagreement arose which then led to the other issues being dragged out into the open. For the 1871 Durbar the Governor of Bombay Sir Seymour Fitzgerald had accepted an invitation to attend and to being seated to the left of the Maharaja, which was not normal protocol. Before the 1872 Durbar he made it clear that he wanted to be seated on his right. The Indian Prince refused to accept the condition and the Governor refused, quite literally, to budge from his choice of seat.[2] Then an invitation came in November 1872 for the Maharaja to attend the Viceroy's Durbar in Bombay. He did not want to receive any possible reprisal because of his own stance and so did not reply. His courtiers or Durbaris felt this would be taken as an insult and advised him to go. At this time Dadabhai was in the State raising

1. Geakwar is the surname or title of the Maharaja of Baroda. It was once a caste name and means 'cowhead' or 'cowgate', i.e. protector of the sacred animal. It was taken to be the family name by the British. Baroda was a moderately sized state of 8226 square miles and two million people. Its relationship to the British Crown was detailed in a treaty and is could enjoy a fair degree of flexibility in the handling of its affairs. A British resident was required to sit in the Maharaja's Court. The towns where Dadabhai's forbears lived and the town of Navsari were situated in Baroda state. The Maharaja was one of only five rulers accorded a twenty-one gun salute.

2. The Maharaja probably wished to sit on the Gadi, which was the cushion reserved for rulers. similar to a throne being the seat of Kings.

support for the East India Association and was asked to help resolve the impasse. He was invited to give an answer to the Maharaja, which he did do, but that was then turned down and so he left. He was then called back for a personal audience with the Maharaja. At that meeting Dadabhai proposed that the Maharaja accept the invitation, but then excuse himself because of the illness of his wife, the Maharanee who had just lost a baby son. Upon this being agreed the Maharaja gave his apologies and Dadabhai also advised him to send a conciliatory letter to the Viceroy and Secretary of State over the seating arrangements for the Governor. The Viceroy's reply was negative in tone and the Secretary of State did not receive the copy of the letter

The Maharaja was so pleased with the advice that he offered 50,000 rupees to Dadabhai. He refused, but the Maharaja pressed the matter further and ended up by suggesting a trust be set up for the children of Dadabhai, as he would not accept the money for himself. Unfortunately, gossip still pursued Dadabhai and on 6th August 1873, he had to make a public statement, to state that the money was used for his children and that he had not sought for payment when he had first been approached for his counsel. The issue of the seating arrangements was never resolved because back in Baroda, the scene was hotting-up for the Maharaja. A new Governor had come to Bombay and a new resident, one Colonel Phayre, had come to Baroda. The British did not like the growing evidence of misgovernment by him and his cronies, and he was now faced with pressure to act and clean up the affairs of his rule. By then a Commission of inquiry was waiting in the wings and there were moves to have the Dewan (Prime Minister) and his deputy suspended. If the Commission came in, the Maharaja would in effect lose his autonomy, his position and his income.

So when the Maharaja's next request came to Dadabhai, to take up the position of Dewan, he was torn between leaving that sinking ship to manage its own affairs and returning to help it. Because the Maharaja turned to Dadabhai in a very quick period of time his Durbaris felt they may be left out of events and so lose their privileges and status. They went to Colonel Phayre and told him that a man like Dadabhai would keep his own counsel and not consult with the resident as he should. Colonel Phayre overreacted and he said he would physically bar Dadabhai, if necessary. *The Times of India,* not a paper to hold views contrary to the establishment, when it heard of his comment went so far as to say he may have 'lost his head.' Against this two-pronged attack and the anticipated problems in the State, Dadabhai took time to consult with Sir Erskine Perry who in turn raised the matter with Sir Bartle Frere. Both felt that although it was a heavy task, in the long term it would prove a good choice because his aim was to bring in good government to the State. Dadabhai felt the same and accepted the fickle ruler's plea to help despite knowing of the obvious pitfalls in advance. The Maharaja informed the resident of his intention to bring in Dadabhai in December 1873. For ten months after that Colonel Phayre proved to be a hostile man to deal with and it was his report to Bombay that delayed the official appointment of Dadabhai. This delay meant that the Durbaris and others could try to remove Dadabhai as long as he was only there on a temporary appointment. Why Dadabhai stayed on is probably revealed in his comment to his close colleague when he said, "...we have not come to serve the man; we have come to serve the cause".

An insight into Dadabhai's daily life is handed down to us through the report of one of his lieutenants at this time. He woke early, had a brief bath and personal toilet in the morning, no breakfast and was at this duties until lunchtime. Lunch was a hasty affair of around 3 to 4 raw eggs and although there was no need to worry about salmonella in those days the risk of such a diet in such a hectic day would have given his opponents considerable joy. He then worked on until early evening and had a meal at supper time, before carrying on to complete his average of 16 hours per day. In 1873 he was 48, but this daily regime was to carry on into his 70s.

He had to work hard because apart from three trusted lieutenants, Homi A Wadia, Bal Mangesh and Kazi Shahabudin, he was surrounded by the intriguers and schemers at the Maharaja's court, and the Maharaja himself was no ally. Dadabhai knew he had to begin by acquainting himself with the situation at the court, as much to protect his own back as to deal with the present structures. He had Homi appointed as Chief Magistrate and Head of the Criminal and Police departments, Bal as Chief Justice and Kazi in charge of revenues.

The Commission of Inquiry had reported that a reputable person was needed at the helm. On top of this it had become clear that it was expected that ministers would have to be deposed by the Dewan but the Maharaja was not to be deposed of except on the special orders of the British government. It also said "the resident should for a time at least be vested with special authority to intervene, if necessary, between the Maharaja and the Minister". This was not a good move given how Colonel Phayre was trying to torpedo the official confirmation of the appointment of Dadabhai. The Commission had drawn out the catalogue of malpractices that the State and therefore by implication the Maharaja had pursued. On receiving the Commission's findings Dadabhai had proposed to reply by saying it was accepted that new ways were needed and that the past should be overlooked in order to get on with improving the future. The Resident was informed of this and said Dadabhai should also try to defend the Maharaja's reputation. Dadabhai refused which did not go down well with the Mulharrao.

At around this time another incident took place where Dadabhai had to go out on a limb. The wife of a sirdar had left home saying she had been badly treated by her husband. She was a Gaekwar and had gone to a house with some guards refusing all pleas to reconsider her decision which was partly based on her standing as a member of that family. Her husband said he would use force if necessary to take her back and Colonel Pharye had agreed. Dadabhai therefore took the Maharaja's seal in the middle of the night and sent a message to the woman to say that she would lose her inheritance if lives were to be lost over her choice. She immediately changed her stand and returned home. The Maharaja had been asleep and could not be awakened at the time, but was not pleased when he heard of Dadabhai's action.

However if blood had been shed, the British may have intervened, which would have shown a vote of no confidence had been made of the Maharaja. The difficult position for Dadabhai was that he had the Maharaja blowing hot and cold over him, and at times like these, listened to what his courtiers said against Dadabhai. More time had to be spent by Dadabhai at defending his name, than in running the Principality. Also the Maharaja was changing his mind again through the persuasions of his courtiers and was going to try and contest the Commission's findings. He then changed it back to Dadabhai's way, so as to keep him, and if only he realized it, keep his Principality for a few more months.

One of the main reforms that Dadabhai wanted to get brought in was the ending of the corruption that destroyed all justice and just about any fairness in the Court Administration. He perceived that the selling of justice and of Nazarana or 'favours', could be stopped if he could only get his methods in the ascendancy. Nazarana being the 'present' made to the Maharaja by anyone taking up a position in his State. The harder Dadabhai tried the more his enemies wanted to see him leave. However, when corrupt police officials began to be charged in Mr (latter Sir) Wadia's court, the practices began to decline. In a way the Maharaja was his own worst enemy. He vacillated over all decisions and would have in all likelihood brought back the old corrupt officials one day and dismiss Dadabhai at whim. He showed his duplicity, when despite knowing why Nazarana should be stopped, he stated that he wanted his share again, at which point Dadabhai again gave in his resignation. He had in any case begun to feel the strain of the appointment and his health had deteriorated.

The Maharaja then called on Dadabhai to forget his resignation and offered to talk about new conditions on all payments, including who authorized what and the removal of certain corrupt officials. In August the Maharaja was still considering these points when the Commission of Inquiry sent a letter to him from the Viceroy. He asked a trusted Dubaris to read the letter to him. It stated that he was allowed to retain his Principality provided he put the administration onto a sound basis by 1875 or else he would be deposed.

Dadabhai was next informed that he had in effect been confirmed in the post. Colonel Phayre heard the news soon afterwards and swore to several Durbaris with him 'Girainga, Girainga!' ('I will bring him down, I will bring him down!'). Dadabhai had become an obsession for him, and he obviously believed that Dadabhai was a personal as well as a political enemy.

On 23rd September 1874, the new Dewan was invested and despite his earlier pronouncement even the resident seemed to have changed his stance and accept the appointment. Behind the scenes though he apparently had been prompted to understand that the government strongly approved of the candidate and he chose to employ different tactics. The agenda for Dadabhai was clearly to clean up the principality within 17 months, by the removal of the old vested interests and to secure the permanent achievement of such a change.

On Dadabhai's appointment, there was a remission on a quarter of land assessment, which was a wholly appropriate concession for the overburdened peasantry. Nazarana was made illegal, as was 'veth' or forced labour and torture. The Durbaris began to get hostile and the resident who had not really changed his colours, once again seemed to menace the actions of the Dewan. Correspondence ensued culminating in a letter written by Dadabhai, through the Maharaja, to the Viceroy, Lord Northbrook and the government to ask for the removal of the Resident. By this time the government was ready to consider its Resident was too hostile to be its representative and took steps to remove him. The Secretary of State for India at that time was Lord Salisbury, and he vindicated Dadabhai's stance over and against that of the British Resident. Because the Governor of Bombay had not acted sooner and stopped his official's behaviour, a special Commissioner, Sir Lewis Pelly, was placed by the Government in Baroda, so that in effect Bombay's jurisdiction was suspended. The Maharaja felt it was he who had got rid of the Resident and was ebullient at this unprecedented action.

The Principality's finances were in no way a surprise, they reflected its general condition and hence were in a poor state. The remission on land assessment created a larger deficit and in addition claimants cases were being agreed and they were being compensated from the Principality's coffers. Dadabhai's suggestion that the Maharaja use his own money for the time being to help pay these off, was not accepted. Sir Lewis showed that he would not interfere nor allow petitioners to make their claims to him before they had gone to the Dewan, in order to establish where the authority lay.

Dadabhai produced a list of four courtiers who he wanted the Maharaja to remove. Some of them had been receiving payments going back many years. The Maharaja dilly-dallied, and was entranced by the nest of vipers in his court and would still listen to them as much as to Dadabhai. He agreed to three but not to the fourth one. The test of will was impossible and Dadabhai finally decided to resign no matter what new deal was promised by the ruler. He and his close staff did so, and Dadabhai them met Sir Lewis to give his reasons and to state he could stay on for a reasonable time, if a successor was to be appointed, to provide some continuity for that person. Shortly afterwards Sir Lewis told Dadabhai that the Maharaja had previously been suspected as the instigator behind a poisoning attempt on Colonel Phayre (who had blamed guess who?). The matter had always been a bit cloudy, and until then the Maharaja had not been implicated personally in the poisoning attempt which had taken place on the 9th November and had been done through a concoction of arsenic and diamond dust. Dadabhai and his colleagues therefore decided to depart sooner and leave the Maharaja to his own webs of entanglement.

The Maharaja was glad to see Dadabhai leave on 11th January 1875, but within the week he was pleading with Dadabhai to return. It turned out that his personal secretary who was the fourth courtier mentioned above, provided the damning evidence against the Maharaja concerning the poisoning attempt. Although not charged with the poisoning, the Maharaja was apprehended and held for notorious misconduct and gross mismanagement. Despite uproar in Britain over the consequences, the Maharaja was deposed by the Authorities. This was a clear departure from normal government policy, which was to allow the 'Native States' the right to at least appear independent, and in some cases to have control over many internal affairs. The corrupt Maharaja kept asking Dadabhai for his help throughout this time; but Dadabhai knew by now that he would always be treated to two faces from the Maharaja.

Another, not directly related member of the princely family, Sir Sayajirao Gaekwar, was initiated as the new Maharaja and proved to be a dynamic leader, taking the Principality into the 20th century. He reformed some of the Hindu ways of life and instituted social reform. Primary education became a compulsory right of all his people in the nineteenth century as he saw that they had to understand and accept his new ways if those were to prosper. He made sure untouchables could attend school, and brought in some measures to emancipate women, such as outlawing polygamy.

The strain on Dadabhai's personal health from this period took more than the normal recuperation period for recovery and the effects were to lead to a lowering of his general health, which may have stayed with him in later life. (For Dadabhai a government health warning, to the effect that 'this government can cause damage to your health' should have been attached to the appointment). Released from his duties, Dadabhai could recuperate and his strength slowly came back. He maintained a firm hold on his principles during this time as Dewan, and because of that was in a better position to see what needed to be done and even to recognize that in a way, success had been achieved. He had been contending with corruption, lying and deceit, vice, injustice and greed. Just by showing and maintaining a sense of duty, of justice and love for the truth, he was in the circumstances gaining a triumph. He had kept faith with the teachings of his faith, and it seems that those teachings had kept faith with him. As he said in a letter of 1887, "to lead a right life is in our power; with that we can meet all troubles and surmount and survive them." And in a letter of 1879 he related that "Prosperity has not elated me, and I hope adversity will not (depress) me, as long as I can feel that I am living a life of duty." Sir Lewis Pelly was to state that "Until purged by the administration of Mr Dadabhai Naoroji, the Criminal and Civil administration of the State of Baroda was notoriously venal and corrupt."

CHAPTER SIX

PRIVATE AND PUBLIC AFFAIRS

Due to his prolonged absences, his personal family life could have suffered, but it did not. That was partly because Dadabhai, although absent in body, was present in his letters and in spirit. Partly as well because the family life and traditions of the Naoroji family were kept through the presence of the uncle and other family members, as was the accepted norm for the community. Taking the role of Head of Household for someone else in a culture such as India's has provided a remarkable testament to the strength of continuity in family life, where extended family life gives a sense of honour to such arrangements. Honour to those undertaking the task, but also, perhaps in a more subconscious manner, honour for the dependants. For they can recognize and feel that they are not an afterthought, if someone of recognized seniority is over them and caring for them. Of course such arrangements are not the whole answer, but they do provide a basic strength that helps explain why Dadabhai's long absences did not lead to a gradual distancing between himself and his family. Their material well-being relied to a large extent on the gift that Mulharrao Gaekwar made to Dadabhai for his services in 1872.

In the Naoroji family's case, a lot of effort was still required to maintain the family throughout his absence. Primarily the responsibility for this task was to rest on his friend and former pupil's shoulder, Muncherji Merwanji Dadina (1832-1913), who though he had his own family and career as a teacher and then auditor to cater for, also took over the household duties and the more general parental concerns for the Naoroji children. He liaised with Gulbai over the tasks they should share, although Gulbai's influence was much more a background role. This was partly because her own personality was more of that ilk and partly because of the role that women played, even though she was probably better respected than many other women. Unfortunately the details of this time have not been kept but it is possible to derive an insight into the relationships of this large family from the records that exist.

It is possible to tell that strong ties were formed because the two families were connected by marriage when the children reached adulthood. Dadabhai's only son Ardeshir(Adi), had been engaged to Muncherji's daughter, Virbai (Vir), whilst they were in their teens. Later Dadabhai and Gulbai's eldest daughter Shirin was engaged to Muncherji's son Framroz, and the second daughter Manekbhai (Maki) to the other son Hormusji (Homi).

Adi and Muncherji had their differences. Adi was more easy going and of an independent, spirited nature, whereas Muncherji was a more orthodox Parsee and hence more conservative in his nature, but affectionate as well. Adi and Muncherji found little to agree upon, and in an exchange of letters with Dadabhai Adi had pressed for a rise in his allowance to Rs 7 against Muncherji's decision of Rs 3. Dadabhai took the view that Rs 5 was enough but then gave in and accepted Rs 7 over Muncherji's head. Shirin called him a 'chokhha marwadi' or 'a veritable Shylock' during this period. The disputes became a serious matter after Adi had first injured himself in the leg through an accident with a gun and then damaged some furniture in another firearm incident. Letters went back and forth between Muncherji, Dadabhai and Adi. The younger man was asked not to hurt the feelings of older members over their views of more orthodox rites. Presumably the incident with the guns was representative of their general disparity of opinions.

However, once this was cleared up Adi stated he wanted to marry before completing his final exams. He had been working for the Indian Medical Service, but a further accident, this time with a gun carriage had given him a bad left leg and arm and put paid to this goal, although he was still trying for a medical qualification. Muncherji's response was a flat no. He felt that Adi should get his exams over with and then marry and await Dadabhai's return to India in any case. Dadabhai proved to be rather an absent father at this time, because he wrote to Muncherji indicating that his presence in Britain would be required for some time and so he saw no reason to delay the marriage. Hence he heard of his son's marriage on the Diwali of 1880 some time after the event and in fact did not return until Adi had a daughter a year later and had also passed his exam. Adi obtained the Anderson scholarship for proficiency in surgery and surgical anatomy and he joined Bombay's Grant Medical College, so proving himself of good worth, and that in spite of his physical handicap. He and Virbai (or Vir) set up home in Cutch, three hundred miles North of Bombay, when he obtained a position as a Medical Officer.

Muncherji had another tough duel on his hands some years later, when his son Homi wanted to go to Britain before marrying, which was against his father's wishes. Dadabhai in his correspondence sided with the youngsters, despite Muncherji's misgivings that Homi could return with an English wife. Homi did not and went on to get his qualification in mechanical engineering. Maki used the time to qualify in medicine and got the LRCP and also the FSPG at Edinburgh in 1887 and then pass a further qualification (the LM) at Dublin.[1] She and Homi eventually married in 1897, when she was 29, despite Muncherji having again impressed on Dadabhai the need for further consideration and asking for his support through a mutual letter writing friend, Dinsha Wacha in a letter of 18th September 1897. All this must have left Muncherji with a feeling of where did I go right when so much of what he said was not followed; but matters turned out to be positive in any case. Dadabhai did not get Maki to follow his advice either at that time as he asked her to go into practice in Britain when she had qualified, but as Gulbai had asked her to be near her she returned to Bombay.

Dadabhai was not as distant a voice as he may seem to have been in these proceedings, as there was a weekly correspondence with all the concerned parties. Dadabhai began this when Adi went to the Grant Medical College in Bombay. Dadabhai wrote: "You know that I have only three ideas in my mind for the remainder of my life .... I mean my desire to pay my moral debts for the failure of 1866 .... The other two ideas or desires are, as you are well aware, my children's happiness and a remedy for India's poverty." When Adi's eight children (three sons named Jal, Kershap and Sarosh and five daughters named Meher, Gosi, Nargiz, Perin and Khorshed) had become older, Dadabhai was in correspondence with all of them too and he obviously longed for the weekly news from home to come in the post. In their letters to him they all called him "Dad". In some ways he was more involved with his children and grandchildren than are some present day fathers. But Muncherji's role was never an easy one and his dedication over all those years cannot be diminished. Gulbai's role is a silent testimony to

1. Maki therefore achieved a first amongst Asian women for studying in Britain. Other pioneers include Nolini Bonnerjee, the eldest daughter of W C Bonnerjee, who received her education at Croydon High School in 1887-1889, and then became the first Indian woman to study at Girton college, Cambridge, before gaining her degree in medicine in London. Her sister followed her soon afterwards and then practiced as a doctor in Liverpool and also undertook a lot of welfare work. She worked for the Indian famine fund and set up clinics and women's centres when she returned to India in 1922. Cornelia Sorabji, (described as a "Parsee Christian lady" as her father was the Reverend Sorabji Khursedji), was the first woman to enter the Deccan College in Poona. Despite the obvious dislike of her male counterparts at her being there, she gained scholarships in each year and finally gained a first class honours in the BA examination held at Bombay University in November 1887. She was a fellow and lecturer in English literature at a Gujurati University when she came to Somerville college, Oxford to study Law in 1889. She was appointed as legal advisor to the women kept in purdah by the Bengal administration in 1904, following a scheme she set up to allow legal advice to be made available to them, because of their isolation. There was a steady but never numerous succession of Indian women and men who studied in Britain up until independence, especially in the Higher education circles. It was undoubtedly true that the rarity of these students meant they were more accepted by their white counterparts.

herself as through will those years she remained with her family whilst her husband was away. Manekbhai (the grandmother) died in 1875, which was a great blow to Dadabhai and he had to bear it with fortitude. On the other hand, he could see his young and it appears quite spirited family, growing up and carrying on to do well both personally and within the security of the extended family. One grandchild, Kershap, Adi's second son, deserves mention, as he went to Christ College, Cambridge, then joined the Middlesex regiment as an ordinary soldier and saw action in 1915. He was promoted to Lance Corporal and then Sergeant and he was involved in several brave actions. In a charge he was wounded, but survived and was later given a temporary commission once Indians were allowed to hold one outside of the Indian regiments. Hence he may have been one of the first Indian Officers to command British troops in a time of war.

On his 50th birthday, Dadabhai was one of the first four Indians appointed by Sir George Clerk to be a member of the Bombay Town Council, which had been wholly British in its composition. He returned to the question of the finances of India at a local level, following the spend- thrift years of Arthur Crawford, a previous Commissioner who had been suspended. Dadabhai delved into one costly project in particular, the Vehar loan, which was commanding very high interest payments on a government loan. Dadabhai wanted to find out how it had happened and as a member of the Council, began to feed new information about the loan to his fellow members, thus forcing the officers who administered it to find their own figures to complete their counter arguments. Dadabhai's arguments went into more details than was expected and he impressed his fellow Councillors on the scale of the research that he had carried out at a meeting held on 25th January 1876. He also worked out the amounts of water that the scheme was supposed to carry as being fourteen gallons per head and not the stated seventeen gallons per head, after he had reviewed the original scheme proposals. It transpired that the loan from the Government was overcharged by around £60,000 and the Accountant General had to acknowledge the mistake. In the end it was not so much the officers of the Administration, as the original drafters of the earlier Act that brought in the loan, who were probably the real culprits for the sloppy management of this loan. But Dadabhai's one-man effort was far reaching and was the real impetus to getting change, which came about several years later. He raised the issue of this particular loan in 1886 when he visited a Mr W Pedder at the India Office during his search for a parliamentary seat.

When he resigned from the office on 26th August 1876, he was given a special vote of thanks which was without precedent. Coming from the other members of the Town Council, such a vote had to be genuinely felt and gives an objective perspective on the value of his endeavours.

He returned to Britain soon afterwards and immediately began to delve into the finances of India under British rule. In 1877 Queen Victoria became the Empress of India (Kaiser-i-hind) which was a move prompted by the British Prime Minister, Benjamin Disraeli. In 1878 Dadabhai produced a booklet called 'The Poverty of India', which basically showed that the Jewel in the Empress's Crown had a production rate per head of population of about half of the estimate given and was hardly enough to meet basic needs.

He showed that India was in perpetual debt to Britain, and would have never been able to make a balance of payments that showed any surplus and this was without taking into consideration the additional interest charges on all the loans that India had to accept. Dadabhai pointed out that during the crusades all Europe had paid tribute to Pope Innocent III. An English Bishop of the time had written out against that enforced poverty and the resultant disease that existed. He especially highlighted that situation by contrasting the well off monasteries, who had ties with Europe, with the wealth held by the Crown. The monasteries received up to three times the King's income, through the Pope's dealings and arrangements. This drain, he claimed, made England far more backward intellectually and politically than it should have been. The parallel was obvious. Dadabhai said India needed industrializing and that required capital. But the capital would need to come from the richest nation on earth. As it already administered the subcontinent the question was, why did Britain not let capital flow into India on easy enough terms? To quote, ".... with pressure of taxation nearly double in proportion to that of England, from an income of one fifteenth and an exhaustive drain besides, we are asked to complete with England in free trade." An example of the unfair conditions placed on India occurred in 1879 when Lord Lytton the Viceroy abolished the import duties on cotton, i.e. from Britain to India. Dadabhai said the real reason was to quash the infant factories in India and presumably protect the British industry in Lancashire.

Dadabhai's paper was the first such publication on this issue and hence its structure was well informed but primarily that of the layman. Nonetheless it was the best of its kind and aroused interest. The estimates he gave were fairly well corroborated in 1882 by Evelyn Baring (Lord Cromer) and Sir David Barbour, who gave 27 shillings per head to his 20 shillings. Even by 1901, an increase in agricultural and industrial output could only give the Viceroy, Lord Curzon, a figure of 30 shillings per head.

Dadabhai's work on the inept financial handling of an entire country kept him busy for many years, and 1877 to 1881 is marked down as a quite period in his public life. He still got aroused by certain events in India, especially during the Viceroyalty of Lord Lytton, which tested his faith of British justice. Although not taking an active part, he decried the Vernacular Press Act or 'Black' Act of 1878 which curtailed the freedom of the Indian press. Then when the Second Afghan War broke out in 1878, it was paid for by the Indians. Primarily the war was fought for the British Empire's ends, and this goaded Dadabhai along with others to point out the unfairness of this arrangement.

Some people of that time, noting his quieter profile and advancing years, now reckoned he had reached his apex, but Dadabhai, who was 55 in 1880 was not yet ready for any retirement type of lifestyle.

He did have the running of a small cotton firm bearing on his mind during this time and this period was a difficult one in terms of the business staying profitable. The financial needs of providing for himself and his family drained him because for the years 1876-1881 in particular he gave a lot of time to the East India Association. Whenever he was in India he would correspond with his partners on a weekly basis, as there were many problems to resolve and orders to place. Amongst the goods they traded in were roller skins, machinery, watches, bracelets and anatomists plates. However there was little he could realistically do in several situations as is indicated in a letter dated 26th August 1881 from Dady Cama who had the power of attorney during Dadabhai's prolonged absences. He wrote " I am very sorry to see that there are very remote chances of your getting money from Mr M.....your losing the money should not make any change in our business relations. My arrangements will remain as they are...... As the case now stands, you will never be able to make up the former loss, coupled as it is with this great deficit of Mr M. Would it not be therefore advisable to wind up this firms business immediately so that people who may have dealings with you may run the least risk?" Although in another letter written on 7th October Dady had said that he agreed with Dadabhai that some good business might result if he kept his name with the firm, he also asked Dadabhai to give a final decision on whether he would keep the firm running by the end of the year. Shortly afterwards Dadabhai decided to win the firm up, but he kept on trading on his own and would place any order he won in Bombay direct to the Camas, unless such an action would have definitely lost the transaction.

Many of Dadabhai's letters to the Camas during this period were in fact a mixture of business and requests for the information that he was trying to unearth in order to make his case on India's condition. These letters starkly show up the doubling of priorities that Dadabhai was

70

trying to keep going and show how he was as interested in buying the latest copies of the Blue books (or Government statistics), as in the accounts of his own firm. His means of support were never more than sufficient and he had to make part of his living by continuing to place orders with the Camas for many years. It should be noted that the split from that family's firm in 1858 was not done because of a personal dislike, but for reasons of principle and although it is not recorded why Dadabhai was trading with them at this time he did include members of the Cama family in the firm he had set up in 1859. Another reason that may explain why he continued to be involved in business with the Camas is that many members of that family were actively involved in the reforms that Dadabhai was committed to achieving. The family had given to several causes over the years and hence despite being quite business minded were not the more typically conservatively minded Shetias of the Bombay business community. In politics they had much in common with Dadabhai's liberal views and that significant point could be why he continued to trade with them over the years, despite the obvious differences of view that had led to the parting of the ways in 1858. Nor does he seem to have let the fact that he would have had to work through them on their terms deter him, as he could exercise choice over the type of goods that were traded.

Being relieved to a large extent from his business meant he could concentrate on the financial question day and night. He probably ordered more 'Blue books' (or financial records on India's economy) than anyone else alive, plus copies of old reports and budgets. He also raised questions once more on the admission of Indians to the Indian Civil Service. He was also posing questions to Parliament through Sir David Wedderburn[1], on the salaries and pensions of European employees in the different departments of the Indian Government. Perhaps his public campaigning had dissipated for a while, but the background drive for reform was still in gear, though nothing notable was achieved during those years.

Dadabhai had used reports on the Punjab in Northern India to establish his general figures. He now entered into prolonged correspondence between 24th May 1880 and 4th January 1881 from 32 Great St Helens in London, with Lord Hartington, Secretary of State for India and his advisers, on what they made of the figures. Their main spokesman pointed out what he felt were flaws in Dadabhai's calculations and Dadabhai retorted and so expert clashed with expert. There was in fact some genuine confusion in the form of analysis and

1. The Wedderburn family came from a twelfth century Baronetcy and the Wedderburn name was one of the most well known in the border country. An ancestor had fought for Bonnie Prince Charlie at Culloden in 1745.

conclusions of both parties, probably because no one in government had really kept the information in any comprehensive way.

Dadabhai wrote the following excerpt to the Secretary of State on 16th November 1880, "Europeans occupy almost all the higher places on every department of government, either directly or indirectly under its control. While in India, they acquire India's money, experience and wisdom, and when they go, they carry both away with them. Thus India is left without, and cannot have, those elders in wisdom and experience who, in every country, are the natural guides of the rising generations in their national and social conduct and of the destinies of their country; and a sad, sad loss this is! There may be very few social institutions started by Europeans in which natives, however fit and desirous to join, are not deliberately and insultingly excluded. The Europeans are, and make themselves strangers in every way. Far, far is it from my earnest prayers and hope that such should be the result of the British rule. In this rule there is every element to produce immeasurable good both to India and England." Dadabhai continued by reminding the Secretary of State that he could guide parliament to acts "worthy of the English character, conscience and nation." He quoted a long list of men in Britain who were willing to press for the exercise of proper administration and hoped their example would enable statesmen of strong moral courage and firmness to attempt to put through the proper changes.

Dadabhai began to feel concerned that a despotic tendency was entering the British administration's psyche. They claimed that on the plus side the benefits of the administration were there in the form of educational reform, the proper organization of the sub-continent and especially the lack of corruption, the building of railways, public works and an infrastructure. These they were certainly doing and no one could claim they were not benefits, when the effects were so obvious. However, they neither settled in the land, nor left, but rather settled on it, carefully protecting India from the rest of the world, but then being free to take away its treasures, quietly and almost legally. They were not, as the ruling power, facing up to the negative aspects of their rule. To quote Dadabhai again, the British were "now beginning to train up feelings of impatience, pride and high-handedness. They who keep constitutionalism alive and kicking were gradually adapting a style of rule that was as despotic as the Asian rules they justifiably denigrate. And what of the opium trade, hoisted on the Chinese (through India) - the opium trade is a sin on England's head and a curse on India for her share in being the instrument." Basically the better British system, when compared to some previous rules, should have been producing better results, but the fruit of British labours was beginning to go sour.

72

Dadabhai wrote against the Indian famine Commission's report of the time, which attempted to give some justification for the overbearing taxations. The cry of the local population of (not) "more Europeans", who of course gave more burdens for the Indian, became more pronounced as the drain continued. Dadabhai warned that the "heart rending, blood boiling condition of India" needed change otherwise England would "in reality be the most disastrous and destructive foreign invader of India .... This unfortunate fact is to be boldly faced in England; .... I am writing to English gentlemen, and I have no fear, but that they will receive my sincere utterances with the generosity and love of justice of English gentlemen." However, Dadabhai had to contest that moral point before Committees, and Commissioners and the House of Commons for years to come. For 25 years it proved a thankless task, and the administration grew more intolerant of people like Dadabhai.

When he published his 700 page 'Poverty and un-British rule in India' in 1901, it became a major work, and a follow on to his 'Poverty of India.' It was widely read in India and Britain and although it was a tedious affair it reflected the command Dadabhai had at marshalling together facts on the financial situation in India.

In this field Dadabhai was the foremost exponent both in the depth of his knowledge and in propounding reform through economic change. His 'Poverty and un-British rule in India' was still being referred to in a publication written for the United Nations "Human Development Report" in 1990. That publication reckoned that Dadabhai's work was less well known, but was probably more ambitious than the pioneering works on poverty of General Booth (the founder of the Salvation Army) in 1889 - 1892 on conditions in London and also when compared to the work of Rowntree in York in 1901.

Because his continuous calls for getting his arguments accepted were stone walled for many years, Dadabhai became more embittered at the British attitude over this period of time. As has been said they seemed to get tougher on the more moderate, but trustworthy and sincere criticisms made by people like Dadabhai than on anyone else. Nevertheless he still hoped this un-British, British rule would end, and revert to its older way of fair play and respect of justice. "A blessing to India and a glory to England, a result worthy of the foremost and most humane nation on the face of the earth", was still an indication of the tenor of the book in 1901, despite Dadabhai's feelings of a harsher rule having crept in.

At about this time, Dadabhai found a very staunch ally in a noted socialist of the time, and founder of the Social Democratic Federation, Henry Mayers Hyndman, who was to remain in constant communication with Dadabhai for the rest of his life. The acquaintance came about only by accident, when Mr Hyndman chanced to see a copy of Dadabhai's earlier work in a bookseller, where it had had its cover ripped off. Hyndman was researching into the British Administration's handling of India at the time and he began to write to Dadabhai and ask him for various facts and figures. Both men felt that if the Authorities persisted in their present policies it would lead to disaster. Dadabhai found Mr Hyndman's support valuable over the years and Hyndman often drew on Dadabhai's knowledge and experience for his articles, letters to the papers and leaflets. Hyndman and Dadabhai's correspondence roamed far and wide, and was to look at all aspects of world events and people's lives before their decades of letter writing came to an end.

At the beginning, one of Hyndman's observations was rich in wisdom. A great master of satire, Lal Mohan Ghose was to visit Britain to present petitions. Hyndman wrote, "If you see Mr Lal Ghose, pray counsel him to let bygones by bygones. Englishmen will not be abused, however wrong they may be, except by themselves. He may do much good by pushing for reorganization." Later on they entered into debate on how to effect changes, which brought out Hyndman's approach, which was for revolution as opposed to Dadabhai's approach which was for reform. Although they would never agree on such a basic difference, their support to each other never diminished.

CHAPTER SEVEN

INDIAN POLITICS

After closing his business in 1881, Dadabhai returned to India to the era of 'Ripon the Righteous.' This was the Vice-Royalty of Lord Ripon who had replaced Lord Lytton. Two resolutions were passed at that time. One was designed to let the country's revenues be spent with greater assent to the people's wishes. The other was to enable the people to receive more of the fruit of their labours. One of the important principles that went with these resolutions, was that "the people should be taught and left to self government."

Ripon had written in 1883 that there was 'the hourly increasing ..... necessity of making the educated natives the friends, instead of the enemies of our rule.' He had also written that for some people and he included himself, being a Viceroy was a question of choosing 'the policy of those who have established a free press, who have promoted education, who have admitted natives more and more largely to the public service in various forms, and who have favoured the extension of self-government.' The contrast to Lord Lytton, his predecessor, was pronounced and it proved an impossible effort for many Anglo Indians to reconcile themselves to the new style of government. Hence Lord Ripon would find in time that the opposition of Sir James Fergusson or Sir Ashley Eden, General Richard Strachey or Sir Henry Maine on the India Council, became virtually an open enmity. Within the Administration, Ripon did receive the support of other men such as Major Evelyn Baring, The Finance member and Courtney Ilbert, the Law member along with Sir Charles Aitchison. Support also came from outside the administration as the Indian Community warmed to Lord Ripon, and this included those of many varying backgrounds and opinions.

Due to this change of philosophy on how India should be ruled and the resulting upheaval Dadabhai was asking people to begin to use his caption that the 'living stores' or human resources as well as the material stores of India, should be home grown, and that this was an opportune time to reiterate this call. He had included educational advancement under this caption and in 1882 was pleased to see that an Education Commission had been established. Lord Ripon also introduced a Local Self-Government bill in 1882.

Lord Ripon was a Viceroy who showed his sincerity to the Liberal cause in the acts he did and these were sometimes to his personal cost. He wanted to do more than the public opinion of Anglo-India would allow. Hence forging ahead with plans for local self government would have made it possible to have then gone on to prepare a way for far reaching changes. But as Alfred Lyall, the Lieutenant-Governor of the North Western Provinces (1882-87), put it, "the general idea, if only moderately developed, is good enough." Lyall spent a good deal of time helping put the measures into practice but in a scaled down and what he saw as a workable compromise. Both men were looking to a time when Indians would be able to hold responsible positions, but their views on timing were different.

The Bombay branch of the East India Association under Dadabhai, asked for an extension of Lord Ripon's tenure of office on 17th February 1883, from the Queen Empress. A little later on 24th April 1883, the same body supported the Ilbert Bill which overturned earlier rules that affected Indians judging court cases. These had stated that no Indian magistrate could inquire into any charge against a white British subject, and that only an European subordinate could do so and hence bring a charge to bear.

In principle the Queen's proclamation of 1858, or the 'Indian Magna Carta' as Aitchinson called it, should have underwritten the Ilbert bill. But the European community reacted with a virulence that surpassed the previous antagonism, as it saw its right to administer the justice system on the basis of racial origin, was to be challenged. This was especially the case with the planters and landowners who probably had more to fear with regard to some past abuses coming before such courts.

Lord Ripon had received good support for some time from members of his staff, but it also proved to be the case that the men in his administration, such as Grant Duff of Madras, or Lyall, did not always prove to be true allies and only a few supported Lord Ripon throughout this time. Amongst the prominent figures who continued to give support were Lord Cromer and John Bright MP. Lord Ripon's reforms were stopped when he eventually left office in 1884 after many fights both within and without his Cabinet. During his tenure of office the Viceroy was literally vilified and abused at times and unhappily more so than a corrupt of unfair or ignorant office holder would have suffered. The 'Confederacy of Blusterers' used all means possible, and at one time a group in Calcutta prepared to storm Government House and send Lord Ripon back to Britain. When so much advice was directed at the Indian Community on non-violent agitation, it made no small impression of the hypocrisy of such statements when the members of the ruling community of the country would use whatever means they saw as fit and proper. The Bombay meeting of the East India Association of April

1883 was set up as a counter to this lambasting and a public meeting was also held at the Willis's rooms, St. James in London on 1st August 1883, in support of Lord Ripon's 'native policy.'

When he left, Dadabhai and many others ensured he had a departure unlike any other, which included a Memorial to the noble Lord, and culminated at a large public meeting in December 1884. That meeting was attended by Sir Jamshedji Jijibhoy and other leading Shetias, but was addressed by men like Dadabhai, Telang, Pherozeshah Mehta and Naoroji Furdunji. In fact when a Shetia rose to speak he was hissed and prevented from finishing. However, Ripon had instilled a greater sense of common purpose to the two sides and as the *Times of India* reported on 19th December 1884, "a strange and significant innovation. Nothing like it, (i.e. public demonstrations) has ever been seen before, and it must, we think, be acknowledged for the first time in Indian history that the people of India have learned how to demonstrate and agitate as a whole, irrespective of caste or race."

Dadabhai and other people remembered him long afterwards as a conscientious reformer, who had tried despite the opposition.

The first Indian Judges were appointed in 1883 and Dadabhai was made a Justice of Peace in 1883, which may well have been a much better position for an Indian to occupy, given the influence of Lord Ripon. In general terms, Lord Ripon had set the conditions for more equality in the law, a betterment of the economy of India and some form of local government.

These changes took years to establish and in 1888 for instance, the Public Service Commission which looked into the recruitment of Indians in the Higher Civil Service, came about as an after effect of Lord Ripon's original proposals, albeit in a rather luke warm manner. In its recommendations was one for 108 posts of the Covenanted Service to be transferred to the lower graded, but wholly Indian staffed Provincial Service. At the end of the day the total real change in available positions amounted to one, as some of these charges had already been pre-planned to come into effect. Dadabhai gave evidence to the Commission during its deliberations on the materials available for consideration.

Apart from trying to progress such reform through legislative means, Dadabhai had also considered other methods which he could apply to the causes he supported. Being an able writer and communicator Dadabhai began a journal in 1883 called the *Voice of India* which asked for a fair hearing and justice for India. Dadabhai was still sure large parts of British opinion were willing to render these to India and he wrote in the prospectus of January 1883 that he believed 'the English Middle classes should take a correct view of the Indian position.' He knew there were several British friends who would show their desire to get India's needs recognized by their lifelong support, but both they and India had virtually no public platform. The journal was to report on what was printed in the Indian press and to make the British in Britain more aware of the concerns, feelings, customs and also the prejudices of Indians. Dadabhai financed it for some years, until a Mr B M Malabari took it over. On 1st January 1890, it was incorporated with the *Indian Spectator*, which remained as an important Indian publication until Malabari's death in 1912.

The value and power of the press was already well known to many of the reformers of India and to their opponents by this time. As had been noted, Dadabhai was directly involved in setting up several newspapers in his time and as the *Voice of India* said in March 1889, "Wherever the influence of the native press penetrates, his name is a household word." Although the circulation levels of the papers were never very high, their readership could be estimated to have a ten fold relationship to their circulation as each edition would often be read out to an audience of eager listeners by those who were literate.

The short-lived Vernacular Press Act of 1878 had really had the objective of stifling the native opinion that grew from the indigenous press. Thankfully it was repealed by Lord Ripon in 1881 and so freedom of speech was maintained. Apart from Dadabhai, who often received support from most of the native press, many Congress politicians of the next twenty years also got favourable treatment. It is sometimes hard to estimate how much influence the press has on political or popular movements, but there is no doubt that Dadabhai gave it a lot of importance at times in terms of the energy he expended on the news sheets and on the newspaper business.

Dadabhai's public career was also interspersed by other local communal matters from time to time. Although a Parsee he was, as said before, a member of a grouping within the Parsee Community who were called the Dordis, which literally meant "rope made of coir." These types of rope were given a special name because the threads were twisted to give it extra strength; Dadabhai once said, "you may burn a Dordi, but you can never take a twist out of it. So it is with me. When once I form a decision nothing will dislodge me from it." The way the name was acquired however had nothing to do with this tenacity of purpose. It was held as true that many years previously a priest had gone to dinner, but had arrived rather late. He had tried to conceal himself by moving around the room, whereupon someone said, "why are you twisting and turning like a Dordi?" There again tenacity of purpose was not the monopoly of the Dordis, who belong to one Parsee line, and both the Noshakras who made up a Navsari priestly group, and another group, the Mobads of Udwada were equally firm in their resolve.

There were other groups too, including the Sanjanas of Sanjan, the Bhagrias or 'Sharers' of Navsari, the Godavras around Anklesar, the Khambattas of Cambay and the Bharuchas of Broach. Along with communities in Vankaner and Variav, these were the main centres of the Parsee community, and many Parsees today, though dispersed across the world, can trace their origins as they still bear the family names of those times.

Sometimes intercommunal rivalry came to a head as it did with the Noshakras and Mobads at Udwada, through their proximity to one another. They had a dispute over their respective rights and duties at the consecration of a Tower of Silence,[1] at Kherguam near Babar in that part of Western India.

It is also interesting to note that the most scared fire of the Parsees is kept at Udwada, and that the most senior priest hails from Navsari.

The case went on for some time and was heard at the court at Babar. Though a Dordi and hence belonging to the Navsari side, Dadabhai was approached to resolve the dispute, as all parties would accept him as being impartial and willing enough to see the proper resolution of the case. Dadabhai did resolve the matter in favour of the priests of Navsari and such was the respect for him that no one felt any need to dispute this judgement.

On the municipal side, Dadabhai was again elected as a member of the Corporation of Bombay (1883-1886) along with a few other reformers such as Naoroji Furdunji and J P Kapadia. Of this group only Naoroji Furdunji managed to be elected by the Corporation members to the Town Council, which remained in the hands of the Shetias. Dadabhai was not put off by this obvious feat of power-broking and he carried on with the Veshar debt question. He was able to show that the government was demanding Rs 500,000 more that it should have done from the Corporation and re-iterated that the supply of water averaged fourteen gallons per head and not the claimed seventeen gallons.

However at the end of 1883 his health took a nose-dive and he had to take a full rest for six months, first at a place near Bassein and then at Tithal near Bulsar. He in fact wondered if he should stay on at the Corporation as his workload was greatly reduced, however the debt was a problem he could no longer just allow to lay fallow.

1. A Tower of Silence or Dakhma is the traditional burial method used in Zoroastrianism. It is literally a Tower, whose roof pitches inward to a central point. The ridges of this 'roof' are large enough for bodies to be laid between each ridge. The bodies are eaten by vultures or decompose and the bones slide towards the centre, where they fall through an opening onto a floor below the roof. In hotter, more spacious countries, the towers are often miles away from inhabited places, but are not so common in our cosmopolitan world where they would be too close to other humans. However, in places like Iran where the Zoroastrians are a persecuted minority, Towers of Silence still exist, though the bodies need to be protected from defilement.

But it was the Ilbert Bill that provided the biggest spur to his public agenda, because it reinstituted the Indian community's desire to set itself a new agenda for reform. The East Indian Association had deteriorated in Dadabhai's absence of several years but the agitation against the Bill by the Anglo-Indian community, did more to arouse the Association and other groupings back into life than any amount of internal efforts.

What is more the members wanted a more politically virile Association, and so on the 31st January 1885, a launch was made of the Bombay Presidency Association with Dadabhai as a Vice-President and Dinsha Wacha as Secretary which continued on from the Bombay branch of the East Indian Association and the Bombay Association.

Mr (later Sir) Dinsha Wacha (1844-1936) remained as Secretary for thirty years and was to be in constant Communication with Dadabhai for all these years. In August 1885, despite being known for his stance and his unrelenting purposes in India's cause, Dadabhai was invited by Lord Reay, the Governor of Bombay, to join the Bombay Legislative Council as an additional member, along with Mr Ranandes, another notable leader and prominent judge of the time. By doing this, Lord Reay was fulfilling a promise to have Indian members included on its ruling body, which was a fairly unique appointment at the time.

The first outright political campaigning by Indians began at this time, when the British Government called a general election, mainly over the issue of home rule in Ireland. The Bombay presidency wanted the candidates who supported India to receive its support and sent over three men, Narayan Chandavakar, Munmohum Ghose and Rama Swamaj Mudaliyar, to campaign for a chosen list of candidates. These included Sir J Phear, Captain Verney, John Bright, J Slagg, William Digby, W S Blunt, S Keary, S Laing, W C Plowden and lastly an Indian candidate, Lal Mohun Ghose. He was the first Asian to stand for any seat and had previously studied law at the Middle Temple, then returned to practise in Calcutta and, due to his efforts to get Indians into the Civil Service, had come to Britain in 1879. He stayed on and taking up a political agenda to aid his efforts, stood as the Liberal candidate for Deptford. Conversely, certain individuals were expressly repudiated by the Bombay Presidency for their claims to represent India, including Sir Richard Temple, J M MacClean, Sir Lavis Pelly, A S Ayrton and Sir Roper Leithbridge. To specify by name who to support and who to campaign against, showed the increased willingness of the community to get involved in the hurly-burly of Politicking. The three speakers were heard by thousands during their campaign, but, unfortunately, none of the candidates they supported got in, whilst a few of the others did gain their seat in the House. At the same time the Shetia members of the Presidency Association were very discomforted by this active political involvement and left en bloc.

But the new mood may have set Dadabhai thinking along the lines of parliamentary representation. Nothing definite has come to us from that time, to confirm that these events were a spur to Dadabhai, but circumstantial evidence makes it very likely that he had been prompted to consider standing. In September 1885 the *Indian Mirror* stated he was contemplating the idea. However, at the same time Dadabhai was also taking part in another new movement of that era, as he actively supported and helped create the first Indian National Congress.

It was the Bombay Presidency Association which had a lot to do with the formation of this national body. *The Times of India* on February 2nd called the Presidency "truly national" and saw it as "the leading political Association of India." Dadabhai, along with Pherozeshah Mehta, Dinsha Wacha, Gopal Krishna Gokhale and D A Khare, were leading members of the Presidency who became leading members of the Congress. At the first Congress meeting, which was hosted by the Presidency Association, 18 of the seventy two delegates were from Bombay and they put up four of its nine resolutions. As a founding member, it took up a lot of Dadabhai's time and, given the Bombayite weighting in its membership, he would have been involved in its preparations as it was held at the Gokuldas Tejpal Sanscrit School, Gowallia Tank in Bombay on 28th December 1885. That first meeting was to help the drive for political reform to become an established and legitimate aim for India. Dadabhai spoke on the drain on the economy and on admission to the higher levels of the Indian Civil Service.

At around that time, 95 percent of all posts in the Service which paid no more than Rs 75 per month, were held by Indians, whereas at the Rs 500-600 mark they made up around 15 percent and at the Rs 1000 mark, they could be counted on an individual basis. Hence Dadabhai addressed Congress with the need to press for Indianisation of the administration as "the most important key to our material and moral advancement. All our political reforms will benefit us but very little indeed if this reform of all reforms is not made."

In particular through the influence of Dadabhai and others, Congress wanted to get more Indians admitted to the covenanted Civil Service which consisted of around a thousand higher graded posts at that time. Dadabhai when moving the fourth Resolution on the 30th December said: "The Resolution which I am proposing does not in any way involve the questions whether the distinction between the covenanted and uncovenanted services should be abolished or not." It read: "That in the opinion of this Congress the competitive examinations now held in England, for first appointments in various Civil departments of the public service, should henceforth, in accordance with the views of the Indian Office Committee of 1860, 'be held simultaneously, one in England and one in India, both being as far as practicable identical in their nature, and those who compete in both countries being finally classified in one list according to merit', and that the successful candidates in India should be sent to England for further study, and subjected there to such further examinations as may seen needful. Further, that all other first appointments (excluding peonships and the like) should be filled by competitive examinations held in India under conditions calculated to secure such intellectual, moral, and physical qualifications as may be decided by Government to be necessary. Lastly that the maximum age of candidates for entrance into the Covenanted Civil Service be raised to not less than 23 years." Dadabhai moved and the Congress then adopted this resolution as the fourth on the agenda and continued to do the same at each succeeding year. In the next year, a Public Service Commission was set up to investigate the Congress demands and made a recommendation when it advised that 23 was a better age for student applicants from India. It did not however make other recommendations in line with the Congress resolutions, and the employment of Indians remained a debatable issue right up until Independence.

Hence the influence of the men from Bombay was considerable in the early days of Congress, but Dadabhai in particular stands out because he had also played a leading role in the earlier Associations formed in Bombay since 1852. The Bombay grouping as a whole espoused the more moderate, thought out and questing style of campaigning which marked Congress's style until the 1900s. The press of the era gave a lot of support to Congress and up to a third of its founding members had journalistic connections. Hence it was made up of people who were prepared to encourage debate and challenge the institutions, with the whole of India as its potential audience.

As has been noted, Dadabhai took part by giving several speeches, including one calling for a Royal Commission, because he recognized that it was the only vehicle for reform that could be authoritative enough to achieve real change. He got the resolution passed on the Royal Commission after having put to the delegates that "It is evidently the desire here, that a full and impartial inquiry by fair and high minded English statesmen, with an adequate number of natives on the enquiry body, should be carried on in India itself." That first Congress also pushed for the reform of the Imperial and Provincial legislative Councils, and continued to pronounce this demand until the 1892 Indian Councils Act was passed.

W C Bonnerjee was the President that year and again in 1892, but the Secretary, Mr Allen Octavian Hume was perhaps its most conspicuous supporter, even over the Bombay people, as he had spent many years in India, from being a district officer just before the events of 1857, to becoming Secretary to the Government of Indian's Department of Revenues, Commerce and Agriculture. He had retired in 1882 and a few years later, wrote an article to find fifty volunteers. To quote him, " .... If fifty men cannot be found with sufficient power of self sacrifice, sufficient love for and pride in their country, sufficient genuine and unselfish patriotism to take the initiative and if need be devote the rest of their lives to the Cause - then there is no hope for India. Her sons must and will remain mere humble and helpless instruments in the hands of foreign rulers ...." Dadabhai was one of the fifty odd volunteers, along with other Indians and British supporters, including William Wedderburn. Hume was to remain in India for the rest of his life and he was the General Secretary of Congress until December 1908.

Why he sought to establish such a body has been explained in many different ways including the commonly repeated safety valve theory. This is that by having a body of their own the natives could vent all their dissatisfaction through that body and be kept away from direct approaches or reproaches on the Authorities. Some feel that Hume was influenced by the people he knew in the government to follow that direction. Although it is true that Hume did have highly placed government contacts and they were part of his circle of advisers, he did not rely on them alone. In 1881 he became a disciple of a Madame Blavatsky and her theosophy movement which claimed it could bring its followers nearer the more mystical authorities. She purported to be in touch with gurus whom she called mahatmas. They were supposed to be incredibly perceptive and knowledgeable individuals who lived in a kind of unseen secret brotherhood. They gleaned what they knew from thousands of "chelas" across the land.

Although Hume fell out with Madame Blavatsky in 1883, he maintained his belief in these contacts and even entered into 'correspondence' with them. He feared their reports that discontent was at boiling point in the land. He wrote to people such as Wedderburn and Lords Ripon and Dufferin, who became Viceroy after Ripon, to put this last point forward, but when he was pressed for his sources by Dufferin in 1887, he could not produce them in any factual way. It seems likely that his interest in eastern religions kept him believing there was something else happening outside of the normal intelligence available to people, and this influenced him to set up the Congress. Although he eventually stopped relying on the gurus and chelas to inform him of their surmising of the situation across the country, he recognised by then that he should persist in his efforts to establish Congress as the representative body for the natives.

Both Dufferin and Reay, who was the governor of Bombay, were more liberally minded than many in the administration and had initially supported the proposals Hume put forward, despite having some misgivings over his reasoning. Initially he could use his direct contacts with them to bring Congress to their attention. Hence to begin with, the relations between the Governor and Viceroy and the reformers were apparently amicable, even too friendly in some people's view. The Lord (Marquess) of Dufferin had apparently advised Hume in 1885 not to keep it restricted to social reform, but to widen it to the political education of the people. He had invited its delegates to a garden party at Government House, purportedly to show his support for it at the second Congress in Calcutta. At the third in Madras, Lord Connemara, Governor of Madras, did the same. But it is also clear from his personal letters that from mid-1885, Dufferin had begun to dislike the notion of a Congress and had begun to write letters warning of its effects. He in particular mentioned Hume, but also warned against the "Bengal Baboos and Mahratta Brahmins", and he was not alone in this feeling that sedition must be in the minds of many of the clerks employed by Europeans. In time they came to feel his idea was too much of a hot potato for the political unrest it could throw up. Because Congress may never have started without Hume he was in a sense its most important member at the time.

In later years, the Congress's tenor and authority became more stringent as the membership changed. Therefore Congress began in a small way and apparently as a sop of the authorities, but it was having to stand on its own feet from very early on in its life. It is only by making a beginning that something is achieved and it may be argued that an important adjustment in the thinking on self rule began from the time that it held its first meeting. When Bonnerjee had been asked by the Russian traveller I P Minayeff what was the reason behind having an Indian Congress he said "growth of national feeling and unity of Indians".

By the 5th November 1888 Hume knew enough of the feelings of the authorities to be able to write, "another secret which I learned only this week; Lord Dufferin is now against us." The Authorities began to keep a close eye on Congress in case dissent should be fermenting amongst the better educated and well informed groups who made up the majority of its members as they were often the same individuals who were complaining about the unfairness of the system. Dissent could easily move into disorder if their words struck home with the majority of the Community. The authorities began to wonder if Congress would begin to Campaign for Home rule for India in the same way as was happening in Ireland. But as Dadabhai stated, in 1888, 'With regard to Home Rule .... I am a warm Home Ruler for Ireland but neither myself nor any other Indian is asking for any such Home Rule for India. You must see from the Report of the Congress that our demands are far more moderate, in fact only a further development of existing institutions (the Legislative Councils'). At the same time when he had said as President of the second Congress that a "National Congress must confine itself to questions in which the entire nation has a direct participation", he could have been taken to mean India's self rule. However this directive was laid down to make clear that social reform, which would involve more intercommunal matters, was not to be the theme for Congress, which was broadly in line with Lord Dufferin's advice of 1885.

Until 1892 Congress limited its demand to reform of the Legislative Councils and the India Councils Act of 1892 increased the number of additional members of the Imperial and Provisional Legislative Councils from six to ten and from ten to sixteen respectively. However on the Imperial Council, the number of unofficial Indian members was small, (five out of twenty four in 1909), and it only met for around thirteen days a year.

In terms of countering the Congress a letter sent in December 1900 by the then Secretary of State for India, Lord George Hamilton, to Lord Curzon shows up the hardening of the attitudes held by the authorities. It showed that in private they were in an antagonistic mood, even though in public their tone was far more temperate. He wrote, "Naoroji has been bombarding me with letters written in his high-faluting sentimental style ..... I thought it just as well to give him plainly a piece of my mind in very courteous language, which I have done ..... I think I shall publish it later on, as it is very desirable to bring home to the educated natives who may sincerely desire to co-operate with the British government as far as they can, the absurdity of nourishing these dreams and hallucinations in connection with India." Unfortunately this attitude seemed to gain sway amongst the majority, but never all, of the rulers. Over time, the general mood changed from one of dismissiveness to distrust and then on to rancour and strong disapproval. In the case of Lord Hamilton, he was noted as one of the harsher types of British overseer and so he did show less tolerance and more aggressiveness to the point of being a courteous bully.

It should be noted that, amongst the 'educated natives', there were always a good number who did not hold with the style of Congress, often for reasons internal to Indian society, and so their choice was to side against Congress, which meant the chances of divide and rule were a reality. Inescapably though, the idea that British India was the land of the Indians, meant that all sides came to face the reality of the situation and so their end goals began to crystallize in the early twentieth century in ways that were unthinkable to those who lived through the last fifteen years of the nineteenth century. There were always negative feelings on both sides, but they became stronger during this time, whereas positive attitudes were more prevalent at other times in the history of events. For Dadabhai, the situation he found himself in was a deteriorating one, but never a hopeless one.

CHAPTER EIGHT

TO FIND THE CONSTITUENCY

On 13th March 1886 the *Hindu* of Madras announced that an Indian was to stand for Parliament, namely Dadabhai Naoroji. It now seems evident that Dadabhai had been in communication with friends in Britain to see if a candidature was a strong possibility. He had received a reply from Martin Wood on 12th September 1884, (an ex-editor of *The Times of India* for 1864-74), that after Lal Mohun Ghose had declined to stand at Woolwich, there was every reason for Dadabhai to try for the position. Martin Wood (1828-1907) continued to play a supporting role to both Dadabhai and the Congress throughout this time. It has been suggested but not proven that after an address made by Dadabhai to the Bombay Presidency Association in September 1885 on "India's interest in the general election", that he made his mind up to take up his own words. As he said "it is in Parliament that our chief battle has to be fought", but this may also have been one in a series of events in his life that culminated in his choice of action. Dadabhai departed from India without any suggestion of his purpose, which was to follow up on openings like the one from Martin Wood. This did not stop the speculation on the reasons for his departure and the response from the native press to this move by Dadabhai was one of joy and excitement.

The *Hindu* also reported that "As an authority of Indian economic questions there is none equal to him in all India. He has devoted over a quarter of a century of his life to the study of India's subjects, and by pressing his views on the Secretary of State and upon influential Englishmen in England he has turned his knowledge to the best account possible. Old as he is, Mr Dadabhai is a man of remarkable energy, and his great patriotism has won for him the confidence of his contemporaries of the Hindus and Mohamedans, as well as Parsees in every part of the country." This expression of all round support seemed to be real, albeit that a few active campaigners also felt it was a double-edged sword to stand for Parliament, as all his work in India could then come to a standstill.

Dadabhai's personal diary for the months of April and May show a busy round of meetings with people from many different backgrounds and positions. He was not just in Britain for his political future, and wanted to use his geographical proximity to the Indian office to pursue issues like the Bombay municipality's water works loan. He also kept himself involved with the East India Association and the Indian nation's needs were always present in whatever conversations he held at this time.

Coming from a country which many in Britain did not think could produce men like Dadabhai, meant he had to get himself known and appreciated in a short time. On the other hand those who had wanted reform and had been working for it would now be able to point to at least one notable Indian in their ranks. Hence through Dadabhai's presence they could show their opponents that what they worked towards was representative of the desire of the Indians themselves, and also answer some of the unsympathetic critics who questioned the capabilities of the Indians.

Having to choose a party to which he would then have to give his allegiance went against the grain for Dadabhai, as the *Indian Spectator* printed on July 18th, "He goes the whole hog in spite of his constitutional dislike of such a course." Dadabhai's meetings with officials of the Liberal party were courteous and pleasant enough, but their help for his point of view was demure and lacked conviction. He also met with a Mr Peddler and a Mr Waterford of the India Office; Mr Godley, the Under-Secretary of State of India; Sir George Birdwood; Dr Codgreve; John Bright; Mr (later Lord) Alfred Milner; Lord Ripon and several newspaper editors. Their advice spanned from encouragement to condemnation of his standing as a candidate. He was approached by the Irish home rule movement who wanted to nominate him to an Irish seat, but they later retracted their suggestion because of a fear that it would alienate Irish supporters. Dadabhai soon found out that the Irish question was more important to most people than whether an Indian should stand for parliament. Dadabhai made his position on the Irish question quite clear from early on; he supported the idea of a separate parliament for Ireland and would continue to do so for the rest of his political career. Nonetheless his first passion was for India and it was clear from before he came to Britain that he would represent that Nation wherever he could, if he was elected.

Several suggestions were made on where to look for a constituency, such as Woolwich, but nothing definite seemed to appear. Members of the Scottish group felt Scotland had a better track record for their Liberal approach to causes like his and asked him to come North. On the other hand the very pro Conservative St Albans constituency was put forward for his consideration. Dadabhai was learning to adjust to politics and not make a quick move to anyone's direction, but not be so defensive that he would not be available for offers. His name was also taken up by some regional papers and various groups invited him to become a member, including the Cobden Club. The National Liberal Association forwarded his name to several groups on its list.

Then on 18th June Dadabhai's nomination was accepted unanimously by the Holborn Executive of the Liberal Association. In effect they head-hunted for him as the nominations from the National Liberal Association basically gave recommendations or information to local executives, but carried little weight in the normal course of events. This was a vote of confidence in Dadabhai and showed the genuine support he could expect.

He entered into the fray and campaigned hard, determined that he would be seen as the local candidate and not just be known for his other pursuits. He knew that Holborn was stoutly conservative and therefore his hopes of winning were poor, but he wanted to make a real effort and go for the election.

From his residence at Hogarth Road, South Kensington, he began his campaign with nightly addresses, followed by reams of correspondence and visits. In one of his letters he must have written to Florence Nightingale, because she then wrote to Dadabhai to express her support to him.

> London, June 23, 1886
> My dear Sir,
> My warmest good wishes are yours in the approaching election for Holborn, and this not only for your sake, but yet more for that of India and of England, so important is it that the millions of India should in the British Parliament here be represented by one who, like yourself, has devoted his life to them in such a high fashion - to the difficult and delicate task of unravelling and explaining what stands at the bottom of Indian's poverty, what are Indian's rights, and what is the right for India; rights so compatible with, indeed so dependent on, loyalty to the British Crown; rights which we are all seeking after for those great multitudes, developing, not every day like foliage in May, but slowly and surely. The last five or eight years have made a difference in India's cultivated classes which has astonished statesmen - in education, the seeds of which were so sedulously sown by the British Government - in power, of returning to the management of their own local affairs, which they had from time immemorial; that is, in the powers and responsibilities of local self-government, their right use of which would be equally advantageous to the Government of India and to India (notwithstanding some blunders); and noble because a careful beginning has been made in giving them this power. Therefore do I hail you and yearn after your return to his Parliament, to continue the work you have so well begun in enlightening England and India on Indian affairs. I wish I could attend your first public meetings, to which you kindly invite me tomorrow; but alas for me, who for so many years have been unable from illness to do anything out of my rooms.
> Your most ardent well-wisher,
> FLORENCE NIGHTINGALE

The meeting that Florence Nightingale referred to was one of the first of several similar held meetings at the Town Hall, Holborn. This one took place on 24th June 1886, and at that meeting Dadabhai shared the platform with James Bryce, Under-Secretary of State for Foreign Affairs. The Holborn Guardian reported, "On Thursday night there was a grand Liberal demonstration at the Holborn Town Hall, in favour of the candidature of Mr Naoroji, and we venture to say that a meeting of such dimensions and enthusiastic unanimity has never taken place in Holborn Town Hall before."

From newspaper reports and other material, it is possible to build a picture of his talking style and content. He talked straight forwardly and used simple statements. His speech that June night was on Home rule for Ireland, which was in line with the official Liberal stance, and on his concerns for India's millions. A transcript of the speech shows that if 'India' was substituted for 'Ireland', it could have been a speech that had been delivered by the Indian Nationalists of the 1930s or 40s. Dadabhai's main campaign issue was to seek election so that measures could be brought in to secure Irish autonomy. As well as this he also stood for a change in the Land Law affecting Town and Country dwellers. Supporters for the Irish cause were strongly recommended to give Dadabhai their votes by their leaders.

Dadabhai continued the same theme for the rest of that week at other venues in the constituency. The *Pall Mall Gazette* recorded that he was certainly a worthwhile person to represent the millions living in his home country and wrote that, "if 254 millions of Her Majesty's subjects in India are ever to be represented ..... it would hardly be possible to find one more worthy of the position or more fitted than the honourable Dadabhai Naoroji ...."

Other newspaper reports of the time included one by *The Times* of 26th June, which said, "like Ireland, India has grievances to be redressed and it was right that her representative should have an opportunity of bringing those grievances before the people of England. Apart from the special knowledge which he would bring to bear upon the Indian question, Mr Naoroji by 20 years residence in England, has made himself fully acquainted with English political questions and by returning him to the House of Commons, Holborn would prove itself one of the grandest constituencies in Great Britain." The Christian Million stated on July 1st that, "he is a 'Gladstonite' .... (named after the Liberal leader at the time). Apart altogether from party politics we think the House of Commons would gain by his election and are gratified by the cordial welcome Mr Naoroji received from the electorate of Holborn."

Articles in the *Weekly Times, The Echo, Weekly Despatches, York Herald, Rochdale Observer* and *Freeman's Journal* in Dublin and other papers of that week were also favourable. The *Freeman's Journal* on 3rd July commented upon his previous track record at Baroda, by reporting on a favourable introduction made of Dadabhai by another speaker who said that he " ... ruled with great distinction for some time over two millions of people (cheers). In fact, his administration was so beneficent that it called forth from the British Governors of India the warmest testimony of admiration. Well, he contended that a gentleman who had struggled so long for the rights of his own country, and who had shown such distinguished capability as a statesman, ought to prove himself a worthy representative of Holborn." The *Pall Mall Gazette* also included a reference to his time as Dewan, when it wrote about his background and it concluded that, "In Holborn the ex-Prime Minister of Baroda is creating a great impression on the constituency, and convincing many, both in and out of Holborn, that whosoever is left out of Parliament, Dadabhai Naoroji ought to be inside" (3rd July 1886).

This article served the purpose of giving Dadabhai some background and some context for the electors to judge him upon. To most people he had began as an unknown quantity and this, as much as anything, could hamper his election campaign.

Another contemporary source noted that his origins had puzzled the British elector, who could handle a Mr Jones or a Mr Brown and would have thought no more about him had he been British. There was certainly no handicap or poor presentation to be picked upon which would be the expected performance of most Indians in those times. The press in general seemed to find his nightly speeches entertaining, succinct and well presented. They did have difficulty getting his name right; hence 'Funny Folks' on 3rd July expressed the wish for a "Pronounced" success to the candidate "with a name difficult to pronounce."

In India two men in particular, Malabari and Dinsha Wacha campaigned for him and tried to raise money for his expenses. It is true that some thought it all a waste of time, but others did not see campaigning for a lost cause as a negative move. Dadabhai had money problems, and wrote later to Malabari to say that, "My wants therefore are not only the expense of one or two elections, but also the means to enable me to live in England in suitable style." When he had sent this letter to Malabari he had hoped for a positive response from the Indian community. He found that just as support had been lacking, so it continued to prove meagre and money problems were to remain with him for many years.

With such problems Dadabhai and his small band of supporters were already thinking of the next election, even whilst he was kept fully preoccupied with the present one.

9 1

Unfortunately amongst the ones who felt he would be better occupied if he did not remain in Britain were included many leaders of the Indian National Congress, such as Pherozeshah, Telang and Wedderburn. In time the latter became one of those who was more sure of the line of action that Dadabhai pursued as were the Sheriff of Bombay, Sir George Birdwood and H M Hyndham, who wrote to him in this manner.

For Wedderburn the next year saw him with more time on his hands as he retired from the Secretaryship of the Government of Bombay in May 1887. He had marred his own prospects in his working life, because of his interest and advocacy for the Indian people's needs. He joined Congress on his retirement and was its President in 1889 and 1910. He gave both of his health and wealth to that cause both in India and as a Member of Parliament of Britain, up until his death.

Dadabhai was up against money and influence in his opponent Colonel Duncan. Dadabhai had little of either and on top of that Holborn had also changed its political complexion because of a change brought in six years previously. As was reported on December 26th 1885 in an article headed 'The Old Borough of Finsbury and the New Borough of Holborn', the writer pointed out, "Liberal it has been from first to last, until divided into sections and having to meet an unhealthy and I may add unholy combination of Jews, Irish, Parsons, publicans, an alliance not aiming at one purpose, but all striving for different interests, that portion of it the virgin borough of Holborn has now stained the good chronicle by returning a Tory ...."

In line with all the 'Gladstonians' of the Liberal party, Dadabhai was known to support Home rule for Ireland and probably suffered because of splits amongst supporters over the stated Irish policy. It was not a good election for the Liberals and they suffered nationally. Hence in a safe Tory seat, Dadabhai did well to get 1950 votes against the Colonel's 3651. Lal Mohum Ghose also contested as a 'Gladstonian', again trying to secure the seat of Deptford but suffered from the same setback as did another Indian candidate named Rajah Rampal Singh. The election date was 7th July 1886 and so Dadabhai had only a short time for his electioneering and unless it had been a safe seat, he could never really have expected to win.

As the *Holborn Guardian* reported on 10th July, "The Liberal candidate, Mr Naoroji, had a very uphill battle to fight, especially in view of the fact that the contest was on the old register, and perhaps thousands of votes had left the district due to clearances. The Honourable Mr Naoroji during the short time he had before the election, made himself immensely popular; and we believe we are right in stating that at another election Mr Naoroji will be found fighting the cause of Liberalism and progress in the Holborn Division."

9 2

This only spurred Dadabhai on to preparing for the next general election. He began by campaigning for a better seat and had learnt that he needed to get a better party machine to support him, though Holborn had done their best. He had wanted a personal secretary, but slender resources, both then and now, still count against a candidate's ability to campaign.

At the end of 1886 and because of his standing for India at the Holborn election, which had helped give a unity to Congress's members, he was asked to attend the second Indian National Congress in Calcutta as the elected President. He gave a speech more remarkable for its restraint and moderation. He still pushed for more representation for Indians where it counted, and for simultaneous exams in India and Britain. On the first issue his efforts were taken up by Charles Bradlaugh MP in 1889. He brought in a bill, then withdrew it on the understanding that the Secretary of State, Viscount Cross, would propose his own one in the following year. Unhappily, Mr Bradlaugh never lived to see a bill proposed, and Congress and Dadabhai had to contest the same issue all over again some time later. On the second issue, Dadabhai gave evidence to the Public Services Commission soon after the Congress, which was set up partly due to the pressure that had arisen from the resolution that Dadabhai had inserted in the programme of the first Congress.

However, on this issue the Muslim minority feared a Hindu majority in positions of authority, if the simultaneous exams were to be introduced and they opposed the change which John Bright MP was proposing as a bill. To see it torpedoed from within caused Dadabhai much anguish and distress and he wrote to several Muslim leaders of the time, to prevent it happening again, including in particular a member of the Commission, Mr Kazi Shahbuddin. Efforts to restrict or oppose the Congress also came from other Indians. In 1887 Dadabhai wrote to Malabari of the *Indian Spectator*, "Now, my dear fellow, what an amount of unnecessary mischief you are doing. By all means fight for the merits of your cause (of social reform), but why unnecessarily discredit and discourage other important movements?" Malabari was not generally negative to either Dadabhai or Congress and in fact took over the control of the *Voice of India* from Dadabhai in 1890 as had been mentioned before. His real complaint at this time was probably the way that Congress had played down on efforts for social reform. In the previous year, as President, Dadabhai had sought to maintain a unity amongst all the groups in Congress and has steered it away from pursuing matters of social reform. He felt that the various religious and national groups present represented a danger if *Congress* took up the wrong issues, and said, "there are essentially matters too delicate for a stranger's handling

- matters which must be left to the guidance of those who fully understand them ..... which are wholly unsuited to discussion in an assemblage like this in which all classes are intermingled."

Dadabhai arrived back in Britain and in August 1887 he was arguing the point on what were the causes for Indian's poverty with Sir Grant Duff, who had been running India down. Dadabhai had retorted with his range of economic arguments that pointed to the British Government's policies being the cause for India's economic ills, not Indian laxity or poor management.

There was no one better to champion the arguments and defend the nation. However, he also had to continue campaigning, but was hampered in this because he did not receive as much concrete support from India as he really needed. On the contrary, one 'friend' continued to owe him £2000 for several years. In fact, even whilst he was in need of funds, Dadabhai was also involved on a more personal level in continuing to either give support himself or campaigning to raise support for other people.

One family who remembered him for his efforts were the wife and daughter of a Major Evans Bell, who died in 1887. He had helped the Maharaja and the state of Mysore for many years, whilst he was still fit to hold his position. In fact, whilst he had been Assistant Commissioner at Nagpur in 1855, he had incurred his Chief's displeasure because of his efforts, and had been dismissed. He was liked by Lord Canning however, and appointed Commissioner of Police at Madras in 1861 until his retirement in 1863. As said earlier, his book of that time entitled "The Empire in India, 1864" may have influenced Dadabhai's own writings on the Economic Drain theory, and Civil Service entry for Indians.

His wife now wrote to Dadabhai to say he was dying and to ask him for some help in return. He went to see her and gave her a cheque and an address to use, as well as asking several Princes to help. None did but Mrs Bell was to remember Dadabhai's help for many years, both for herself and in the memory of her husband, who had become run down partly through his exertions when he had been based in India. Another cause that Dadabhai responded to at this time was to make representation to the Shah of Iran for the Zoroastrians in Persia. The 'Reis and Rayyet' reported on 6th July, ".... Mr Dadabhai Naoroji presented the Shah with an address from the Parsis, thanking His Majesty for the improved conditions of Zoroastrians in Persia."

During 1887, Dadabhai met the Central Finsbury executive in the early spring and felt a favourable response was forthcoming. Central Finsbury (also termed Finsbury Central) was a North Central London constituency, next door to Holborn, and had a different type of electorate which included the watch and jewellery district in Clerkenwell, as well as poorer areas of Finsbury and also contained 5 percent of the prosperous Muswell Hill area. Dadabhai wrote to Malabari on 2nd March to report on progress. He was actually second to the Earl of Compton, the son of the Marquess of Northampton, but the seat became vacant by the resignation of that candidate. Between March and August that year, the Committee held 8 to 10 ballots to try and get just four names agreed. On 15th August a vote was taken of the proposed candidates and Dadabhai secured forty-nine votes to forty-five for a Mr Richard Eve, twenty-three for a Mr F Ford and seven for a Mr Dodd. The following announcement appeared in the Daily News of 17th August 1888 because the result of the ballot was considered to be final. "Liberal candidate for Central Finsbury - The Hon Dadabhai Naoroji has been selected by the Central Finsbury Liberal and Radical Association as their candidate at the next election for Central Finsbury. Eight names were in the first place submitted to the members, with the result that in the last ballot, Mr Naoroji proved successful polling 49 votes, Mr Eve being second with 45, and Mr F A Ford third. Some dissatisfaction at the outcome of the ballot was expressed by a section of those present.

The final ballot was not a snatch ballot. Some eight or ten ballots had taken place in the course of nearly six months, from March to August."

As reported in the *Holborn Guardian*, the Secretary of the Association and Eve, Ford and Dodd had congratulated Dadabhai on his win of the 15th August. But the next day the Secretary, Mr Edward Jacobs, said another meeting was to be held. This caused delays and it was actually a year later before one of the scrutineers claimed that the reason for the change in the decision was that Dadabhai's friends had rushed from the room before the final ascension vote had been taken, and so the Chair, Mr Hampson, had postponed that vote. But the point still remains that if they had stayed, he would still have won and the formal vote was really a rubber stamping. A revote was called for, despite the fact that the Secretary had written to confirm Dadabhai as the candidate and Mr F Schnadhorst, the highest ranking organizing officer of the National Liberal Foundation had repeated this result in a letter of 18th August. Dadabhai was indignant and refused to attend the second meeting held on the 3rd September. He was also upset that the Liberal headquarters group, who had never helped him with the Holborn seat, were not going to do anything positive in this predicament.

Mr Eve won the vote of 3rd September and Dadabhai immediately said, "they have thrown the gauntlet at me and I have picked it up. I have informed them that I will go to the poll ...." He also wrote on the 5th September to say, "that if I gave way at Central Finsbury I should have not

9 5

the remotest chance of being accepted by any other constituency, as my withdrawal would show that I had no firmness in maintaining my just rights and position." He said that he would contest the seat, and so he called a public meeting for the 10th September, to explain his stand. Thus began a battle that should never have happened, but by then the die was cast. The Secretary of the local group also wrote to him to rescind his previous letter of congratulations, and this presumably made it clearer than ever that he was left on his own.

Finsbury Central was not a particularly easy seat to win in any case and as figures for it and the neighbouring Finsbury East constituency show, the vote was always a close run matter.

Conservative & Unionist Vote as a Percentage of the total Poll

	1885	1886	1892	1895
Finsbury Central	44.7	50.1	50.0	56.4
Finsbury East	50.2	49.2	46.8	53.2

In fact as the following list shows, the outgoing incumbent Captain Penton and his Conservative colleagues actually did better in these two constituencies and the recently realigned Holborn one, than did the Liberals. The listing is from Whitaker's Almanac:

July 1886   Finsbury Central - Captain Frederick Thorp Penton (C)
            Finsbury (East) - James Rowlands (L)
            Holborn - Colonel F Duncan (C)
Nov 1886   Holborn - Gainsford Bruce QC (C)

July 1892   Finsbury Central - Dadabhai Naoroji (L)
            Finsbury (East) - James Rowlands (L)
            Holborn - Sir Charles Hall QC (C)

July 1895   Finsbury (East) - Henry Charles Richards (C)
            Clerkenwell (Finsbury Central) - Hon William F B Massey
                                              Mainwaring (C)
            Holborn - Sir Charles Hall (C)

Finsbury Central had been a working class area, but was changing due to an expansion of business and industry from Central London. It still held a lot of the watch and jewellery trade in its boundaries and had continued to include a detached portion, outside of the London Country Council boundaries several miles further north at Muswell Hill, which was the 'detached villa' area. This anomaly occurred because the Knights of St John, who had owned half of Finsbury Central had also owned a deer park in Muswell Hill. It had apparently remained with Finsbury Central despite the previous Boundary Commission's changes.

96

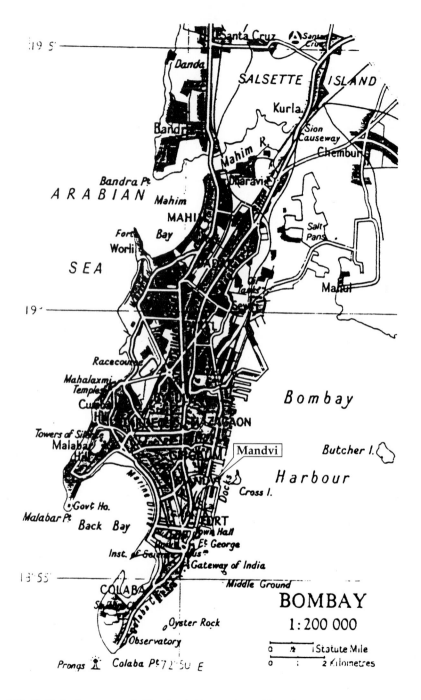

Dadabhai's birth place was probably Mandvi in Bombay, although claims have been made for a Mandvi several hundred miles further north on the coast

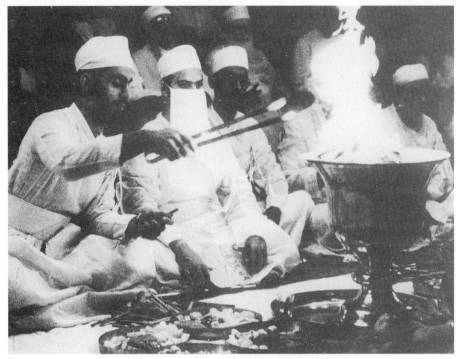

A Zoroastrian temple and some of the officiating priests. The Priesthood is passed from father to son and Dadabhai's father was a Mobad (Priest)

The Zarathustrian tenet - "Good Thoughts, Good Words, Good Deeds"

A sketch of Dadabhai made when he was 20

A Parsee girls school

KARSON DAS MULJI   SORABJEE BENGALEE

KHARSHEDJI N. CAMA   DADABHAI NAOROJI

*Four members of the original editorial group of
Rast Goftar including Dadabhai*

*William Digby was a friend of
Dadabhai's and they maintained a
correspondence for many years*

During the American Civil War, cotton supplies from America dropped and exports from India boomed. Dadabhai was actively involved in trade at this time. The picture shows part of the docks at Bombay (circa 1890)

A cartoon that appeared in 'Hindu Punch', January 1889. Its caption read: "WHO IS THE BLACKEST", a momentous question answered by the great master painter Herbert Gladstone. (In the meantime Mr Herbert Gladstone is to be thanked for an entirely new light upon the question. "I know Mr Naoroji very well" he says, "and I know Lord Salisbury by sight, and I am bound to say that of the two Lord Salisbury is the blackest." Perhaps this revelation may lead the Prime Minister to investigate the colour of the Parsee race.)

Dadabhai depicted as the dark side of the moon - "Naoroji Sahib, 'That comes in likeness of a coal' - Titus Andronicus, iii, 2."

Captain Penton was Dadabhai's Conservative opponent in 1892. He filed a petition to get the election result scrutinized and it was not until December that Dadabhai's result was confirmed

James Rowlands was a contemporary of Dadabhai's and MP for Finsbury East. He and Dadabhai proposed and supported each other on three Bills

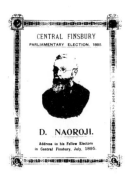

Cover page of Dadabhai's election address for 1895

Dadabhai's booklet published in 1904, showing an increasing sympathy for Socialist views on his part

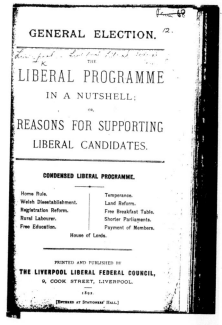

The Newcastle programme which Dadabhai adopted as the Liberal candidate for the 1892 election

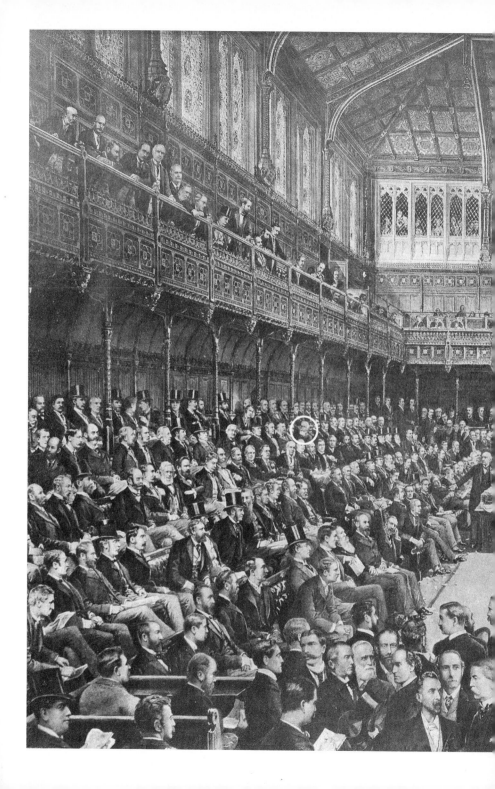

Dadabhai in the House of Commons (circled). Gladstone is at the dispatch box

Dadabhai at his desk. His letter writing capacity was enormous and he would have spent hours of his time in his small study

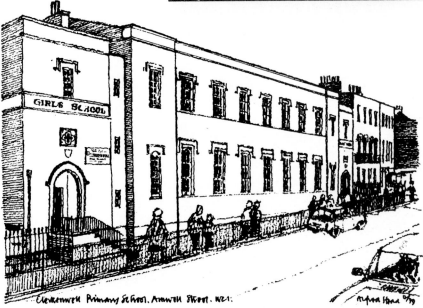

Amwell or Clerkenwell Primary School where Dadabhai spoke against boundary changes on 27th January 1893

Dadabhai spoke at the Foundation Stone laying ceremony for the Clerkenwell Vestry Hall (now Finsbury Town Hall, pictured below) on 14th June 1894 and gave the Vote of Thanks at its official opening on 14th June 1895

The Reception Committee of the 5th Indian National Congress of 1889 held in Bombay, which appeared in the Album sent from India and includes notable Bombayites who were friends of Dadabhai

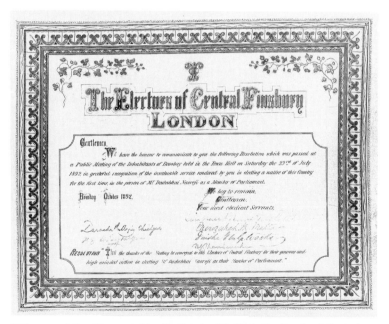

Title page of the Album sent by the People of India to the People of Central Finsbury for electing Dadabhai as their MP

Dinsha Wacha, Dadabhai (seated) and Gopal
Krishna Gokhale were all Presidents of the
Indian National Congress. Both Wacha and
Gokhale regularly corresponded with
Dadabhai as if he were their mentor

Mohandas Karamchand Gandhi as a young
man in western dress

Dadabhai in the traditional Fetto, Parsee headgear

A Parsee lady weaving the Kusti or sacred thread. She will either be the wife of a Priest or a lay woman entrusted for this task. The Kusti consists of 72 threads, divided into six strands, and is wrapped three times around the body over the Sudreh or sacred shirt worn next to the skin. It is untied and retied by the weaver while reciting their papers

Outside view of a Zarathustrian (Zoroastrian) fire temple in India

Sir Mancherjee Bhownaggree, who was the Conservative MP for North East Bethnal Green (1895-1906). He is pictured above outside the House of Commons and right in a portrait by Mrs Radcliffe Beresford of 1928

Shapurji Saklatvala addressing the crowds at Trafalgar Square

The carving that appears on the base of a statue erected in memory of Dadabhai in Bombay, 1927

Dadabhai in 1913, aged 88

Commemorative plaque to Dadabhai erected on Finsbury Town Hall (March 1993). A nearby street was also renamed Naoroji Street in 1996. The picture shows (l-r) Cllr Dina Kleanthous, Chair of the Race Equality Committee for Islington Council; Omar Ralph, author; Dr L M Singhvi, Indian High Commissioner; Chris Smith MP, Islington South and Finsbury; Edna Griffiths, Mayor of Islington; Rusi Dalal, President of the Zoroastrian Trust Funds of Europe and Cllr Derek Sawyer, Leader of Islington Council

CHAPTER NINE

No 'Black Man'
in Parliament

adabhai campaigned from door to door, gave talks, held meetings,
replied to letters and took an active interest in the constituency.
He intended to put the constituency first and foremost and was
beginning to gather the public's support and liking. Then on November
30th he went to bed a small figure in British politics and woke up the
next day to take centre stage. Lord Salisbury, the Prime Minister of
that time, gave a notorious speech at Edinburgh, when trying to explain
the reason for the Conservative majority's drop in the Holborn election.
He said, "It was undoubtedly a smaller majority that Colonel Duncan
obtained; but Colonel Duncan was opposed by a black man; and
however far we have advanced in overcoming prejudice, I doubt if we
have yet got to that point of view where a British constituency would
elect a black man. I am speaking roughly", continued Lord Salisbury
amidst laughter and cries of 'hear, hear!', "and using language in its
colloquial sense, because I imagine the colour is not exactly black, but,
at all events, he was a man of another race." These words simply kicked
Dadabhai into fame, and rebounded on the aspersions embedded in the
speech of his Lordship.

Dadabhai did not mind, but in India it gave great disquiet and
offence. The majority of the British public were also shocked by their
Premier's attack. This was not a media hungry individual, but their
Prime Minister giving well chosen denigration to all those people who
lived under the British Empire and who were very aware of the racial
divides he was stirring up. He seemed to want to elicit and not just
acknowledge racial prejudice and, although he would not admit to his
fault later on, Lord Salisbury had blackened his own character far more
than Dadabhai's. Even close associates were surprised.

Others rallied to defend Dadabhai, because even on the question of
his physical appearance it was obvious Lord Salisbury had never seen
him, and in regard to his abilities and character and his 'Englishness'
(i.e. his sense of fairness and honesty), he was publicly extolled as
having always been a fine example of the human race. Schnadhorst
had written to Dadabhai's friend William Digby on 18th August 1888,

stating, "In my opinion, although a Parsee is much handicapped in an English constituency, Naoroji is not only the better man and politician of the two (compared to Eve), but is more likely to win. Naoroji will be more liked the better he is known."

The papers by and large rallied behind Dadabhai. *The Star* for instance, pointed out in a blunt manner that, on the basis of skin colour, then "Surely Lord Salisbury of all men should not be the Prime Minister", as Dadabhai was lighter skinned! Other papers such as the *Accrington Times*, the London *Daily News* and the London *Graphic* considered it right that someone should be able to speak for India in Parliament. The *Warrington Examiner* in 1889 stated, "In India there are 250 millions of people; and it is monstrous doctrine that they are not to have as much as one representative in the House of Commons. The right policy is to strengthen parliament by the admission of men who know something of the pressing wants of people..... They do not ask for Home Rule yet; but they do demand, and have a right to demand, that they shall have some voice in the government of their country." The *Weekly Despatch* voiced the broader concerns over the state of the Empire when it said, "The mischief done by Lord Salisbury is irreparable. That sneer will be quoted in every paper and pass from month to mouth in every bazaar in India. There is indeed only one way in which its fatal poison may be counteracted. If some British constituency were to send Mr Naoroji to Parliament by acclamation, then the Indian people would see that Lord Salisbury spoke not the voice of England, but merely expressed his own caddish contempt ...."

But an attack came from Sir Lepel Griffin, who intoned words similar in intention to Lord Salisbury's, in that he sought to make Dadabhai appear unrepresentative. Sir Lepel was Chairman of the East Indian Association which Dadabhai had helped set up and a past Chief Secretary of the Punjab. He said Dadabhai was "an alien in race, in custom, in religion; destitute of local sympathy or local knowledge, no more unsuitable a representative could be imagined or suggested. As to the people of India, Mr Naoroji no more represents them than a Polish Jew settled in Whitechapel represents the people of England. He is a Parsee, a member of a small foreign colony, probably Semitic in origin, settled in the west of India. The Parsees are the Jews of India; intelligent, industrious and wealthy ...."

Given that right wing Tories sought to use divide and rule on Dadabhai and his supporters, these comments made in a letter to *The Times* by Sir Lepel appear entirely out of order with the position of common trust and aims that it was assumed he had held with Dadabhai.

Lord Salisbury tried to vindicate rather than apologize for his words, and further stated, ".... that the Liberal candidate was not only of a different race - widely separated from us - but that it was marked by his complexion that it was so, so that the whole constituency knew it, and that, in the existing state of English opinion, was a very strong factor in the decision which they gave .... The British House of Commons .... is a machine too peculiar and too delicate to be managed by any but those who have been born within these Isles."

Of course political capital was also made of the matter by the Liberals. One of his grand daughters and a daughter of Adi named Gosi remembers some events from this time in her childhood when she was about six. She relates that Dadabhai was small, with a beautiful face and was fair of skin. Therefore Lord Rosebery, (the future Prime Minister), used to have Dadabhai join him on the platform and had cards made up showing Dadabhai and Lord Salisbury, who was rather dark featured, asking "who is the blackest?" It is perhaps better to point out that letters did pour in, from ordinary members of the public. They came from those who were friends and from those who were strangers, to give Dadabhai their support, and to detest the words of Lord Salisbury's sneer. It was becoming a blessing in disguise, because that sneer brought out into the open a hidden bias that was, and still can be present in an election. It also showed that many in Britain did not want it stamped on them, their country or their sense of duty to all the peoples of the Empire and most importantly, wanted to do something about it. Another person who was undoubtedly affected but not outspoken over the comment was Queen Victoria. She was most aggrieved by Lord Salisbury and his intonations about her subjects, and this was not at all in line with her own view. She rebuked Salisbury over his remarks, but did this in private rather than in the public domain.

The smear allowed two sides of British opinion to be more openly expressed, rather than sticking to the usual form of keeping such strongly held views quiet. Yet it is sadly true that these views can play a part in deciding elections. To bring them out is a risk, because it could clear the air or damage the standing of a candidate. It takes a cool head to not be overcome by the passions of such a time and Dadabhai and his friends showed that they could rise over the situation, by never reacting in a like manner.

In recent times we have seen Race Relations change from meetings to develop good will, to a multifaceted enterprise, spanning Education and Commerce, Politics and Community relations. There is no one who has not had cause, at some time, to think about what its effects are and in consequence to have formed their own judgements on the matter. It is however a bit surprising to have seen only a handful of ethnic minority candidates elected to the British Parliament in the last few years given the change in the attitude of the British public when compared to a hundred years ago. But in some ways, we are only seeing the wheel of history come around once again. It is almost uncanny to see how many issues that are pertinent and unresolved in our generation, were already debated and challenged by the people who inhabited Britain and India at that time.

For weeks Salisbury's 'Black man' was flooded with invitations. The National Liberal Club held a special banquet on 21st January 1889 to mark its disapproval. Lord Ripon gave the toast and support continued to come to Dadabhai from unexpected quarters, which may have been encouraged by Lord Ripon's commendation of Dadabhai when he said, "Mr Naoroji was a specimen of the men who should be called upon for advice .... He was well entitled to represent the culture, intelligence and public spirit of India, and when he found his way into the House of Commons he would make a most valuable Member, and an admirable representative of the Indian people." Lord Ripon concluded by asking that "those who were accustomed to put themselves forward as friends of unity", should be, "facilitating the entrance into Parliament of this native of India."

Dadabhai was also now a nationally recognized Liberal figure and Schnadhorst and Arnold Morley, both central figures in the party, got him to speak at many meetings. The irony of this was not lost when the *Bristol Evening News* pointed out: "The British public now know more of Mr Naoroji than they ever knew before and Lord Salisbury may console himself with the reflection that he has done more than any man living to secure the return of a native of India to the British House of Commons." Dadabhai's position as a candidate was thereby considerably strengthened.

But Schnadhorst also wanted to restore the Finsbury Central Liberal party from the present wound caused by its division, and asked for arbitration at the Central Finsbury level to resolve the dispute. Seeing as Dadabhai had already refused this he did not change his stand. He felt the acceptance of arbitration would be a cowardly and suicidal act - as he had said before who would have him after submitting like that? He knew he was causing consternation by his stance, but as he said, after he had told his supporters, himself and now the electorate one thing, how could he change his views, even if it meant a split vote and the Conservatives getting in.

In India the machinations of the Liberal party caused dismay and distrust, and as the *National Guardian* of 5th October said, "We cannot expect the opponents of native advancement .... to feel anything but satisfaction at the split which threatens so largely to diminish Mr Naoroji's chances of success...."

However, in June 1890, Eve got another constituency and bowed out, Dadabhai was therefore formally accepted. Then in January 1891, the manifesto for a rival Liberal candidate hit Dadabhai like a thunderbolt. A new Association (not elected) put up Mr F A Ford, outwardly with the recognition of the leaders of the Liberal party. Seeing as they had once again turned tail on their position of Dadabhai's candidature, he felt bitterly rejected, which showed in his new correspondence with them.

William Digby who had been Secretary of the National Liberal club from 1882 - 1887 wrote to Schnadhorst on 22nd February 1891 to say Dadabhai seemed to have been chosen. Schnadhorst replied on 4th April 1891 that no support would be of any benefit. Digby replied on 26th June 1891, why when nationally feted by the Liberal party at public banquets, did the party not tell its own members to stop this petty playing around and accept Dadabhai? Schnadhorst, at an interview in July, said the central organization could only regret the dual candidature, but that if Mr Ford should retire, it would try to get his supporters to support Dadabhai. Schnadhorst kept Digby's and his own memorandums quiet and out of the public eye for a few days, but he also remained too quiet over the action he had promised vis a vis Mr Ford for several weeks and never apparently approached him to get him to consider standing down. During all this period Digby was a close confident of Dadabhai's and they kept up a regular communication. Digby was the founder of the Indian Political Agency and its first Director from 1887-1892 and also editor of the *India* from 1890-1892. Hence the two men worked hand in hand over many issues and although Dadabhai's candidacy was the primary issue of this time their correspondence also shows a common set of aims that gave Dadabhai the moral support he needed. This was because Digby by his actions proved that others believed in all the initiatives Dadabhai had taken to relieve the stress and hardship suffered in India. Dadabhai would have fought for his candidacy without a William Digby as his friend, but with this support, from a notable Liberal of that time, he was better able to withstand the effrontery of others in the Liberal party. The Indian press voiced its increasing disillusionment with the internal wranglings that were wearing out their candidate. Dadabhai himself wrote to Dinsha Wacha that, ".... I must go on for the sake of India .... I cannot allow it to be said that bullying and persecution can easily drive an Indian away from his resolution."

Ford appeared to get backing from headquarters and Dadabhai felt he had to make the facts public on 28th July 1891. The letter he wrote went to the *Daily News, Daily Chronicle* and the *Pall Mall Gazette* and appeared in the *Weekly News and Chronicle* of 1st August 1891, and is reproduced here.

"TO THE EDITOR

Sir, As there seemed to be some misapprehensions and as a consequence mis-statements in some of the papers, I shall feel obliged by your kindly allowing me through your columns, to make a brief explanation of the circumstances of my candidature in Central Finsbury, in connection with the Liberal Headquarters at 42, Parliament Street.

When I was selected as Candidate in August 1888, an attack was, by a party, made upon the selection.

The Liberal Headquarters then wrote to me, "Pray do not be influenced by the attack made upon you." They gave their unqualified decision that I had been fairly and carefully selected, and said that it was their duty to support me, and promised to do anything to support me in every possible way.

A few days after this, at an interview, my resolve that I was in duty bound to go to the Poll was not only fully approved of, but it was impressed upon me that as there was not case to go to arbitration, if I gave way at all, I should not have the remotest chance of being accepted by any other constituency, as any weakness on my part would shew that I had no firmness to maintain my just rights and position. Further, my proposed reply to a request to confer with a deputation from the party referred to, that there was nothing to confer about, was fully approved.

Since then I have all along replied upon the honour of the above pledges, and will do so to the close of the Poll.

When the Marquis of Salisbury made a remark about me in connection with the Holborn contest, the whole Liberal Party... including our Great Leader...The Press, and the National Liberal Club, by a Banquet under the Presidency of the Marquess of Ripon shewed generous sympathy towards me and my countrymen. The Marquess of Ripon in his speech on the occasion, among many other kind and appreciative expressions, said of me, "he (Mr Naoroji) had given valuable advice to many a public man in England upon Indian questions of a variety of kinds.... He (Lord Ripon) felt justified in saying that their friend was one of the most eminent of living Indian statesmen... Mr Naoroji was a specimen of the men who should be called upon for advice...and when he found his way into the House of Commons, he would make a most valuable Member. Those who were most accustomed to put themselves forward as the special friends of unity could hardly find a better mode of approving its reality than by facilitating the entrance into parliament of this Native of India." The Earl of Rosebery spoke about me (I write from memory) at the great Edinburgh Meeting, as "the eloquent advocate of his countrymen."

A few months after, some misunderstanding arose at headquarters, but is unnecessary to go into it, as after Mr Richard Eve retired (for which I am thankful to him) the highest Organizing Official (in July 1890) renewed the assurance to Mr Griffiths, the Hon. Secretary of the Central Finsbury Liberal and Radical Council, Penton Hall, of support to me when the time came, that no second Liberal Candidate would be encouraged by them, and that they would endeavour to leave the road clear for me.

Later in October 1890, a friend (William Digby) informed me, after a conversation he had at Headquarters, that no step calculated to make my candidature more difficult would be approved there.

In accordance with these promises, I am informed from highest authority that Mr Ford in becoming a second Liberal Candidate after I have been in the field for three years, will receive no assistance at all from Headquarters, nor had he received any such assistance or approval in any way whatever. I am informed that the Head Organizing Officials are maintaining a neutral position, but I feel no doubt, that in remembrance of their pledges and promises of support, they will be with me, and that united in the work to which in Central Finsbury during the last three years I have been devoted, we will win back the seat and thus add another to the recent Liberal triumphs".

Because it was moderate enough in its tone Digby sent Schnadhorst a copy to show that along with giving Dadabhai's version of events there was a readiness expressed in the letter for a reconciliation. Weeks later Schnadhorst curtly said the matter was closed. The rift amongst the Radicals and Liberals in Central Finsbury widened.

On 23rd October a Mr William Harcourt wrote to Dadabhai to say that "Lord Ripon, with whom I have been staying, tells me that you have been good enough to say that you would not be unwilling to meet me and have a little private talk." On November 2nd Mrs Bell who had become a long time supporter of Dadabhai, passed on that William Harcourt had provided some private correspondence which stated that Lords Ripon and Reay wanted Dadabhai. In addition, several National Liberal Club members had told the Central Liberal Association, the National Liberal Federation and the National Liberal and Radical Union that they had better recognize Dadabhai soon. A special resolution was also passed at the Indian National Congress in December 1891 (see Appendix 7).

By then Lord Ripon had more control over the Liberal party offices as he was Director of the Liberal party. He tired to get Dadabhai another secure seat, and Dadabhai's correspondence mentions about a visit to Reading in January 1892. Nothing transpired from this possibility and with little direct support coming his way, Dadabhai put out a pamphlet on 23rd March 1892 for internal distribution. Dadabhai had felt he had earned the respect of Senior Liberals and was both shocked and surprised when he had received a letter on 22nd March 1892 from Arnold Morley, in which the mention of arbitration was first made. Others tried to push him towards arbitration once again. Dadabhai in a letter of 29th April said that Morley had made it clear that the management of the party would no longer be 'Neutral' in his case if he did not agree to arbitration.

Dadabhai heard that his continuing determination to keep his independence meant that the London Liberal and Radical Union was now determined to dispose of him. He wrote to Malabari at this time, stating that his devotion to the Liberal Party remained and having Lord Ripon and Mr Gladstone's support had meant a lot to him and he still believed the British people would give him justice. But he could not say this publicly in such terms, and the matter weighed heavily on him. Lord Ripon appeared to lose ground with party officials. Dadabhai was in a critical position and sent a discreet statement to show that what had happened was unfair. Then out of the blue he wrote on the 11th and 12th June that a Mr Caustin was trying to rectify the situation. In the end Mr Ford withdrew rather than split the vote. Dadabhai had at last been give a fair chance, and his supporters held an enthusiastic meeting on 15th June.

He put his all into the final push and published the following manifesto, which was very much in line with the Liberal party's election manifesto of the time - Home rule for Ireland; for London the endowment of the London County Council; proper application of charitable endowments for the benefit of the people; women to be qualified to contest for seats in the Country Council; contributions by owners of property for public improvements; rating of vacant properties or land; representative parish and district councils; direct popular veto of the liquor traffic; extensions of the Factory Acts; free breakfast tables (which was a measure aimed at freer trading conditions); graduated income tax on incomes over £300 and higher rates on a sliding scale; inexpensive Industrial courts; all labour questions to be handled justly; and all main Indian reforms to be met. As reported in the local papers, his campaign was based on "the double causes of politics and humanity."

Gladstone, Rosebery, Ripon and Reay sent Dadabhai their best regards now that the split had healed, so did Mr Eve, who had never opposed Dadabhai on a personal basis. Martin Wood also continued to give his personal support to Dadabhai's candidature.

It has been hinted that Dadabhai and others and the Irish nationalists had entered into negotiations to form a somewhat clandestine electoral pact, when he had been searching for another seat after the Holborn elections. The idea had been for safe Irish seats to be made open to Congressmen in return for which the Irish party would receive financial help from wealthy individuals. The evidence for these negotiations is scanty and not really corroborated and in any case never led to anything. But it may be that a secondary effect was that Irish voters were more willing to vote for Dadabhai or were given some direct encouragement from their leaders to put their cross against his name.

Josephine Butler, the great women's rights reformer of those times, wrote to Dadabhai at that time. She said that she was supporting him because of his "uncompromising friendship of womanhood", and that he always upheld the necessity of equal laws for men and women, and for his moving appeals on several occasions. She went on to say that his insight into all that was unfair to women was not surpassed by countrymen of her own, and that his standard for the integrity of marriage and the purity of the home, are what the Christian could desire in accord with Christ's teachings. She would pray for his success - this letter is perhaps one of the most illuminating ones that has been brought to light as it shows the often unseen but obviously strongly held principles in Dadabhai's life on equal rights for men and women.

The new Maharaja of Baroda, His Highness Sir S Gaekwar, came to the aid of Dadabhai at this time. Dadabhai's rival Captain Penton was an influential landlord, who had carriages supplied by Lord Salisbury and other aristocrats for the election day. He was the present Member of Parliament and had a track record as a Captain in the 4th Dragoon Guards with whom he served in Egypt in 1882. He was a son of a Colonel Henry Penton of Pentonville, which is an area of Finsbury Central and Pentonville Road still exists as a major thoroughfare.

The Prince gave Dadabhai 20 coaches to help him in a like manner.

A Barrister, Mr (later Sir) Mancherji Bhownaggree was there to help Dadabhai, and in the process he learnt what an election campaign required of the candidate. This was good preparation as he himself became the next Indian in Parliament, when he became Conservative member for Bethnal Green, for two terms from 1895 to 1906. He was a popular member of Parliament in what was a working class area, but he opposed much of what the Indian National Congress stood for, and proved to hold a very different stance to that of Dadabhai, which made him unpopular in India.

Digby, Keir Hardie who became the first Labour MP on 4th July, John Burns, James Rowlands and Griffiths (the Local Secretary) gave a lot of a assistance to Dadabhai's campaign. Burns put the Labour vote Dadabhai's way and stayed with him throughout this time.

Ford's supporters now rallied behind Dadabhai, not in a niggardly way, but positively as did Mr Ford and his wife. Mrs Bell and her daughter were indefatigable in meeting the challenge of all sorts of calls, as was the daughter of Charles Bradlaugh (deceased), Mrs Bradlaugh-Bonner. Florence Nightingale, who had maintained an active interest in India for several years, was supportive, but confined to her rooms through illness. A Miss Colenso and Mrs Wynford Phillips enlivened a public meeting held on the eve of the election. The support of women was therefore a key part of Dadabhai's campaign, and it was strengthened through their endeavours.

The Conservatives tried to emphasize that Dadabhai was a fire worshipper and quite a few 'Christians' refused to vote for him solely on that premise, although if they had checked up on the facts they would have found this assertion was untrue. "A fire worshipping Asiatic" said the *Spectator* magazine. One retired officer referred to Parsees as only a bunch of traders, who would be massacred if the British ever left India. The *St Stephen's Review* gave an oblique appreciation, by saying that at least Dadabhai was not the worst, but why "was not in the whole of the division an Englishman, Scotsman, Welshman or Irishman as worthy of their votes as this fire worshipper from Bombay."

On election day, 6th July 1892, and in spite of these comments, Dadabhai got 2959 votes to Captain FT Penton's 2956. This narrow majority reversed Captain Penton's five vote majority of the previous election and was not so uncommon in those days. It also got Dadabhai the nickname 'narrow majority' as an easier pronunciation of his own name.

Cheers erupted through the night sky for Salisbury's 'black man.' They were heard for miles, as thousands had gathered according to reports. For weeks Dadabhai got messages of congratulations from all four quarters of the globe. Gladstone commented on his great satisfaction at this victory on 7th July. A Scottish Home rule group wrote from as far as Melbourne, because Lord Salisbury's remark had been made in the Scottish capital, at a meeting hosted by a Scottish peer (Lord Hopetown). The implication on the Scots was one that they wanted to reverse, in the name of many Scottish people. Dadabhai wrote a letter of thanks to his electors which is given here, and was posted from the National Liberal Club, Whitehall Place, SW on 7th July 1892.

> Dear Sir,
> I desire to take the earliest possibly opportunity of tendering to all the electors of Central Finsbury my most grateful thanks for the honour they have conferred on my by placing me in the proud position of Parliamentary Representative for Central Finsbury.
> I also desire to offer my deep acknowledgements to all who have aided me in my work at much self sacrifice and trouble. Having had so much voluntary assistance from many quarters, it would be impossible for me to thank each individually. I pray, therefore, everyone to accept my heartfelt thanks.
> When I first came among you, more than four years ago, I promised that, if elected, the interests of Clerkenwell will always receive my first and principal consideration. That promise shall be by me faithfully performed, as well as all the pledges in my programme, and I trust your entire satisfaction.
> You have in electing me generously and nobly helped India to obtain a voice in the Imperial Parliament, and I offer to you, on behalf of my countrymen, our most sincere and heartfelt thanks.
> I remain, every faithfully yours.
> D NAOROJI

India was surprised by the election result and tumultuous over this son of the land, who had always taken up their cause and was now elected to the seat of the Imperial government, returned by a British electorate. Their thanks went to that English constituency for having done this, and their feelings for British rule were enhanced by seeing an Indian actually being elected. Bombay in particular was rapturous, but even more telling in a way were the Indian opponents who sent heartfelt congratulations to Dadabhai (see Appendix 7).

Dady Cama wrote to the Lord Mayor that the followers of the Prophet Zoroaster were taught to share their joys with others. He therefore sent 100 guineas for the poor box at Mansion House. The City press was moved to say "There are some things among the Parsees that we should do well to follow."

Some comments on the reason for Dadabhai's election victory come from his granddaughter Gosi. She remembers a visit by a MP, Ben Spool, to India when he said that it was the Irish vote which swung things Dadabhai's way. He also stated that he felt the Liberal party had almost undermined him, by playing a "trick", which could have meant they did not support him fully as a candidate. Public meetings were held in India and the voters of Central Finsbury were feted as much as Dadabhai. Pherozeshah Mehta a leading Indian politician and associate of Dadabhai's said, "Many people profess to be sceptical as to the patriotism and political sagacity of the electors of Central Finsbury (cheers) - in choosing an Indian for their representative. But I think you will agree with me, gentlemen, that they have rendered a service of incalculable value, by proving by their generous action, that the instincts of English political wisdom are capable of triumphing over the direct prejudices of caste, colour and creed, (cheers)."

Another proposed "that the thanks of the meeting be conveyed to the electors of Central Finsbury for their generous and high minded action in electing Mr Dadabhai Naoroji as their Member in Parliament." A magnificent carved box was then sent to the people of Central Finsbury, which contained a unique album of photographs of India taken in the 1890s. This album is still held by the Finsbury Library.

It was now that a rumour began and both the *Globe* and *Echo* made much of a supposed £28,000, though Dadabhai had never received anything like this amount in financial aid. Captain Penton filed a petition with the authorities, demanding a scrutiny and recount of the election. The recount was held on August 8th and Dadabhai's vote rose to 2961, whilst Captain Penton's stayed at 2956, giving an increased majority of 5 votes, which was the same as Captain Penton had had for the last six years.

Dadabhai was accused of corruption or other unsavoury acts amounting to seven charges in total. Personally he had no reason to fear for his conduct but what was unsettling was that one of his helpers, Homi Dadina, unaware of the Corrupt Practices Act, had 20 coaches and money to use on the day to ferry supporters to the polling booths. Some of Captain Penton's supporters went and asked him for carriages to bring voters. Dadina offered them lifts and gave some money for a drink in gratitude for their efforts, being genuinely unaware that such an ambush could be used. The voters were then picked up, to vote for

Penton! Henry Cobb, Dadabhai's solicitor, questioned Dadina and Dadabhai told him to tell it as it had happened. It was felt that Dadina should take a long holiday, rather than be made to face cross questioning. Captain Penton's case was filed on 26th November, and the court hearing was fixed for mid December. The local papers felt that the election of Dadabhai had done much good and as *The Echo* said, "There are plenty of urban Landlords in the legislature, but only one bred and born native of India. Under such circumstances, Captain Penton can be better spared than Mr Naoroji."

After five months of waiting, Captain Penton's case came up in the courts before Mr Justice Cave and Mr Justice Vaughan and *The Times* carried reports of the case held on 12th, 13th and 14th of December. Neither side was clear about where it stood as a lot of the evidence required knowing why individuals had cast their vote.

As each voter was called up, their right to vote was challenged and either approved or disapproved. Captain Penton's side challenged about 100 votes and Dadabhai's side challenged about 70 votes. As *The Times* stated, "Yesterday (14th) the trial of this petition proceeded and some curious and puzzling questions arose – the parties, as before mentioned, being quite in the dark as to how the parties they objected to voted until the voting papers are produced, after the vote had been declared bad, and some of the voting papers being lost or not identified. Before the end of the day, however, (after the midday recess), the petition was withdrawn." Now Dadabhai, the constituency party and India could breathe easily again.

On the confirmation of the election, a very enthusiastic meeting was held at the Foresters Hall on the Clerkenwell Road on 23rd January 1893. Leading MPs and London citizens and 2000 others attended for one of the biggest meetings ever held at the Hall, to sound out the way forward. It was noted that Dadabhai's election represented not only India's interests, but was also in the best interests of all Britons who wished its progress and prosperity and who had often wanted to show that British claims for popular government could actually happen in truth. Dadabhai and others spoke for Indians at that meeting, in terms of their desire to be British subjects, having equal birth rights with all other British subjects.

But it was just at this time that Dadabhai was facing his severest problems on the financial front. On 20th July 1892, Mr Malabari acting as a close associate, had written to ask Dadabhai how he was faring with his finances. Dadabhai was already having problems then and yet had kept up with the electioneering and then the court case, and also with his constituency matters, rather than giving time and effort to making money. Any funds from India were undermined by a system

108

that lead to the rupee being devalued. The story that Dadabhai had received thousands of pounds from a Maharaja, only added salt to the wound, and probably put off any contributors. If only he had had a penny for every time this rumour mongering went on, he would have been a wealthier man.

Dadabhai had kept his personal expenditure low, but he needed a cash flow to print material, subscribe to journals, reports, travel, and he continued to give to philanthropic institutions and individuals, primarily those based in his constituency.

Mr Malabari used the *Indian Spectator* in late 1892 to state that Dadabhai was getting very little support from India. Dadabhai was upset because he always wanted to raise monies through private donations, not by public appeals. However, by the 24th February 1893, he was prepared to return home, through having no money. Literally an MP who was a Member of the Poor. But then in the nick of time, £1000 came from Baroda. Other Indian states followed later on, and Dadabhai's mind was able to concentrate once more on parliament, but the result had been a close run matter, which almost ended his political career.

CHAPTER TEN

PARLIAMENT'S BUSINESS

Having been elected the question now was, once in Parliament how to get real change implemented for India? There were difficulties as well as advantages at being in the House of Commons. In the early days of that Parliament, only a few members, around twenty in total, had any real interest in India, and half of these were strongly conservative and smelt dissension in any liberalizing force. The few of the other camp who balanced them had the real desire and the intimate knowledge of India that was necessary to being about change, and a number of these were already Dadabhai's friends, including W C Caine and Samuel Smith. There were around six hundred and seventy members of Parliament in total.

The previous experience of Dadabhai's friends reflects some of the growing awareness that members of the British public were beginning to show over the events that were occurring in India. Dadabhai's election to the British Parliament was not so much the pinnacle of achievement but rather the most significant step on the progress that was being made. It was now possible for a new Indian voice to be raised, which spoke for India and would be heard inside Parliament, to complement all those that were being raised from the outside.

An Indian Parliamentary Committee was formed at a dinner held on 27th July 1893 around the founding members, who were Dadabhai, William Wedderburn (Chair) and newly elected member for Banffshire, W C Caine, J H Roberts (Secretary), J E Ellis, W S B Mclaren, J Swift-MacNeil, C E Schwann and S Smith. Their aim was to establish a caucus in Parliament, which would support Indian's claims. It began with around twenty members and slowly grew to one hundred and fifty-six (see Appendix 5). Liberal Members of Parliament were predominant in its earlier years, but Labour members joined the 'Indian opposition' as it was called up until 1915.

It became a cause of worry to the Authorities and troubled the Anglo-Indian community no end. When *The Times* attacked it, *The Indian* noted this was a good sign, because it was therefore recognized as a significant force in the House. An 'Anglo-Indian Defence Association' was set up to act against this grouping. Undoubtedly the Indian Committee was a major reason behind Lord Salisbury and Sir Lepel Griffin giving their support to a Conservative Asian Parliamentary candidate in the election of 1895, Mr (later Sir) M M Bhownaggree, because he held Tory views and was willing to give vocal support to them in Parliament. They were trying to be more effective at sabotaging the weight of opinion in the House and amongst the general public that the Indian Opposition was using to further India's cause. Over a decade and especially in the Liberal Government of 1906, the Indian Parliamentary Party, as it was also known, was able to do more for Indian issues in the House. It continued the aims of the earlier members who had first met in 1893, and similarly but in a more distant connection, also continued the work of the grouping set up by John Bright MP in 1853 and 1883.

Amongst the pro-Indian MPs, Mr Caine had sought out his own knowledge of Indian affairs by a hands-on experience, and he had visited India on several occasions. He noted how at that time the really self-governing bodies were confined to a few municipalities, and he praised the efforts and the work of the Bombay Corporation as an example. In a leaving speech on 7th February 1889, after one of his visits, he spoke in favour of the Indian National Congress and was immediately taken to task by the *Times of India*. He was not therefore viewed in a benign way by the establishment and the Anglo-Indian community in particular did not like his visits to 'their' country. That year the Congress had been attended by Dadabhai's son Adi in his absence, and was presided over by another of the pro-Indian lobbyists, namely William Wedderburn.

Samuel Smith MP had spoken before in the House of Commons on the Indian budget issue. He, Dadabhai and others had repeated the principle both in the House and elsewhere, that it was only fair to tax India to such an extent if the British Government would recognize that with taxation went representation. The campaigners were also used to the fact that they would be routinely disregarded in the House. Mr Smith also came into contention because of his views (e.g. with Sir M E Grant Duff, Governor of Madras 1881-6) on matters of government in India.

Dadabhai was a member of Gladstone's last Liberal administration, and the Grand Old Man of British politics wanted to have one last go at achieving Home rule for Ireland. There was also the list of reforms proposed by the Liberal party in the Newcastle Programme of 1891 and Dadabhai supported his leader on all these main issues although Gladstone was not that enthusiastic about the Newcastle Programme. Because the Liberal government had no overall majority, it relied heavily on the Irish vote to give it a slender majority in the House of Commons,

Dadabhai's position was moderately enhanced as every vote counted and that meant senior members of the party listening to what was said by the backbenchers. However India was not very high on anyone's list of priorities and it was Ireland that would always catch the attention. In consequence Dadabhai found that he was on the backburner through placing India as first on his order of priorities. Although India did command time and attention in the House it was seen as being someone else's business and did not get the level of debate or importance that should have been accorded it. As had been said previously, when it came to matters concerning India, he had a few firm friends like Samuel Smith and W C Caine, and allies of a political nature in Lord Kimberly, Secretary of State for India, and his deputy George Russell (see the Appendices for a list of the parliamentary business).

On his first visit to Parliament, the native press made fun over the fact that his fairer complexion would give Lord Salisbury's colleagues a hard time in identifying him. After taking a secular oath, Dadabhai gave a rather over complimentary maiden speech on August 9th which probably arose because he felt that after an unusual election like his, he wanted to put down some kind of marker and also thank his electorate. The next day *The Daily Telegraph* gauged the speaker as an "eloquent and fervent recruit to opposition (?) ranks."

On the whole Dadabhai was a capable speaker who kept his messages plain and concentrated in their content, often returning to just a few themes. His delivery was apparently cool and easy to hear, making him a reasonable speaker who often prepared many notes and liked to use quotes made by contemporary politicians. The Hansard records of his Parliamentary Speeches show that he was not really a debater, and in the context of Parliament he was long winded. In the particular case of his maiden speech whilst he did not overdo it on length he did not do very well on the content and would probably have wished that he had waited a little longer. The content of his later speeches show a lot of well researched argument, but as Parliament is not noted for listening to a balanced view, Dadabhai rarely kept the other members glued to their seats. What he did sometimes do was to challenge other speakers or be challenged himself by raising issues in the House. But as Hansard shows unless he gave a prepared speech, most of these challenges were quite brief and he must have spent a lot of time listening to other debates. All the same he was an active Parliamentarian and he soon began having to field and face a host of questions and filled over a page of the order book of the House of Commons with notices of motions calling for information on India. He did not want to be labelled as the 'Member for India', which title the Indian press in particular gave him. But given that his favourite quote was the one made by

Macaulay, "the heaviest of all yokes is the yoke of the stranger," he could not lay down the drive and determination in himself in wanting to remove such a condition. Therefore he had to accept his own yoke of promoting Indian's affairs which meant he had to carry the label as well.

Early on in the administration, a dispute arose over gold and silver values, which were diverging from one another. As the leading financial and trading nation in the world, Britain wanted to preserve the gold standard on a modified basis. India's rupee, which was a silver based currency, had already been devalued by other measures and could be hit harder by these proposed changes. Dadabhai had already written to confute the 'bimetalists', and the situation was not helped by the Viceroy omitting any explanation of how the financial consequences of the modification would affect the Indian people. This omission was shown up clearly in a resolution in February 1893 and in a subsequent report for a select committee, which was set up on 23rd March 1893. These were primarily established to see how the falling rupee was affecting the government and its paid officials, but not considering the effects of these changes upon the people. Dadabhai gave evidence to this Indian Currency Committee of 1893 and to another one set up in 1898.

During the deliberation on the issue Dadabhai had the chance to pose the questions that, as he had earlier stated, neither the Viceroy nor the members of the different branches of Government were up to investigating. He also used the opportunity of the time to move on to giving a thorough explanation of the poverty faced by India. He stressed how the unfavourable rates of exchange that the modifications could bring in, when placed on top of existing arrangements, such as loan repayments, would pile one hardship on top of another. He talked in Parliament for some time on the issue, and being a sound researcher and in this particular instance, an able presenter, was listened to attentively, after some initial outbursts. He completed his presentations by proposing an amendment. This was lost because of the cost factors involved, but not without first earning some new respect for its author in the House.

During his time in Parliament, Dadabhai was able to get access to papers that he had previously been barred from seeing. Hence he kept up his researches and was able to argue very knowledgeably with anyone. A surprising number of MPs thought India was rich and so had no interest in the Indian budget debates. Dadabhai kept up with the issue of the rupee, later publishing an article in a journal named *Commerce*, to state that the Government compelled the indigenous Indian tax-payer or ratay to pay proportionately more from his rupee income than the British residents who were paid in pounds sterling in Britain. Dadabhai submitted further statements to the Indian Currency

Committee in 1893, attacking the basically despotic methods behind such a financial drain. In hindsight, his principles were correct and his supposition over the bimetal issue which was that commodities are reckoned against other commodities in the long run is seen as a sensible base. But on the bimetal question alone, he was wrong to oppose a change from a silver standard to a gold one. Hence the Indian rupee was further devalued by the bimetallist approach.

On the general state of the Indian economy, Dadabhai posed questions and raised debate throughout his Parliamentary career. He was the acknowledged master on the subject of economic reforms for India. Basically he told the House that the present system was grossly unfair, especially when India was made to send 'payments' to Britain for the 'blessings' of British rule, when really it was a method of extracting further wealth on top of the tax system. He said, "it mattered not that what the State received was called tax, rent, revenue or by any other name they liked. The simple fact of the matter was that out of a certain annual production, the State took a certain portion."

According to official figures in 1890/91, the debt owed by India was £92 million for railways and £27 million for canals, plus £80 million for other purposes, mainly military. The government claimed that the financial health of India was good because gross revenue and expenditure were roughly balanced. Respectively, the official figures in rupees were 787,597,440 and 807,883,760 in 1887-8, 819,696,780 and 816,596,660 in 1888-9, 846,363,000 and 828,266,000 in 1889-90, 849,321,000 and 846,617,000 in 1890-1. Given that debts also had to be repaid off at around 3-4 percent and that other unfunded debt and guaranteed interest payments on capital outlaid for railway lines and the like had to be paid each year, then adding these figures on (as Dadabhai did), meant the books could not really balance. Also for trade, like cotton, a one-way system existed, which meant India was always importing more than it exported and Dadabhai was pointing out that in real terms, India was not allowed to break even.

He proposed that if India could actually be developed by British investment going into building up Indian-based products, then an indigenous consumer market would also grow as per capita income grew. He asked members to consider that in the long run even if British industry exported a mere £1-0s-0d of goods per head of population, which the average Indian could then buy if his wages increased, the Indian market would equal the rest of the world, to the benefit of both countries.

Nor was he opposed to any taxation, because he could support it for the ends of the policing of India and for services for the Indians. But the expenditures placed upon India were not the same from India's viewpoint as they were from Britain's own worldwide views. He cited military expenditure as a prime reason for the present financial drain on India, along with a highly paid administration, land rent and taxation. He asked the authorities to supply information, which he said "... would satisfactorily show whether, under the most highly paid administration in the world, India is poor or not; a Finance Minister expresses the same opinion as was expressed long ago, (i.e.) Nothing more can be said than that India is extremely poor."

To get changes he proposed in September 1893 that a full Inquiry be set up in India, "... to ascertain whether it is or not that the administration of India is based upon a principle, not only destructive, but very much mistaken." But he also noted a problem to such ideas because, "the Front Bench (of the House), and the India Office are so much associated and identified together that the Front Bench is put in the false position of defending its secret and irresponsible India Office in everything they do." India's politics were intertwined with Cabinet government, and its first aim was to rule Britain's Empire. At that time, his proposal was not taken on board.

On top of his parliamentary business, Dadabhai was constantly going to meetings across the country. The *Indian Spectator* of March 1893 was astounded at the vitality of Dadabhai, given his age. In the course of a month, "we find him on a visit to Liverpool, in connection with the Liberal Federation... appearances at Puton Hall and St George's Hall...", which were trips done in addition to everything else that he did.

Dadabhai tabled a motion for a Bill on 2nd March 1893 on simultaneous examinations for the Indian Civil Service in Britain and India. The Secretary of State could already allow such exams. But Dadabhai wanted to raise a debate, even though the Bill had no chance against other legislation, because the 'in principle' agreement was not being honoured as it should have been. At that time, 95 percent of uncovenanted jobs which were the lower paid posts, were held by Indians, but only two applicants passed the entrance exam for higher posts in 1892. He said the Indian Civil Service was a "triple loss" to India of 'wealth, wisdom and work.' Wealth because salaries and pensions left India, wisdom because Indians did not gain experience, work because it went to Europeans.

His Bill was blocked by the Front bench of his own party. When Herbert Paul MP won a high place in the ballot of bills, Dadabhai had asked him to table a resolution to the same effect and members of the Indian Parliamentary Committee were canvassed. Mr Paul moved it on June 2nd, just after Dadabhai had withdrawn his own Bill. He did that after making clear to his own front bench that they had "taken every means in their power of breaking to the heart the words of promises and pledges from time to time." He confirmed that " the application to natives of the competitive system as conducted in England, and the recent reduction in the age...are all so many dishonest and transparent subterfuges". With Dadabhai and William Wedderburn supporting the new resolution and after a memorable debate on the motion, it was passed by eight votes (84 votes to 76). This was a great surprise and a significant victory for the Parliamentary Committee, Dadabhai and India. That the resolution would then come up against other opposition, especially in the House of Lords, was to be expected, but it was the mild opposition of the Liberal government that had been encountered during the debates that was not so easy to bear. Gladstone himself let the matter ride for a few days and then consulted the Indian Government, which was then given the ideal opportunity to raise further objections. Gladstone was not naive in this matter and few people were fooled by his desire to let everyone be consulted provide the explanation for his motive of going to the Indian Government.

So, despite the resolution being passed in parliament, Dadabhai wrote to friends in India calling for large scale support from there to show the amount of ground swell opinion in favour of making the Indian Civil Service more approachable for Indians. One letter writer wrote back that British teachers with little or no experience, were replacing Indians with fifteen to twenty years teaching background. Dadabhai had put in his original resolution that the exams for the Civil Service should be held after further training had been given to Indian candidates, because most people placed Indian tuition at a lower standard than British tuition, whether in terms of qualifications for jobs or in terms of the examination questions given in assessments.

Another reason for his calling for support in India was that the resolution of the House was not binding on the Indian Government. The Secretary of State wrote and said that although he, Lord Kimberly, was personally opposed, he would forward it to the Government of India. Having got together the Indian Parliamentary Committee, Dadabhai, William Wedderburn and WC Caine wanted to keep up the maximum pressure from their end. Short of open internal civil war in the party, this was the best that could be done.

The Anglo-Indian community had already expressed its dislike for a 'Babu raj' and the government of a 'Bengalee Babu.' Because of the questions that Dadabhai could raise in the House, it now adopted a new tactic and 'exposed' that agitation was being caused by Dadabhai over these issues. Dadabhai merely retorted by saying how he had found the 'agitation method out from the English press and *The Times*', who were not above doing the same thing themselves. In the end the full overhaul of the practice of a simultaneous exam was not achieved, and only a change was engineered. Nonetheless it proved to be a change in the right direction and led to a greater review years later.

Dadabhai still put in the time to keep up a full and proper interest in his constituency role. He kept in contact on a nearly daily basis, and raised questions in the House of Commons on behalf of his Finsbury residents (see Appendix 4). When he left for India in 1893 there was a vote of confidence for Dadabhai due to his good track record. He joined in the life of many different groups in Finsbury, and was an Odd Fellow, a Forester, a Druid and a Good Templar, and attended the Band of Hope Society meetings. The London Municipal Reform League, Trade Unions and Societies, Working Men's Club, the Women's Liberal Federation, and the Women's Franchise League and later on the National Union of Women's suffrage Societies were all personally known to him, either because he spoke to their members or because he gave money and advice or a mixture of all three. The *Weekly News and Chronicle* of June 16th 1894 reported on his speech at the Laying of the Foundation stone of the New Vestry Hall in Finsbury. Dadabhai spoke on the boost to local municipal rule that such a building would give as the Vestry Hall was the seat of Local Government in those days. He was also present on June 15th 1895 when the building was opened by the Prime Minister, Lord Rosebery, in Rosebery Avenue at which Dadabhai gave a vote of thanks. The building is now known as Finsbury Town Hall and still faces on to Rosebery Avenue. The London Chamber of Commerce and the Institute of Bankers heard him speak. The *Weekly News and Chronicle* supported Dadabhai throughout his time as the Local Member of Parliament and reported on prize givings, talks to the Goldsmiths and Foresters Union and the Stone and Zinc Preparers Association (see Appendix 6 for a fuller listing). He toured and retoured all the ward associations of the Party.

He wanted to see fair ground rents and land values fixed which were an important issue for many residents of Clerkenwell. His first motion connected to the constituency was on the Lincoln Inn Fields, which would have given more open space to the locals. The measure was passed in the Commons and then lost in the House of Lords. He introduced a measure on land values with Mr James Rowlands MP (Finsbury East) and supported Mr Rowlands' own measure on election expenses (see Appendix 3).

James Rowland was another radical Liberal, who had been born in East Finsbury in 1851. He was self educated to a large extent at both the Working Men's Ormond Street College and Shoreditch Town Hall. He consistently spoke on the rights of Labour and when he stood again in 1906 he was mistakenly assumed to be the Labour Candidate.

Dadabhai also worked with his colleagues against unequal gas charges and they led a deputation to the Board of Trade. In the period of 1893 to 94, Dadabhai served on the Standing Committee for Trade in the House of Commons.

As reported in the *Islington Gazette* of 27th January 1893, Dadabhai was also President of the Local Government Board, and he sought to use his influence to prevent the detached portion of Finsbury, namely Muswell Hill, from being transferred to Hornsey. In fact it would have been in Dadabhai's political interest to have seen Muswell Hill go, as it represented a Tory stronghold in his constituency.

Dadabhai and Mr Rowlands also fought for their constituents' rights through proposed amendments in the London County Council (General Powers) Bill. On 29th May 1894, Dadabhai is reported in *The Times* for moving a second reading in the House of Commons, and both he and James Rowlands also campaigned over the powers of the House of Commons in that year.

On the India front the year of 1894 had actually began with a poor start for the reformers when the Government of India made it clear it did not wish to have simultaneous exams for the natives. However, as an MP with responsibilities for Central Finsbury and through the work of the House of Commons, Dadabhai was kept very busy. He attended six hundred and fifty-four out of seven hundred and four divisions (votes) in the House and found a 'pair' or opposition member of Parliament who could match his vote for the fifty times he could not be present.[1] It was a very good track record and only beaten by the Chief Whip. Dadabhai also maintained a lot of local correspondence and took an active interest in the business of his constituents. He may have been a son of India but he was also motivated to fulfil his role as a British MP and that meant doing his best for those who had elected him to the responsibility.

In the House his efforts for a full ranging inquiry into India's expenditure meant he took another step forward with his colleagues. On the Indian budget debate, Samuel Smith moved a resolution in August 1894, pointing out in his speech that Indians could make no appeal of their own. Others rose and pointed out that Gladstone had seen the emancipation over the previous sixty years of the Irish, the Jews and the Slaves, which begged the question about what would happen for the Indians.

He continued by saying that the Liberals, through the resolution in the Act of 1833 of Macauley and Lansdowne, had made promises, "That no native of the said territories nor any natural born subject of her Majesty resident therein shall, by reason only of his religion, place

1. By these means members of opposite persuasions could have their joint votes counted against each other without needing to be present in Westminster

of birth, descent or any of them, be disabled from holding any place, office or employment of said Company (or government after 1858)". Would the member for Midlothian (Mr Gladstone), who at the very beginning of his career had been in the House for the passing of that Act, not wish to see the effects carried through at the end of his career, just as he was striving to do for the Irish. Some other members spoke against the resolution by saying that India had received much benefit from British rule. But as Seymour Kear pointed out in reply, it was not the Government of India that was the main point of the resolution, but rather the people of India. Dadabhai spoke for two hours on the subject to an audience of eighteen. When this became known, several people in Britain and India felt disheartened by the lack of interest in India's needs. The resolution that was moved stated "That in the opinion of this house, a full and independent Parliamentary inquiry should be made into the condition and wants of the Indian people, and their ability to bear their existing financial burdens, the nature of the revenue system and the possibilities of a reduction in the expenditure, also the financial relations between India and the United Kingdom and generally the system of government of India".

To these comments, Sir Henry Fowler, Secretary of State for India replied that he was not against the idea of an inquiry, but what he would personally ask for was a full and independent inquiry. He proposed that policy on India was for the House only, but if the motion was withdrawn, he would undertake the appointment of a select committee at the next session, to inquire into the financial affairs. Samuel Smith agreed, as long as he and his supporters were free to ask for an extension of the scope of the Committee's deliberations to include the authority to look into the tax paying capacity of the Indian people. Hence they did not press on with their resolution.

The financial drain was a consistent problem for the reformers, and later in that parliament, on February 12th 1895, Dadabhai also raised the question of the apportioning of expenditure between Britain and India, stating that Parliament should also look into that financial feature too. He again powerfully asked for righteousness, pointing out that the slaves worked for their master's profit were also housed and kept by them, and yet the Indians worked for British profits, but were not housed by the same token. In the Queen's speech of that year, he had added that, "the short and whole of the matter was whether the people of British India were British citizens or British helots." The Secretary of State had been asked in the House if a Parliamentary inquiry was the best method, as they only last the life time of the government, and MPs and governments can be gone almost before the inquiry could sit. The Government was already in trouble in 1895 and Gladstone had resigned the leadership in 1894, so an alternative method to a short lived Committee was preferable. A Royal Commission, smaller but very efficient and impartial and permanent in its dealings would be a better option. The Secretary of State was asked if he agreed with this alternative, which he did and so a Royal Commission was appointed. Dadabhai then withdrew and sat down triumphant.

The Royal Commission was appointed by Royal Warrant on 24th May 1895, six weeks before the Liberal administration was dissolved. Lord Welby was Chairman and Dadabhai was invited to join as were William Wedderburn and W C Caine, but no other Indian was approached.

In his time in Parliament, Dadabhai raised ten questions on particular matters concerning India which was about the limit his time would allow. He contested and won on the appointment of a 'native' to the Professorship of Sanskrit at Madras College. He tried to get a further hearing on a case of the forced early retirement of a British Colonel, but had no joy. He asked that Indian school teachers who had been fired for signing a petition, have their case reviewed. He also raised questions as on the treatment of Indians in Madagascar, on a suspected plot to blow up the Official Resident in Hyderabad ,on the speed limits for petrol driven vehicles (at 4 mph), and on Post Office employees involvement in political elections. Sometimes he met with success and sometimes he did not.

There was another matter that was being fought at this time both inside and outside of parliament. That was over the way that the Governments of both that time and previous years had manipulated events to secure a state monopoly of the growth, manufacture and sale of opium. This trade had originally been started by the East Indian Company, when its profits in India declined because of the growing cost of maintaining an administration. It found that the tea trade with China, which grew from the Commutation Act of 1784, could be paid for with opium from India and the tea trade was its major profit-making enterprise.

In 1894, the income from the tax revenue was eight and a half million rupees. In those days the proposed solution was for the complete disengagement by the British Government from the opium trade. This had flourished for fifty years in China with great numbers of the Chinese becoming addicts, through the supply gates of India and hence with the aid of Britain. There was and always had been a public outcry against this drug traffic, but all the governments, including the one of 1892, pleaded an inability to do without the opium revenue. In those days a generalisation of the official view was that in moderation these drugs had no ill effects. Dadabhai had asked back in October 1886 at a meeting for the suppression of the Opium trade, "How could that which

120

was a poison here, be harmless in another portions of the Empire?"

The Christian missionaries who saw the effects first hand were angered by the root causes of the trafficking and were often remonstrating their concerns back in Britain. On 10th April 1891 they won a victory when the then Conservative government agreed to saying the system supporting Indian Opium was morally wrong and that licences should be withdrawn. Dadabhai was glad, but also unhappy when on 31st October 1892, the Secretary of the Society for the suppression of the Opium trade sent a proposal letter to the Government, making China the main object for reforms. Dadabhai wanted the issue of Indian poverty to be addressed as the Indians received a share of the trade from the British. He wanted to prevent either nation "depending either upon poisoning other people, or upon the charity of the English people." When Alfred Webb raised the same question to spark off reforms in June 1903, Dadabhai's response was still the same.

The Reverend Goodere Mabbs had approached Dadabhai for his advice when planning a concerted attack on the policy of the Government, during his electioneering period. After the election Dadabhai threw himself in with the Indian and China league as it was called. It sought to raise other moral questions too and in time India's financial reform, and 'native participation' in the Indian Government became part of its brief. It was in essence another group for the suppression of the opium trade chiefly organised in this case by Christians, and aimed at getting people in Britain involved in the overall campaign against the opium trade.

In reply to these pushes, Gladstone made a speech in the House clearly aimed at stopping the Government enforcing the trade on China and he set up a Commission of Enquiry to further this end. But this move did little to change the effects of the trade because China was still to be allowed to receive all the trade that she wanted to receive on a regular basis. The anti-Opium party was not happy with the Commission's methods, because in the end not one of their members was called as a witness and its report of 1895 stirred up another debate on the 29th May 1895. By then the Government's successive defeats over many policies and the general untidiness within the Liberal Party as a parliamentary group prevented it taking the issue any further.

There was another consumption problem that Dadabhai had also taken up both before and during this time as an MP. He, along with Samuel Smith and W C Caine, wanted to see the eradication of excessive alcohol consumption and had set up an Anglo-Indian Temperance Association back in 1888. As a young boy, Dadabhai had developed a firm temperance attitude due to a childhood errand he had undertaken. Prior to each evening meal, the family had some wine and so one day when there was none, his mother sent Dadabhai to the 'local' to collect it. He had been so chagrined and embarrassed by what he saw and heard that he never used such a premises ever again, and he chose to abstain from drink for life.

Drink cost the British nation around £130,000,000 in Dadabhai's estimation, and was far more of a major issue than it is now. In rough terms, drugs and drink have changed positions in the priority they were given by the public of that time when compared with the present generation.

Public opinion in Britain had led to a wave of temperance enthusiasm for many years prior to this time. The Indian drive was an offshoot of the movement. Dadabhai knew that the Indian people were not heavy drinkers by comparison, but Britain had introduced the excise system and hence the liquor shop into the country. The Association got a motion through parliament in April 1889 to reform the Indian excise administration. This had been a major reason for the growing consumption over there, which led to more crime, destitution and death and was part of the economic drain. But despite this high profile approach to combat the problem, a home-grown movement never really took off in India.

During his parliamentary career, Dadabhai found a fair measure of support, both for his ideas and because of who he was. Around 1894, he had also found reasons to be disillusioned in the Liberal Party's willingness to help India. To the press of the day, after their initial interest in his news appeal prior to the election and in fact because of it, Dadabhai became far less interesting when actually in the House of Commons. Of those who watched his career, *The Times* remained a bit aloof or superior to Dadabhai's efforts, whereas *The Guardian* was more sympathetic. In India the press remained glued to his progress and detailed much more comment on matters parliamentary. Primarily he remained a hero of the Indian nation and of its press, and conversely was portrayed as the bane of the Anglo-Indian community through the press it controlled. In Britain, the press really showed its comment on the situation of an Indian in Parliament by its lack of column space.

Outside Parliament, people were not so interested in consequence, and it was only those involved in a cause like Hyndman who followed Dadabhai's efforts to use his parliamentary seat as a means to an end; though Hyndman himself did not have much confidence in the Parliamentary system. He pointed out that the House of Commons was a spent force and that he and his colleagues spent their time encouraging the people to think, so that they would then act for the overthrow of the capitalist state, whether its rulers be Tory, Whig, Liberal or Radical. Dadabhai was glad that Hyndman's interest on India was keen, but revolution did not fit in with his views, despite being an Indian patriot. Dadabhai preached moderation to Hyndman. But Hyndman could no more reconcile himself to this pedantic way than Dadabhai could to the revolutionary way. Despite this difference, the two remained steadfast friends for life.

Nowadays, Dadabhai's views must seem almost too complacent with the uncompromising stance of the establishment, but in his day he was seen as a radical creating unrest in the Indian nation. In fact it was probably British reneges on British promises for real democracy that stirred up the Indian nation so much that in later years they might consider the overthrow of the system through the efforts of the younger radicals. Unfortunately, the older radicals could not win, because they were too disruptive for the Authorities to trust them but in the eyes of some of the younger generation they were seen as being too pro-establishment.

Other active reformers of the time included Martin Wood who kept up a correspondence with Dadabhai, as did Josephine Butler. Both of them also wrote articles about the financial drain placed on India and on the corruption it engendered and the 'Imperially imposed horrors' such as licensed prostitution, drink and similar exploitations. So there was always a fairly small but committed band of individuals who were making some views heard in Britain towards the end of the nineteenth century. Dadabhai was obviously a leading light of this grouping and fitted in or led on the various issues they raised which were primarily to do with reform, there not being any identifiable large scale nationalist movement in India at that time.

However, despite being away from India, the Indian National Congress was always in Dadabhai's mind, and even when campaigning he wrote several articles or letters each week, and received the same. It obviously all got noticed, because his articles aroused a negative reaction, mainly from the Anglo Indian press but also from the indigenous press at times, as well as letters of support and favourable articles which resulted from his spoken and written views. Dadabhai's own propaganda campaign which he kept up during his years in Britain was having an effect, both at home and abroad. In India, the effect of having a campaigner who could lobby and speak directly to a government which was thousands of miles away was an invigorating experience for the new Nationalistic movement. In Britain the thrust of his campaigning was also directed to making the people more supportive of reform and in consequence more amenable to the aims of the Indian National Congress.

He also helped push for reform of the Congress itself as he did when the arrangements for the 2nd Congress were being made. Three changes were made to its organisation. These were to see that before the Congress meeting public bodies in the country were given enough notice to vote for their own delegates to attend. In addition, circulars were then sent to the delegates suggesting matters for the agenda for their consideration. Finally at the Congress itself members of the public were to be able to attend as spectators and listen in on its deliberations.

Dadabhai also fought to pressure Congress's integrity of purpose because, as said earlier, Malabari the editor of the *Indian Spectator* had made a series of attacking articles in the early days of Congress which he printed in 1887. He had come out against the way the Congress decided not to get involved in intercommunal affairs. He was a social reformer and he saw it as the most important vehicle for Indians to resolve their own difficulties. But any social reform would necessitate changing the norms or customs of one community or another or of their interrelationship to each other which could have been divisive to Congress's aims. The tone of Dadabhai's letter to Malabari (as shown earlier) was in the form of a gentle rebuke but there was also a personal connotation to Dadabhai writing to Malabari. He also intoned the approach for Congress to take when he had said at the Second Congress in 1886 that, "Congress must confine itself to questions in which the entire nation has a direct participation, and it must leave the adjustment of social reforms and other class questions to class congresses." By saying this, he had outlined the general feeling, that India must unite and speak with one voice. Others, including Hume, had also been looking to Congress to move forwards in political reform and therefore leave aside the questions of inter and intra-communal strife. Malabari's comments acted as a touchstone to show how these differences always existed, albeit in diverse forms. Perhaps in his case he was also aware of the difference between the older more conservative members of a community and the younger more radical members, who needed a vent for their growing dissatisfaction, which caused him to write in so critical a manner.

Apart from Malabari there were also other Indians who were beginning to feel that Congress was not for them. Some Parsees and Muslims came out to oppose it for different reasons such as the possible interference it could have over their own privileged positions, or the fear of too many Hindus being the powerful figures as Congress grew. Such counter moves from whatever quarter, showed that it must have been considered to be of importance to all Indians. Hence while Malabari's articles themselves, although quite heated were of no great importance and could have been forgotten, they reflected the mounting expectancy on what Congress was seen as being able to achieve for Indians in the public arena.

In fact with regard to the criticism of fractions gaining the upper

124

hand Congress had already been aware of the problem and wanted to take pains to ensure it kept a representative mix of people on its bodies or if it took any public stance. No one could be more aware of the problems that could arise from intercommunal rivalries than the Indians themselves. It made a point of holding its yearly event in different parts of the country, in order to ensure that no grouping was seen to dominate its programme or gain the most capital and kudos for themselves. The second Congress which Dadabhai presided over was held in Calcutta and in fact a proposal was passed to hold the 1892 session in Britain. Dadabhai advised that it would be better to postpone that move until after the general election, and although he and the British Congress committee considered the idea in later years, it proved impossible to accomplish given the financial restraints that Congress had to contend with.

There was a growing impatience and anger in India, mainly amongst the better educated classes which was beginning to affect and energize them to find a unified voice for themselves. Despite the obvious differences between many Indians, they easily recognized the greater effect that was possible if a unified stance was maintained. Congress did not stir up the nation, but it did still seek to make views heard at all levels and in all places, in as unified and as forceful a manner as was possible in those days. As Dadabhai said "the new lesson that Kings are made for the people, not peoples for the Kings" had in fact taken root and was now growing in the soil of Congress, so that the peoples views were coming over, and not the views of various independent leaders.

Hence although Congress has often been dubbed as a 'safety-valve', encouraged by the Authorities to allow people to let off steam without directly tackling the ruling powers, this now appears to be unlikely. From the very start, it sought to raise awareness and to control its own affairs and political agenda. It was because of what it did through its own initiatives that the Authorities were quietly opposed to its existence.

In the very last years of that century, the Congress's membership encompassed all the peoples domiciled in India and was growing as the central point for independent opinion after its small beginnings, when only seventy-two men had been involved.

Whilst not actively seeking internal discord, the Authorities were happy to make capital of the disputes that did arise. So a few years after its establishment, the Anglo-Indian Community's fear of subversion and the fear of some Muslims and Parsees, that a native government would be Hindu dominated, meant that there was a vein of opposition to Congress that could be tapped and this dislike had been expressed quite openly as far back as 1888. This helped form the style of opposition that was orchestrated in a low key fashion for some years, as the fears

125

of some groups were fostered by some of the authorities and both Sir Richard Cross, the Secretary of State, and Lord Dufferin had in 1886 felt that "This division of religious feeling is greatly to our advantage." Outright exploitation of these schisms was not actually undertaken, and in fact Lord Dufferin also stated, "... but these circumstances we found and did not create, nor, had they been non-existent, would we have been justified in establishing them by artificial means. It would be a diabolical policy on the part of any Government to endeavour to exacerbate race hatreds among the Queen's Indian Subjects for a political object..." The oft quoted 'divide and rule' caption is often applied by presuming the divisions are fostered. In this case they were observed by the authorities as possible opportunities, but were never devised by them.

Unhappily Syed Ahmed launched a Muslim crusade against Congress in 1886, and although other Muslims were part and parcel of Congress during those first years of its existence, numerous Islamic Anjumans were involved in moves to oppose Congress. They stirred up public feelings by holding open meetings, leafletting, demonstrations and articles in the journals both in India and in Britain. This movement was noted, sometimes eagerly, by the Anglo Indian Community as a definite counter thrust to all the 'patriotic froth' of Congress, just as it began to gain real headway.

Ironically the feeling of some members inside Congress at that time was that it was losing its vigour. Dinsha Wacha in a letter to Dadabhai on 16th August 1887, said that 'Unity of intention is lacking, it breaks out sporadically at a Congress, but soon, the occasion being over, it subsides - to be restored again for a time on another occasion. The spirit of persistent disinterested agitation all over the country is not visible.' In another letter of 5th October 1888 he also wrote that, 'Bombay is... cutting a very sorry figure in every way. The spirit of political activity which was so visible and strong three years ago is no where. A sort of languor has intervened.'

This cannot have been a good time for Dadabhai because he had written in April 1888 that, 'the result of the Public Services Commission and the split of the Mohamedans, has for the present paralysed me in my work here. Anywhere an Anglo-Indian can shut me up with these two facts.' The Public Services Commission was the one that had been set up to look into the problems of access for Indians into the Indian Civil Service. Many witnesses from Northern India had actually opposed the idea of open examinations, because they feared that it would open up opportunities for the Bengalis rather than for them. All this must have had a dispiriting effect on Dadabhai, who was also frustratingly physically distant from the Country.

One bright ray which may have moved some of the storm clouds away was that Dadabhai's appeals to the British at home were sometimes more threatening to the Anglo-Indian community than the first Congress meetings. In a sense he created a second front and could not be reached by the same methods. In consequence, he was attacked in the papers by some quite eminent persons and from this reaction it appears safe to conclude that he was achieving some success. Dadabhai's role therefore was to help establish the beginnings of India's strivings for recognition from within Britain. He saw this through to the end of the beginning whether by campaigning or by helping Congress through its nascent years. He also saw the beginning of the end.

Dadabhai's guidance to his compatriots of this time was for steady and moderate progress, to meet the opposition and the misrepresentation which they had to encounter, then "later action and good result will soon follow in due natural course" (1889). He had been trying to establish a British agency for Congress for some time, and had offered to distribute copies of Congress 'Reports' to various interested parties provided the costs were met, which was the one material factor that had been holding back the formation of such a body. When William Digby offered to set up the Indian political agency at an office in Craven Street, off the Strand in London, the main problem was overcome.

The Office acted as a centre, at first holding copies of the Gazette of India, and records of the subordinate governing bodies, Blue books and the principle Anglo-Indian and Indian newspapers. The British Committee of the Congress was formed soon afterwards in July 1889, with William Wedderburn as the Chair and involved Dadabhai and W C Bonnerjee, with A O Hume and W C Caine as the more active members, and W S B Maclaren, J E Ellis and G Yule as additional members. Dadabhai had written just before this that, "These Congresses whatever other good they may do or not, are really creating a good deal of interest in India here. If they... take steps after a careful consideration to petition Parliament from time to time... I have every hope that success will at last crown its efforts." It was closely associated with the agency and this small Committee was to keep up with its campaigning well after the attempts of others who were opposed to its ethos had disappeared.

It was able to secure an annual income of Rs 45,000, voted in by the parent Congress of 1889, which was presided over by Wedderburn with another Rs 63,000 being raised by subscriptions. These really were very good amounts and in fact in Britain, Congress actually spent more money than it did in India. The second front had quickly grown from a beachhead to become major port of Congress's Strategy and Dadabhai's efforts over here were quickly justifying his move to Britain.

It produced its own journal entitled *India* with Digby as editor, and aimed to "rouse the English working classes... to a sense of the duties which England owes to India." Because there was a guarantee that so many copies of *India* would be distributed back in India, the circulation in Britain never exceeded that in India. This method of editing and publication outside of India was done to allow for the journal and other ventures to be financed by the British Committee. Gosi Naoroji remembered years later that Lord Reay used to give a sizeable chunk of his annual pension of £1000, towards the running of the British office because Indians were either too poor or too miserly. She also remembered that Lord Reay used to act as a guardian to members of Dadabhai's family living in Britain in the later years, when he was incapacitated by periods of illness.

Dadabhai kept pointing out that the way to get reform was to let the British people know what was happening, because in their hands and the British Government's directives lay the only way for real change in India. To that end, he promoted the sending of delegations to Britain and for invitations to be sent to British statesmen to visit India. Four men, Surendranath Banerjea, R N Mudholkar, Allan Hume and Eardley Norton, conducted one such tour in Britain in 1890, meeting with enthusiastic audiences. Their aim as to try and prepare minds to accept moves being put forward that were favourable to India. In particular along with Dadabhai, Wedderburn and George Yule of the British Congress Committee they pressed for reform of the Councils in India. Banerjea came across particularly well from this platform campaign. Dadabhai's words reported in the *India* of April and May caught both his own slant on the ideas put forward and the general call that was being put out. He said "....we desire to prepare India for a system of government by representation, which every race and every class is entitled to, (cheers), we only say this, there is no man in his senses in this country, who if you press him to it, will not have to admit it to end that, sooner or later, India must be governed on the principle of representation, or we must lose our hold on that great Empire." He later asked for the high cost of the administration to be reduced and for the commercial development of India to be pursued, to enable the people to be able to buy more, which "would be beneficial alike to England and India". After the success of the platform tour it was unfortunate that Hume became the centre of a censuring by many of these same colleagues almost two years later.

On February 16th 1892 he wrote a private letter, in which he gave his personal opinions to members of the Congress. These were that the present system pauperized the people, but that the mild Indians would be aroused by horror and misery to the inevitable results. He warned that the better off should look out for their personal safety in the days ahead. Being a private letter the aim was not to agitate the masses to violent action against a particular target, but to forewarn the Congress of the results if it did not strive harder in its efforts. The press got hold of a copy of the letter and make hostile capital out of it, attributing the former aims to its author. The leaders of Congress reluctantly apologized for the temper of the letter, to prevent it being used as a weapon to discredit the movement, but in doing so they tarnished Hume's personal standing. It was a bitter blow for him and a difficult moment for the other members who tried to both support one of their own against outside attack but also let him know his views could get out of hand at times.

It was partly to counteract the possible effects of such press accounts that the British Committee had gone ahead with the setting up of *India* in 1890, to give itself a voice and provide their version of the Indian news. Dadabhai and William Wedderburn put money forward to help the Committee meet the costs of publication. William Wedderburn continued to provide a lion's share of support for many years. By the end of the century, it was faced with extinction, but was saved by the efforts of Gokhale and the servants of the Indian society. Only in 1921 was the London Organization shut down and the *India* closed. By then the Indian Reforms Committee, in the Hume-Wedderburn tradition, had been set up.

Dadabhai had just been invited once again to come back to Indian by the Lahore Congress Committee, when at Cutch Mandvi in Northern Gujerat, Adi his son died of a heart attack. It was 7th October 1893 and just a few weeks before he was due to return to India. Condolences flooded in, and Dadabhai wanted to keep in contact with his son's family as regularly as possible. There were seven children in Adi's household and a fifth daughter was to be born after her father's death. Meetings like some public celebrations set up for the 17th November were called off, but it was more a case of private grief and public work and in effect Dadabhai did not show much diminution of his daily tasks. On 10th November 1893, he had called on Lord Elgin, the Viceroy-Designate of India, to elicit his support over reforms for India partly as a consequence of the impending return to India. Perhaps as Dadabhai knew that as he was already scheduled to return to India, he was prepared to work up to that date. It also seems likely that as Dadabhai had a tendency to being a workaholic, practical considerations and personal preferences went hand in hand.

Dadabhai was due to reach Bombay on midnight on 2nd December 1893. By 7.00 am the dock was packed with ebullient crowds, who displayed a riot of the colours they chose for the occasion. They were also a very patient crowd who waited until 4.00 pm the next day, which was when the steamer eventually arrived. When he disembarked, he

129

was in his national costume, which was a black coat and turban and red silk trousers. He had to be literally pushed into an open carriage and in the procession from the pier to his house at Khetwady, he stood to receive the inundation of cheers and flowers. By 6.00 pm he reached his house and family. Lord Elgin and the Governor of Bombay, Lord Harris, were eager to greet him as well as members of the councils from Poona, Satara, Belgaum, Sholapur, Surat and Broach, Navsari and other parts of the Bombay presidency. After these official celebrations, he was then able to have a family reunion and mark the passing of Adi.

On December 20th, he took the train to Lahore (approximately 880 miles) and all along that route and at any train station, crowds flocked to acclaim the Grand Old Man of India. Along the way he was welcomed by the new Dewan and Nagarsheth of Baroda.

He stopped at Ahmedabad, the capital of Gujerat state, to recall the shelter and help given to the Parsees almost a thousand years before when they arrived on the shore of that area.[1] At the Sikh's Golden Temple at Amritsar, the officiating priest invested him with a robe of honour, according to the Sikh rituals. He also stopped at Delhi.

There were a few dissenting bodies to all this celebration. The Anglo-Indian Community was the first such group, but a significant portion of the Muslim population also seemed to stand aloof from the events. However at Lahore the local Muslim community broke into a spontaneous and jubilant reception and gave speeches in his honour.

At Lahore, it took five hours for the small group to move from the station to the Congress meeting place. And horses were not used to draw his carriage because there were men who wanted to pull it. Sir William Hunter reported in *The Times*, "The enthusiasm with which the President of this years Congress has been received in India was very striking. Mr Naoroji is not only the first Indian gentleman who has ever been elected to Parliament, he is also an example of an early career of promise... His reception at Lahore has perhaps not been surpassed since the days of Ranjit Singh."

1. It is recorded that on their arrival, they were told that among the conditions for staying they were not to try and convert anyone and not to bear a weapon. They were then made welcome and given land to cultivate by the local Hindu Ruler, King Jadi Rana who gave them asylum and allowed them to maintain the right to continue in their faith. 'Sanjan' day is still celebrated on the 21st November each year. The story goes that on their arrival at his court, they were asked what could they do for the land. The High Priest, Neryosangh, asked to be provided with a bowl of milk, filled to the brim. He then asked for some sugar and sprinkled it into the milk, without spilling any, saying "we shall try to be like this insignificant amount of sugar in the milk of your human kindness." They have since blended in with the original Indian inhabitants, without converting any, and have also retained their own culture, religion and lifestyle over the last 1300 years. A further move was thought necessary from Sanjan to Surat and Bombay, when the Muslims conquered Sanjan in 1490. The closest analogy in Britain would be if the Normans had remained as a separate community, still French and Norse, residing side by side with the British for 900 years.

People of all religions were united in the greeting that was given to Dadabhai. He gave a short presentation to the effect that he asked them to be loyal to the British crown and rely on the British peoples' sense of justice. He reminded them of the need to rise above sectarian feelings and be Indians. He also reported to them on the measure of interest that had been aroused in Britain by the debates on India, expressing thanks by name to those who were helping India's cause and remembered the friends of the Irish, Labour and Radical movements in Britain. It is interesting to know that whilst in India Dadabhai received a message which read, "Do not forget to tell your colleagues at the Congress that everyone of Ireland's Home rule members in Parliament is at your back in the cause of the Indian people." This reinforces a view that between Dadabhai and the Irish nationalists there existed some sort of allegiance and that they were asking him to remember some favour from before. Alternatively it may have just been an expression of solidarity for him during his tour; but why bother to write those words if there was no context to give them substance?

Dadabhai was the natural choice for President at the Congress, and gave addresses on what should be the way ahead. As a nationally based movement, though not nationalistic in those days, these was one clear answer, to seek direct and permanent representation for India with the Imperial Government. He made clear that as India's representative in the British Parliament, he was there to do this because, "whether I am a Hindu, a Muhammadan, a Parsee, a Christian or of any other creed I am above all an Indian. Our country is India, our nationality is Indian."

The issues that Congress felt needed to be resolved were the impoverishment of the country, the cost of maintaining the services, especially the heavy military burden and in general the apparent lack of understanding displayed by the rulers. Dadabhai still wanted his listeners to seek for spontaneous or freely given reforms and justice from the British Government. He noted that if at the end of the day change was forced, it would entail, "loss of grace from the giver and loss of gratitude from the receiver."

Events since that time seem to show that both conditions applied to the manner in which change and reform happened. It would take India and Britain another two generations to achieve a more permanent result. At that time the Imperial government was at the height of its pride and it had to be converted down to a more humble government, whose interest became more national and less Imperial, for Indian's national aspirations to be accepted. That was a unique and sobering experience for both parties, and Dadabhai's words were thankfully not fully fulfilled.

Being in India, Dadabhai could also spend more time on a personal level with Vir, (Virbai), Adi's widow who was still living in Cutch. His personal grief seemed to stay with him, but he found a release too in advising and helping the family that remained. He advised Vir to stay in Cutch and in due time she became tutor to the heir apparent to that State's throne. He also got the Maharaja of Gondal to support Vir and the grand children in due time, so that for instance some of the older ones were able to get a schooling in London later on. Two incidents in the family history came down through Gosi, the fourth child of Adi and Vir. She remembers a cyclone in Cutch in 1892 which she said her brother went downstairs from the living quarters above the hospital to experience. They were eight and six and would have been blown clean away off the verandah if some adults had not saved them. She also remembers when aged about four seeing her family weeping after her grandmother's sister, her daughter and grandson were murdered by a servant who thought that the great chest kept in the family home must contain great wealth, from the days when they used to trade with Ceylon. The grandmother and grandson's heads were smashed in and the daughter died in the struggle. Tragedy and excitement were not the only things that she experienced in what was a happy childhood, but those events remained in her memory. The only other thing she remembered from that time was not connected to the family but was the reaction in the community when a boat sailing between Cutch Mandvi and Bombay, called the "Turner" and carrying a wedding party, sank without trace. Dadabhai as stated earlier maintained good contacts with all his grandchildren throughout his life, either by correspondence or through personal contact. Dadabhai returned to Bombay via Agra, Allahabad, Bhasawal, Jalgaon, Khandwa, Manmad and Nasik and at each stop he received cheers from the crowds who came to see him as well as having official ceremonies held in his honour at which bands played, floral tributes were given and presentations were made.

He left India on 22nd January 1894, knowing that he had begun to give the Indian people new ideas in terms of what they could work for and expect, and had given them an insight too into the attitudes of Britain and its people. He had not given the answers, but as much as any one man can achieve it, he had wanted to stimulate that vast nation to be stirred up, and in particular the younger generation of men and women, who were now following in a path he had trail blazed. He received a delegation of the medical profession and he had also made a special visit to Elphinstone College just prior to his departure, where another of his 'firsts' had been achieved. That appointment had always given him courage and personal satisfaction.

132

CHAPTER ELEVEN

UNSEATED BUT
NOT UNSETTLED

India had often started to seethe at its treatment and as the event of 1857 showed, it could explode with violence. Nowadays, it is believed that the non-violence policy which Congress stuck to, when applied to a combination of political demands and a programme of positive action, probably helped to prevent armed rebellion in later years.

But in 1895, Dadabhai was beginning to feel apprehension that a revolt was likely, after so many pledges had been broken and so little done for the country whose rulers were making decisions over it that did not have the inhabitants' needs in mind. He correctly foresaw that the new generations would start where the present one left off, and that would include the use of violence. He was also sure that the financial drain on India was a root cause of the growing dissatisfaction.

Dadabhai had a lot of work to do to prove that there was a need for India to have her financial burdens eased, and wanted above all to make it a point the Royal Commission supported. He spent weeks preparing for the cross examination of the witnesses who would appear before the Commission and especially the officials, who would be hostile or un-cooperative. He realized that he would in effect be finding himself cross examined, not by members of the Commission, but by any witnesses who were not favourable to its aims or could not be impartial in their evidence. He also had to get friends in India to provide clear, concise and pertinent statements, which was not an easy task, given their distance and unfamiliarity with anything of this nature.

However, before the Commission began to meet, the tide of events in parliament was too debilitating for the Liberal party to continue with their reforming Government. In consequence, they had to call a General Election for July, 1895. What had happened was that the Liberals had lost the vision of the man known as the 'Grand Old Man' of British politics, when the days of Gladstone's leadership had come to an end in March 1894. That Grand Old Man was succeeded by the Earl of Rosebery as leader of the party and as Prime Minister. But the Liberal party suffered from many reverses and difficult votes in the House and it was recognized that to be able to carry on it had to go to the Country. In any case Rosebery had never been happy as leader and he resigned in June 1895 as Prime Minister and as Leader of the Party in the following year. Parliament was dissolved on the 8th July 1895 and the elections were held on the 16th July.

Dadabhai had been heartily approved for appointment as the candidate for Central Finsbury by the United Liberal and Radical Association on March 14th 1895. During its tenure of office under what was called the Newcastle Programme, the Liberal Government had tried to bring in Home rule for Ireland, address death duties, land acquisitions and Labour legislation, and these were major reforms that had to face strong opposition. As observers of the time noted, it had found itself facing the landlords, businessmen and the City. The Lords had opposed it over plans for their abolition and they were still a major part of the process of Government, (and would remain as such until 1911). The Church disagreed with it over dis-establishment and disendowment and, in consequence, the party had not won any favours for itself. Dadabhai had said to Wacha, "the Parson, the Peer, the Publisher and property were fighting a life and death struggle against the coming doom."

In his campaign, Dadabhai pointed out that the interests of Finsbury and Clerkenwell had always received prompt service from him, (see Appendix for his address of 5th July). He had in fact worked hard as a constituency MP and he maintained his attendance record of being second only to the Chief Whip. In Parliament he had spoken 29 times in 1893, 11 times in 1894 and 12 times in the six months of 1895. He was hardly an inactive backbencher, and his track record could speak for itself to his constituents and his local party. The Liberal's Newcastle Programme remained unfinished and Dadabhai continued to align himself to his party's policies. The local party organized meetings and the Liberals actively promoted their candidate. But the country voted against the Liberals, and the honourable W F B Massey Mainwaring, who had support from the Church and liquor interests, won by a comfortable 3588 to 2783, a majority of 805 votes. The change in support for the parties also hit other Liberals such as Mr Caine.

Dadabhai's defeat was a source of keen disappointment in India and apart from the native community and sympathetic Europeans even the *Times of India*, which was pro-establishment made the following observation. "We cannot regard without regret the widespread disappointment which Dadabhai's defeat has caused amongst his friends in this country. He was the exponent of opinions with which we are seldom in accord, for he looked at the British administration of India from a standpoint at which no one who dispassionately considered the requirements and the capabilities of the country could place himself. But we do not think that he ever seemed to his most resolute opponents

134

as other than a straight forward, sincere and disinterested champion of the views he adopted".

Taking stock of the effectiveness of Dadabhai in Parliament for the benefiting of India could be summarized by the observation of the "Amrit Bazaar Patrika's" correspondent in London. He stated that if the friends of Congress proceeded to a divisional vote in Parliament on India, at which the Government made it a matter of confidence in their ability to rule, then no more than twenty or thirty members would vote for India's cause. Dadabhai probably held hopes that the Liberal party would support India when he entered Parliament. After all he knew about their traditions beginning from his days at Elphinstone and leading up to their support at the national level if not at the local level, during his election campaign. But basically they were as pro British as the Conservatives and neither India's needs and pleas nor a general humanitarian concern would change the political judgment they had made as to the views of the British public, to whom India was the "Jewel in the Crown". Something to be held up and admired, but not to be analysed and then reshaped for the benefit of its people. Rather it was to be kept as it was for the benefit of Britain and hence for the British people. India was also something that could be displayed to the world, rather like the Koh-i-noor diamond[1]. This does not mean that there were not those in Parliament and elsewhere who wanted Britain to hold up and display its qualities of fairness and justice and to ensure these were genuinely maintained. But politically their voice was a minority one even though they could strike deep chords in the sentiments and views of the British and also in Parliament.

As Dadabhai and his friends were based amongst the more radically minded minority of his day and as said above most MPs voted along party lines when it came to the crunch, there was an in-built bias against getting reform carried through. In 1902 Hamilton wrote to Lord Curzon, the Viceroy, that for any debate held on India in Parliament then "so long as we are in a majority this does not matter". Although he primarily meant the majority to be the one the Conservatives held over the Liberals, the radicals were like a third smaller grouping who were always in a minority, no matter who was in power. However against these general ground rules, Dadabhai and his allies did score noticeably, especially with regard to the vote for simultaneous examinations for Indians in 1893, and the setting up of the Royal Commission. It is noteworthy that the

1. This was given to Queen Victoria in 1850 by Lord Dalhousie when the British confiscated the contents of the treasuries of the Punjab after that area was annexed in 1849.

Indian Parliamentary Committee (or party) did not dissipate after a few years nor did the Royal Commission to which Dadabhai and his parliamentary colleagues give a lot of time and energy, completely ignore the points made in its deliberations. But within the three years allotted to him, there was never enough time for those views to be emphasised and then taken up and owned by the more conservative minded.

Dadabhai never caused the fascination in the minds and hearts of the British public to become affixed to India as say Ireland and its chief proponents did, but he did ruffle the contentment of those who should have known better about the dire wants suffered by Indians and he did bring a kind of respectability to the Indian cause. Just by being an MP he gained a certain authority and status and acted as a magnet for those who were concerned not just about India as a possession, but for India itself as well. At the 1895 election, Mr (later Sir) M M Bhownaggree, won Bethnal Green on the 16th July for the Conservatives, by a majority of 160 over the Liberals. He could be thankful to have experienced something of politics and campaigning under Dadabhai and had also been involved in public affairs as one of the people who established the Commonwealth Institute. But his policies at the time differed a lot to Dadabhai's, and he was to be seen as a counterpoise to Dadabhai, put up by the Conservative and Unionist party.

Amazingly he was in the Government of Lord Salisbury, who many may have thought had given himself too black a name from his earlier pronouncements to now accept an Indian into his government without appearing hypocritical. Bhownaggree certainly aided the establishment in his early years at preventing the 'Indian Opposition' getting too much in terms of reform and he himself did admire the British rulers efforts over India. He was also a good constituency Member of Parliament and in fact won in a working class area, due to his popularity and hard work in that constituency. But it is in terms of his enthusiasm for the Conservative policy that he is remembered. From his stance in Parliament he earned himself the unfortunate name from his fellow Parsees of 'bow-and-agree', and was never seen by Indian patriots as another Dadabhai, though he did correspond and share certain views with Dadabhai. In fact his own views on the recalcitrance of the British Government to act on India's behalf steadily grew over the latter years of his Parliamentary career and his reputation has had to be reviewed recently[1] in light of the number of times he pushed the Government for action. He did press for technical and vocational education in India, and fought for and serviced Indian interests in South Africa. He stood for a second election in 1900 and won by a greater majority of 379 out of an electorate of 7431. Another candidate, W C Bonnerjee, had

1. See *Bhownaggree: Member of Parliament 1895-1906*, published by Hansib, 1995

attempted to win Barrow-in-Furness in 1895, from the Unionists, but was another Liberal casualty.[1]

Surprisingly, Dadabhai was not dejected by his defeat, because he still wanted to get on with securing India's future and work for the good of Indians and the British and he knew the Royal Commission would provide some measure of hope and a lot of work. He also meant to try again for the House of Commons, and said so in an open letter, even though he was now in his 70th year.

Despite still having problems with his expenses, Dadabhai was now turning down offers of financial assistance. In a letter of 20th October 1895, he talked of "some silent patriot of India who appreciates the future result of my work", and was supplying him with his needs. He carried on in the letter to say that he did not need money, but what he did need was a continuous cry by Indians on their condition. It now seems likely that his Highness Maharaja Shri Bhagvat Sinhji, the Thakore Saheb of Gondal was the benefactor, as he remained a lifelong supporter and friend.

Dadabhai now acquired a permanent home for himself and benefited from the greater stability it gave him. His address was 'Washington House', 72 Amberley Road, London SE and apparently he obtained it from the Swiss Consulate because he liked the name. Three of his grandchildren came to stay with him. They were Gosi and her elder sister and brother. She would have been about fourteen and all of them went to a private school called Tudor Hall in Forest Hill. She did well at poetry and reading to such an extent that her English friends used to get her to help them with their English. Gosi also remembers the attitude of her friends to her, which was without prejudice, but steeped in ignorance. They had no idea that the West Indies and the East Indies were in different parts of the world and expected Gosi when asked to wear native dress, to appear in a headdress, feathers and beads. However they soon took to the saris, worn the Parsee way.

Where Gosi did experience racial prejudice was back in India in her early twenties. She and others had boarded a train and had found seats in a compartment occupied by three or four white women who had objected to her entering and had ordered the Indian orderly to remove the Indian women. The orderly only desisted when Gosi promised that he would not loose his job at the next station. At that point one of the

1. The only other Indian MP up until the 1980s was Shapurji Saklatvala, who won Battersea North in 1922 with a majority of 2021 on a Labour ticket. He lost the next year and then regained the seat as a Communist from 1924 until 1929 on a majority of 542 (electorates were bigger in the 20th century). He was also a Parsee, but a far more fiery brand of politician than were his other two co-religionists. He was refused entry into the United States in 1925, when his visa was revoked on the grounds of him being a revolutionary. Later the British Government refused him the right to return to Indian for any reason such as to visit his very sick sister because of his views and activities.

137

women produced a revolver and placed it on her lap for the rest of the journey. Gosi got so indignant she complained of the treatment meted out by foreigners in her country, to which the white women replied with "sedition, sedition". The last experience of peoples attitudes to her in England was when in her school days she and a friend went to Barkers on the High Street in Kensington, London. As they got in the doorway all the counter boys got down from their ladders or looked up and shouted "miss, miss we're all for India".

There were moves to have Dadabhai knighted and the Shah of Iran wanted to decorate him. Dadabhai wanted to make clear to the sponsors of such honours that the idea was both embarrassing for him and that he felt it would be detrimental to his aims. He wanted to keep away from honours and "personal decoration." Even later in life when his path in life was less cluttered, he still refused the proposals to accept a knighthood. William Wedderburn knew his determination, but in 1911 tried to get him to agree if only for the honour of the Congress party in India. The Governor of Bombay, Lord Sydenham, was only too willing. But Dadabhai was not as self-seeking as so many of us would be in his position, although by 1911 he may have given a moral boost to his supporters that would have been in line with his aims.

When he was being called the Grand Old Man of India in those later years, he said "Is it contrary that I should take a great pleasure in being hailed as the Grand Old Man? No, that title which speaks volumes for the warm, grateful and generous hearts of my countrymen, is to me, whether I deserve it or not, the highest reward of my life." This title and tribute were akin to the title of Mahatma, which became a more popular term in the next century.

The loss of a seat was a blessing in some ways. Dadabhai could work harder on the Royal Commission, with fewer matters to distract him. He did however begin writing in 1896 to the War Office and the Admiralty to complain about the exclusion of natives from the examinations for entrance to the Army and Navy. However it was the need for manpower during the First World War which at the end of the day did most to open up commissions to the natives in the British forces including Dadabhai's grandson.

He knew that his main task was to prepare for the Royal Commission. The Chairman was capable and the members seasoned, but it would be questionable to say that they were unbiased, and Dadabhai found he was in a minority of three with William Wedderburn and W C Caine. The other members were Lord Welby (Chair), R Knox, T R Buchanan, L Courtney, E Hamilton, J Perle, A Scobie, R Mawbrey, G L Ryder, W L Jackson, and D Stewart. A summary of Sir Henry Fowler's expectation on what the Royal Commission was to come up with, was in broad terms to provide an answer to his statement that, "The question I wish to consider is whether that (Indian) Government with all its machinery as now existing in India, has or has not promoted the general prosperity of the people in its charge and whether India is better or worse off by being a province of the British Crown." This gave a clearer idea of the purpose of the Royal Commission and was broadly in line with what Dadabhai and the others had been campaigning over for many years.

In the official terms, which is what the Commission should have taken as its written instructions, the terms of reference were to "enquire into the Administration and management of the military and civil expenditure incurred under the Secretary of State for India in Council or of the Government of India, and the apportionment of charges between the government of the United Kingdom and of India for the purposes in which both are interested."

The first meeting did not go well as the other members tried to narrow the terms of Commission, despite the different payments made by India and Britain to common causes being something that Parliament had agreed should be scrutinized. The Anglo-Indians on the Commission, namely W Jackson, A Scobie and J Perle, were interested in a cost cutting exercise and improving the efficiency of the system. Such an aim had to assume the system was already working well for the people of India and that it only needed trimming. Dadabhai and the others definitely felt that the Commission needed to get to the roots of the system.

Dadabhai wrote copious notes on the case for India and eventually filled over a volume of evidence. He began with a letter to Lord Welby, the Chairman, who received the first one on 17th October 1895. He wanted the rulers to see the present system from the Indians point-of-view for a change. He had already researched and written much on the apportioning of charges and Gladstone had been moved in 1893 to say that India "is too much burdened" and that expenditure, especially military expenditure was "alarming." Dadabhai set out his financial details for the Commission's members as follows.

The drain of money over the last ten years was broken down in the various different types of spending, but it totalled a staggering Rs 359,000,000. After a deduction for the costs of public works loans for irrigation schemes, railway construction and the like, the loss was still Rs 321,440,000. Dadabhai attacked the system of government for this financial squalor, rather than the British people. He also set out his remedies which read in a familiar vein and were for more representation by Indians, more equal distribution of costs including the payments for military policing but not payments for Imperial forays. He wrote, "Yes, let India have a complete share in the whole Imperial system, including the government of the country, and then talk of asking her to contribute to the Imperial expenses."

One major point to be asked was why did India pay for military expeditions made outside her boundaries for Imperial purposes? Big figures could be discussed and were a cool analytical way of looking at the issues that the Commission was supposed to review, but they did not delve into the reasons behind such expenditure. Dadabhai also wanted the human plight of the Indians to seep into the thoughts of his colleagues. He quoted what other leading statesmen had said, such as Lord Cromer who had stated, "In England the average income per head was £33, France was £23, Turkey the poorest £4 - in India he would accept Rs 27", (Dadabhai's figure had been Rs 20), which was a figure given by Sir David Barbour. Comparing taxation and income, India's people, paid roughly 50 percent more than the British people, and the tax paid by Britons often came back to them in terms of public works, assistance, and services. The Indian peoples' taxes did not return to them in this manner. Dadabhai also quoted what Lord Lawrence had said to the Select Committee of 1873 when the House of Commons had last reviewed the situation; he had said, "The mass of the people of India are so miserably poor that they have barely the means of subsistence." These thoughts were left out of the final report.

Dadabhai, W Wedderburn and W Caine had perceived that if the other Commission members kept saying financial issues were to do with Imperial policy and could not be talked about, the three of them might have to resign.

Dadabhai wrote to Wacha and to others in India on November 7th to seek their help in the drafting of a minority report, so that the three of them could express their views when the Commission published its findings. Then Caine suggested that the Commission call two witnesses from the Indian National Congress to present their evidence. Dadabhai asked Wacha to approach and nominate people. Three names were submitted along with his, and these were Pherozeshah Mehta, Surendranath Banerjea and L M Ghose. In Britain, Dr K N Bahadurji was also nominated as he kept an active interest in the national issues. Dadabhai had asked Mahader Govind Ranade, the distinguished judge, to come and give evidence. He agreed but the government of India then made clear it did not want a High Court Judge to give evidence, despite his known impartiality.

Dadabhai sent information to the remaining prospective candidates, to brief them on what to expect should they be the ones who were invited to appear before the Commission. He was also informing fellow Indians on its deliberations by providing regular briefings and this was keeping interest alive. Dinsha Wacha was a noted specialist on the economic burdens and policies placed by Britain on India and his presentations to the Commission were presented well. Along with Gokhale, who also gave a good account as a witness to the Commission, he was considered one of the three best exponents on economic measures of the time, with Dadabhai being the senior of the three.

Dadabhai carried on relaying his notes to the Commission, citing many cases and asking that the requirements of the Act of 1855 which placed a duty on the government of India to supply accounts, should be carried out in a proper way. The cases of military expenditure which he raised, were all the more compelling in the case of the payment for the suppression of the mutiny. Britain had said it opposed making profit out of war, especially when it was to India's cost, but had then saved all its own costs incurred during the mutiny as well as in its other military forays, by charging India.

He also pointed out that in the financial records that were kept for India, loans should really be classified as imports, as the debt payments were already classified as part of the country's exports, which had been giving it an overhealthy balance of payments. India had had to 'import' loans from Britain of £34,350,00 in ten years and 'export' interest payments of £57,700,000. He also pointed to the unfairness of the taxation system when he stated "...but the case is wholly different, when the taxes are not spent in the Country from which they are raised.... they constitute.... an absolute loss and extinction of the whole amount withdrawn from the taxed Country". He continued, "From this explanation some final conception may be formed of the cruel crushing effect of the tribute (imposed) upon India".

Dadabhai was more scathing than usual, at the hypocrisy of the British who would be willing to call the Empire 'our' Empire and talk of our fellow subjects of the Empire, and then kept Indians in low positions with the consequence that they remained unheard in the ruling bodies of India.

He tried warning the Commission members of the end result of turning a blind eye to the injustice behind the present system. He could quote from *The Times* itself of that year, "A man may suffer the restrictions of his liberty with patience for the achievement of his national prosperity....when his public rights and his private interests are alike attacked the restraining influences on which the peace of civilized society depends are dangerously weakened."

Dadabhai also counterpoised his criticism when he could and spoke more warmly of the innovation of Lords Iddersleigh and Salisbury on what were called the 'Native States', which were primarily systems of government that were left to continue under Indian administrations.

Dadabhai felt it ensured that Indians could have a real say in the running of the country and gain experience, and their view of Britain in these cases was that its tutelage was seen as genuinely letting matters progress in Indian hands. He cited one good example of the British administration, with regard to the dynasty of Mysore from 1867 to 1881. He commended it as the pre-eminent example of good methodology and diplomacy, and could quote that, "the good Government of the people and the Security of British rights and interests" were upheld. That was the state that Major Evans Bell had been stationed at for a number of years.

Apart from covering financial matters in five different submissions Dadabhai wrote in a sixth submission to say that the Act of 1870 concerning admission of Indians to the Civil Service had actually been reversed by the time of Lord Cross in 1893. He also wrote of the Admiralty's and Army's attitude of not giving commission for Indians, which went against the terms of the Act of 1833 and of the Queen's proclamation of 1858.

He did not just rest on the evidence of his notes. He told the Chairman that he was willing to be become a witness of the Commission and so be examined. The Chairman agreed and was quite severe in the ensuing sessions, making sure that this witness was thoroughly cross-questioned to see if there were any flaws in his evidence. Despite the grilling Dadabhai was happier on balance to being a witness, as he could then acquaint the other members with a fuller version of the facts and in order to cross examine him, they had to take notice of his notes, rather than just leaving them for entry into the books which could then be filed away.

In the end, the Welby Commission did make some recommendations of a reforming nature. It pointed out that the expenditure that the British Government said India was supposed to support did in fact outstrip the growth of the tax revenue, which was around Rs 5,555,000 at that time and that a revamping of the tax system should be carried out by the Authorities. It also pointed out that the apportionment of military expenditure borne by the two countries could be changed in the future, with Britain taking a fairer share.

This amounted to the trimming exercise that the minority members had half expected and was not the root and branch review they had encouraged. As they said in their own statement, "The report of our colleagues admirably summarizes the book keeping and departmental mechanisms, but it does not, in our opinion, sufficiently consider whether the public expenditure has been so controlled and guided, to promote in the most effectual way the general prosperity of the people in the charge of the government of India."

Dadabhai, W C Caine and W Wedderburn saw other areas in need of reform which the Commission had purposefully omitted from its agenda, and prepared a separate minority report looking at how the Administration really met needs. This report brought in the evidence supplied by Dadabhai's compatriots of other procedures that were then being used in India, which placed hefty burdens on the natives. Many of their statements had been left out of the Commission's findings. It had been more concerned on stating how payments were to be adjusted between government departments, and so the evidence it used was only gleaned from the European witnesses involved in the internal running of those departments. The minority report said it was more crucial to see if the un-coordinated approach of those departments meant that they each raised taxes off the people without ascertaining if those increases were just being piled up, one on top of another. There was no real reckoning on the people's ability to pay, and this led to another point, summarized in the slogan, 'no taxation without representation.' The minority group report said Indians should be on the relevant Councils of the Secretary of State and the Viceroy.

The Commission's proposal was for a Comptroller and Auditor-General to be appointed. The minority group proposed a Select Committee of the House of Commons be set up to inquire into the overall financial condition of India. It could not accept that the major result of the Commission was the appointment of one senior official whose duty it would be to oversee what proportion of payments were made by each country. It was understood by most people that his duties only began once the decision on how much those charges were to be, had already been passed.

Dadabhai was not unhappy with his time on the Commission, despite its obvious failings. He wrote in 1897 that Indian views have been given free expression and the Chairman was helpful in that context. It was really a small advance, but it was what could be expected given the realities of that time. In India it probably prompted the 1898 Congress to begin a campaign to press for the Higher Civil Medical Service of India to be taken out of the military's control.

CHAPTER TWELVE

WHATEVER NEXT?

Wedding preparations for his second daughter, Maki, were getting under way in 1897 as she had completed her studies. She wanted her father to attend the wedding in Bombay, which would mean he would have to break from his labours for some time. He said he could not because of the nature of his task whilst on the Commission, which he knew was a mission that relied on him. In a letter of 15th November 1896 he had put this point across in such a way as to make his attendance seem very unlikely. She was determined to get her father and told him she and her fiance Homi would wait in order for him to be able to attend. Unfortunately she did not have her father at the wedding when it finally took place.

Dadabhai was over the allocated three score years and ten and he had tried for four decades to change the way Indian was governed. Whether Liberal or Conservative, the rate of change that any Government was willing to negotiate on was small, despite the support from individual Britons and groups, and the backing and activity of the Indians. So he wrote to the Queen, using the opportunity of her Golden Jubilee. In a letter sent on 5th February 1897, he congratulated her for that notable anniversary, but a part of his letter also pointed out that Britain's slippage from her promise of 1858 had been considerable. He was also corresponding with another royal at the time, Prince Ranjitsinhji of Jamnagar who was the famous cricketer 'Ranji', to try and get him to use economic arguments in his appeal for India.

Dinsha Wacha and Gokhale arrived in April 1897 and stayed with Dadabhai at Cambridge Lodge, Southfields. Surendranath Banerjea and Subrahmania Aiyar, were another two Indians who had been selected so that they could give evidence both to the Indian Expenditure Committee of 1897 and may be to the Royal Commission. As they were in Britain, Dadabhai arranged a "platform Campaign" for all of them. Their venues included South Lambeth, Sunderland, Clapham, Edinburgh, Hastings, Lewisham, Yorkshire, Gloucester and Ealing.

Later that year at the London Indian Society meeting of 28th December 1897 held at the Montague mansions, a resolution was passed, asking that the "un-British System of Government be thoroughly reformed into a righteous and truly British system." The full statement also included demands for greater famine relief, curtailment of the frontier wars and the costs they entailed and other contemporary issues. Dadabhai was told that the language in the resolution was overtly heavy and demanding.[1]

He could point out that it embodied the words of some foremost British statesmen given in fairly recent times. Firstly Lord Salisbury had talked of the 'political hypocrisy' in trying to govern Indian according to Royal proclamations, and secondly the Viceroy Lord Lytton had commented on the use of 'subterfuge', when he was writing on how the Act of 1833 was not being carried out. Dadabhai said these pronouncements had shown him the style to use in his letter and the resolution. Dadabhai also commented on the gagging of the press, giving the example of the jailing of an Indian journalist and Nationalist, Mr B G Tilak, and then comparing the way that a 'Russian' system appeared to be adopted by the British authorities on Indian journalism.

Hyndman wrote the next day to Dadabhai to congratulate him on his strongly worded resolution. Others were uneasy at Dadabhai consorting with Socialists, but probably did not realize Dadabhai never agreed with Hyndman's ultimate types of agitation. Dadabhai met Hyndman often and of course had said this at their face to face meetings - both were as open and as honest with each other as good friends can be. Hyndman could not understand the supiness that led nowhere, especially as the Authorities appeared to be taking a more Russian mode of government to suppress the moderates, whilst others who relied on more radical ways of expressing discontent did not appear to warrant as much attention.[2] Nonetheless, both camps agreed that the British government was relying more on force and fear. Dadabhai replied that

1. The resolution read as follows, " That all the evils and terrible misery that India has been suffering for a century and a half, of which the latest developments are the most deplorable, famine and plague, arising from ever- increasing poverty, the stupid and suicidal Frontier was and its savagery of the wholesale destruction of villages, unworthy of any people, but far more so of English civilization, the unwise and suicidal prosecutions for sedition, the absurd and ignorant cry of the disloyalty of the educated Indians, and for the curtailment of the liberty of the Indian press, the despotism - like that of the imprisonment of the Native - and the general insufficiency and inefficiency of the Administration; of all these and many other minor evils the main cause is the unrighteous and un-British system of government which produces an unceasing and ever increasing bleeding of the Country, and which is maintained by a political hypocrisy and continuous subterfuges, unworthy of the British name and honour and entirely in opposition to the wishes of the British people, and utterly in violation of the Acts and Resolutions of Parliament and of the most solemn and repeated pledges of the British nation and Sovereign. That unless the present unrighteousness and un-British system of government is thoroughly reformed into a righteous and truly British system, destruction to India and disaster to the British Empire must be the result".

2. On the 19th September Dadabhai wrote to Hyndman "...my desire and aim has been all along not to encourage rebellion, but to prevent it and make the British connection with India a benefit and blessing to both countries which it can certainly be, but which unfortunately has not been the case to India owing to an evil and unrighteous system of Government being persisted in by the executive authorities in spite of the wishes of the Sovereign, the people and the Parliament of this country to govern righteously."

"India can only speak as Indians should." But there is no doubt that stopping the press reports, locking up people or destroying villages in the frontier wars, was a burden for the moderates such as Dadabhai in the last years of the century. He saw that the system had indeed produced a more nasty and vindictive administration who would use such ways if it felt it could keep its rule and sway by those means, which would also be counter productive in the end.

An unhappy event occurred at that time when his close associate G K Gokhale, got caught in the 'Apology Incident.' Gokhale had been one of the leading lights for reform in India, and in that capacity he had been given a story of a rape apparently perpetuated by British soldiers, who were known to be using rough methods to stop the plague in Poona. He related it to a group at the House of Commons, including Dadabhai and William Wedderburn. However, on his return to India, he could not find his informants any more and the Bombay Government had publicly called it a "malevolent invention." Gokhale refused to humiliate the informants by naming them and so had to take the whole blame on himself, and make a complete apology. But then, just as he was facing the humiliation himself, his colleagues and the Indian public criticized him for going too far and of bucking under to oppression. After taking such a step to protect others, to then be criticized by his friends was a bitter pill and meant he could lose his support and standing. He wrote about this personal blow to William Wedderburn and Dadabhai to explain his actions. They saw he was right and Dadabhai exhorted him not to consider retirement from public life and that he thought Gokhale had a lot more to do. The situation was a very painful lesson, but Gokhale was encouraged by Dadabhai's letter and did stay on as a leader in the 20th century. This example showed how Dadabhai, as the Grand Old Man of India, was able to effect the adjudication over some community issues and his role as a father figure was recognized. As the Grand Old Man he had also written to other Indians when praises were needed to keep up morale or provide encouragement, such as one active Congress member named R N Mudholkar for the successful organising of the Congress of 1897.

He also encouraged members of other countries based in London and one person whom he met and befriended at this time was the Trinidadian barrister, Henry Sylvester Williams. Dadabhai introduced him to the National Liberal club and also tried to help him find a constituency for the 1906 election. Williams and a black resident of Liverpool named John Archer were both guided and helped by Dadabhai to further their political careers. Hence they contested in the local elections of November 1906, as Williams had been too late to try for the general election. Both men won their seats in London and Williams was elected as a Progressive for the St Johns ward of St Marylebone and John Archer won as a Progressive for Latchmere in Battersea. Williams had already organised the Pan-African conference in London in 1900 and Archer eventually became Mayor of Battersea in 1913. He was also a pan-africanist and came to be involved with the other Asian MP, S Saklatvala in the 1920s.

In 1898 Dadabhai put two statements forward to the Indian Currency Committee, which was chaired by Sir Henry Fowler. It was considering using gold as the basis for the currency in India, and was a carry on of the earlier bimetallism arguments that Dadabhai had addressed as an MP. He wrote to say that for the natives the change would if anything increase the tax burden. This was because a gold standard would falsely increase the value of the rupee against its actual value, making the amount of tax to be paid to Britain, which was always to be deducted in sterling, rise by the same amount. So to pay a hundred silver rupees which were valued at eleven pence each is easier than to first of all obtain (through purchase or by trade) and then have to pay a hundred gold rupees valued at sixteen pence, as that could have been the new rate. Dinsha Wacha also wrote in 1899 to try and prevent the acceptance of a gold standard as he felt it was mainly proposed to help European merchants increase the cash balances they could use in India. He said the present banking system was working well enough to accommodate their need for ready money and that just by saying gold was now the standard, did not mean the Country would attract enough gold. In fact the opposite would apply and most natives would be left holding silver if they had any and the Government of India could never attract enough gold into its reserves to allow the public to have confidence in a gold currency. Then if that were to happen, most Europeans would take their gold out of the Country and so transport out a lot of its reserves, whereas the natives would try and hoard it, and continue to use their silver rupees for daily life. In the end the Fowler Committee was superseded by the Chamberlain Commission, which took a line in between having a gold currency and a universal silver currency and tried to allow elements of both systems to operate, which was not always successful.

Dadabhai was present at the annual dinner of the London Indian Society on 1st November 1898, and both he and others gave the toast and made a statement for the records to say that the Royal family had a pressing need to see that her Majesty's Royal proclamation made after the mutiny should be carried out by her ministers. They also looked forward to a day when the President of the Indian National Congress would be consulted as a matter of routine by the Governor-General. The former happened and was bettered when Independence came fifty odd years later, but the latter never took place for the Congress leaders known by Dadabhai's generation.

Dadabhai wrote to several New York journalists and papers at this time, as they were taking an interest in India's affairs. When writing to George Freeman, a writer on Indian affairs for the *New York Sun*, he gave some quite prophetic words for the next hundred years, "I am afraid the Race Question will become in time a burning one. The backward races in other parts of the world seem destined to have a bad time. The European greed will be too much for them. But the Indian question will be a terrible matter for England, if she does not look out. Once India is fully roused, and in these days of rapid development of political and moral forces this may come much sooner than we expect, it will be impossible for England to hold her own family." Perhaps for India one should submit 'The Commonwealth' and the whole thing seems to have come about. England (Britain) has lost its Empire, but as it did so with a fair amount of voluntary capitulation, it probably kept sway over a Commonwealth rather than losing its creditworthiness amongst the other nations. The race question is still with us, and only the Lord knows how it shall turn out.

Dadabhai began a campaign in Lancashire during November 1898. He chose that area because of the harm done to India by the manipulation of the cotton trade to maintain the strength of Lancashire's exports. It was not a campaign to hammer home the wrongs of the system, but to tell people that Lancashire could do a lot to help itself and India. If they accepted that in reality the drain of wealth from India that was purported to act as a 'protection' of Indian industry was really an enforced tribute, then India's purchasing power was seriously curtailed. Conversely, to allow capital to remain in India would generate jobs and create a home market. With time that would mean money that people could spend and provide a larger export market for Lancashire.

He spoke in Chorlton, Castleton, Chorley, Atherton and Knutsford, along with W A Chambers, Ramesh Dutt, Bepin Chandra Pal and the British Committee of the Congress. They were greeted with approval for their proposed reforms. Basically Britain could profit from India by trade, provided India was made richer and so could afford to buy more goods. Tribute was akin to plunder. Businessmen agreed with Dadabhai and his colleagues, but how to achieve the change in India? To this end Dadabhai was looking as always to the British people to be awakened to the need for change and then make the necessary challenges through their own representatives.

Dadabhai then organized another campaign to call attention to the hardships of Indians in South Africa. He pointed out the similarities between the 'outlanders' in the Transvaal to the Indians in India. He addressed meetings such as the Manchester Society for the Protection of Native Races on November 22nd and the venues included Stratford, Oldham, Falsworth, and Rossendale.

148

One Indian who began his career in South Africa wrote of his first contacts with Dadabhai in 1888 when he was a law student living in Richmond and then Kensington in London. Before being called to the bar on 10th June 1891, Mohandas Gandhi was advised to talk to Dadabhai about his doubts. In his words "One of my friends suggested that I should seek Dadabhai Naoroji's advice. Though I had brought an (written) introduction to him from India, it seemed to me that I had no right to trouble such a great man. Wherever an address by him was announced, I would attend it. In order to come to a close touch with the students, he had founded an Association. In course of time (I) at last mustered up the courage to present to him the letter of introduction. 'You can come,' he said, 'and have my advice whenever you like'." Gandhi later wrote, "when I reached London, I soon found that Indian students had free access to the Grand Old Man at all hours of the day. Indeed he was in the place of a father to every one of them, no matter to which province or religion they belonged. He was there to advise and guide them in their difficulties.

I have always been a hero-worshipper and so Dadabhai became real Dada to me. The relationship took the deepest root in South Africa, for he was my constant advisor and inspiration. Hardly a week passed without a letter from me to him describing the conditions of Indians in South Africa. And I will remember that whenever there was a reply to be expected, it came without fail in his own handwriting, in his unmistakably simple style. I never received a typed letter from him. And during my visits to England from South Africa I found that he had for office, a garret perhaps eight feet by six feet. There was hardly room in it for another chair. His desk, his chair, and the file of papers filled the room. I saw that he wrote his letters in copying ink and press-copied them himself."

In 1900, another famine and the worst for 25 years, hit India. Dadabhai began his campaign to bring attention to the suffering of the people and also to the causes behind these recurring famines by addressing a group at Edmonton, London on 29th April. He pointed out that millions of people only existed in the average years of the harvests, and so the famines reaped terrible harvests when they came and yet it was all so unnecessary. He also said it was gratifying to note that more attention was being focused on the drain of money experienced in India, which was the major cause for the food shortage.[1]

In June and July Dadabhai was again giving addresses all over the

---

1. He had spoken on the problem of famine before, as it was often an issue associated with India and was supposed to be due to over population. However as he pointed out to the Democratic club in London in May 1894, the increase of Britain's population had been eleven point six percent in the last decade, against India's nine point six percent.

149

country. A famine relief fund was set up and Dadabhai helped with that organization's efforts. At one meeting held at the United Methodist Church, in Walthamstow, London, Dadabhai used the words of Lord Salisbury, "as India must be bled" to warn of the future unrest. He was not just looking for famine relief, but the permanent prevention of famine, which would be possible once money was unleashed for investment in agriculture, and not tied up with unfair loan repayments and other drains.

Hyndman was keeping up with his efforts for Indian and the correspondence of 1900 shows him trying to get Dadabhai to put more emphasis on self assertion. Pious words were not enough, though Hyndman did not think Dadabhai was 'servile', which was the judgement of some Europeans of all the Indian people.

The different tone of Dadabhai's speeches can be gauged from a speech he made that year on 7th July at the Plumstead Radical Club. He said, "Great Britain, during the whole period of her connection with India never spent a single farthing of British money on the Eastern Empire... from the time when Great Britain first obtained territorial jurisdiction over India, down to the present day, it has drawn millions upon millions sterling from that Empire; Great Britain had appropriated this Indian wealth, thereby reducing the population to extreme poverty... The Indians have not the slightest voice in the expenditure of a single farthing... British rule was supposed to confer great blessings upon the Indian race. But what has been the result? Millions of the people were dying of famine and disease, and scores of millions from year's end to year's end never knew what it was to have a full meal!" (from *India*, 27th July 1900).

At another meeting organised by a Dr Mullick and held on 13th October 1900 at the Hotel Tudor, the purpose was to give young Indians a chance to hear from the Grand Old Man. He was just as anxious to see them and give pointers on how the struggle could be maintained. Other speakers pointed out to this younger audience what Dadabhai had accomplished in his former years. The audience were encouraged to carry on with making India's needs known in order to challenge what many, but not all the people now knew to be the injustices of the system.

Dadabhai pointed out that difficulties would come, but that the English press now took a serious interest in the matter of the economic drain and the Anglo-Indians were wary of an uprising of some sort. Hence he thought that reform for India would become a great domestic problem soon. Dadabhai knew that his audience had enthusiasm and he wanted more of the youth to come forward, even though they held some extremist and hence rebellious attitudes. He was not unaware that these attitudes could give rise to violence, and did not support any

150

such actions. His role became one of encouraging them to take up the challenge, but to deter them from using violence as an answer. He did not suggest that they begin with the methods he had used, but rather he sought to provide the necessary guidance and rebuke when needed, that would bear on their temper and methods, but leave the choice of action up to this new generation.

Some of the older leaders like Mehta, Wacha and Banerjea, were concerned because the youth were also frustrated at the lack of real change of the previous forty years, which made violence seem all the more likely as a course of action. What Dadabhai felt was to be achieved was for the youth's enthusiasm to be directed in constructive ways, and to be appropriately encouraged by the elders. He did not want them to become a lost and demoralized or antagonistic and anarchic generation. Dadabhai had said so a year before, after the Anglo-Indian press sought to criticize these same younger men.

Dadabhai wrote in 1905 to Gokhale that young, well educated men needed to become the missionaries for their country, both in India and Britain, and that the British press and public were beginning to wake up to the problem. He, along with William Wedderburn and Allan Hume, had published a review in 1900 in the first fifteen years of the Congress. In it they had stated, "We, who were among its originators, have now well nigh completed our work as pioneers; we have given the lead to the younger men and must look to them to take up in larger measure the burden of the work."

A manifesto was issued with the signature of William Wedderburn, Hume and Dadabhai on 19th October 1900, to the President-designate of Congress. It marked a parting of the ways. The older men recognized that the constitutional methods used before would either now develop into full effect or lead to disappointment, but that the younger men must now take up the burden. The Congress had not used underground methods or secret campaigns, but had still been disapproved and subject to the suspicion of the Authorities. It had nevertheless grown and had been recognized as the focus of public opinion by Indians. Given that nothing like it had existed beforehand and that public movements across the nation had not yet become a familiar way of life for many of Indian's inhabitants, it was the most advanced institution of its kind.

That it lasted and grew was a success in its own right and one that is sometimes eclipsed because of the magnitude of the events that were to come about in the next half century. So although in retrospect the effects it had may seem puny, it was certainly not ineffectual and without it a vacuum would have existed. It was only in the twentieth century that it would not still the new hunger for more say in the running of the country of the Indians, by the Indians for the Indians. That was the hunger that wanted to be fed by action, and would go past the old ways of Congress in a few years to inaugurate new styles of campaigning. But at the turn of the century, no organization but Congress could have been instrumental at influencing the Royal Commission to publish that Indian was overcharged by a quarter of a million pounds each year. This admission showed that to make proper restitution further inquiry was still required, as the full effects of the financial drain had to be assessed and comprehensive remedies then devised.

William Wedderburn had retired from Government to give more time to his particular issue for India and he and Dadabhai and W C Caine pointed out that the financial drain was still a massive problem. It was an issue that would only be addressed through a lot of effort and self sacrifice by those who challenged the Authorities and by a large enough body of like-minded people, if its damage was to be considerably reduced. Although this type of effort was more in the vein of the older generation, the younger groups would nonetheless be able to see the older generation's worthy efforts and in that way they still represented a role model for the future.

There was another facet of their behaviour which was also important as a role model because it showed how to reflect a balance in personal attitudes. A snippet from Dadabhai's schedule shows this up. He was invited on 7th November by the parents of W A Chambers to address a local group at Shepton Mallet. He was able to praise their son's efforts for India and say that although he, Dadabhai, was criticized for not saying enough about the good points of Britain, he felt he could not have bettered his stance for Britain than by having said all along that he wanted the connection between India and Britain to remain. Such a sentiment was probably an anathema in some quarters but to Dadabhai and his colleagues it was not possible to point out only the bad characteristics that were present in those whom they opposed. A balanced view would also recognize their strengths and this attitude of mind in the elder campaigners may have had some effect on their younger counterparts.

After that year, Dadabhai spoke of the only remedy to India's problems being found in two simple things, honour and justice, which would mean Indian subjects being treated in the same way as British subjects. By implication he wanted Indians to also keep their honour and justice, so that they would know how to act once they achieved some real equality.

CHAPTER THIRTEEN

UPPING THE ANTE

The inauguration of the Commonwealth of Australian colonies on 1st January 1901 gave Dadabhai cause for pondering. Why had a small nation of less than five millions been allowed to progress well into the twentieth century? Whereas another part of the same Empire of two hundred and eighty millions had not been meted the same treatment but quite the opposite.

In a speech on 14th January 1901 at the Penge and Beckenham Liberal and Radical Club, he pointed out that he would not dwell on the past but look for the righteous policy to be brought about. He was keeping to what was probably his watchword of "Patience, Perseverance and Agitation" for his cause of "India for the Indians." The idea of self-government as enjoyed by others was now to shape his demands, following the inauguration of 1901. For Dadabhai this was no overnight transformation in his quest but it had begun to grow and he began that year with a mixture of his usual arguments and methods and the culmination of some new ones. Some of his writing from that period shows he was also contemplating that some climax could now be on the cards. He knew that friction had been building up and may need to be expended in a violent way, rather like the earthquake that has to release pressure. He wrote "He who runs may see if the present material and moral destruction of India continues, a great convulsion must inevitably arise, by which India will be more and more crushed under the iron heel of despotism or may succeed in shattering the destroying hand of power." He was posing the question on whether the present state of affairs must end fatefully, whereas his faith that a different cause of events would result, also remained in his thoughts and instincts, and so he concluded with, "May the God of all nations lead the English to a right sense of their duty to India."

He was following a busy schedule of addresses to various meetings. Two that were recorded are the ones he gave at Toynbee Hall, Whitechapel in London's East End, and another one at Reading. The *Reading Standard's* edition of 1st March 1901 gave a description of one day in the life of Dadabhai Naoroji. Despite being seventy-six, he spent his whole day at various meetings in Reading, including his breakfast and dinner breaks. So much activity makes one wonder how he could maintain such itineraries over many days. The *Standard* pointed out that Dadabhai criticized the British Government over its policies and was asking the listeners of his message to do their duty. At such meetings, whether in Reading or North Camberwell of from the pulpit of the Free Church in Croydon and at other venues, Dadabhai found that he was usually responded to favourably. He was, for instance, able to influence the twenty-third report of the National Liberal Foundation that year.

On the 24th May 1901 and 2nd June, Dadabhai addressed Indians and members of the London Indian Society and that led to similar resolutions being passed to the previous years, but with a greater slant to self-government becoming apparent though not blatant. He gave further addresses at the North Lambeth Liberal Club, at Brixton and at Liverpool. He quoted one set of facts at this time to bring his message home to his listeners. Britain had waged one hundred and ten wars up to that time beyond the frontiers of its Empire in pursuance of maintaining the Imperial structure. Colonel Hanna, an officer with much experience in India, had shown that between 1878 and 1896, this 'forward policy' had cost a staggering Rs. 7,141,000,000. Dadabhai was using this fact whilst addressing the public at a number of venues including the young Scot's society in Edinburgh and again at their branch in London.

It was at this time that Dadabhai's book "Poverty and un-British rule in India" was published, to bring home with facts and greater detail than his previous publication of 1878, what were the ruinous effects of the money drain. The publication was quite widely read, and was used as a source book by anyone interested in pursuing that matter, who needed both the accuracy and the necessary background from a reliable publication. As said earlier it has been recognized as a foundational document of some importance and as a model for works that have been published up to the present era.

Later in 1901, the Viceroy Lord Curzon expressed the opinion that India should resent and therefore try and prevent British capital going out of India. He also surmised that when other countries such as America and China had received such wealth, or when the boot was on the other foot, and America had now flooded England with its investments, did the natives of those countries complain? Dadabhai retorted that Lord Curzon had not said that the capital that either went to India or came out of it was not properly British in its origin, but usually Indian. So even when some of it went back for 'development', it was impossible to call it completely fresh capital for Indian's benefit because it had often been accumulated by India having first been despoiled. Dadabhai ended by saying that a substantial amount of fresh capital would make a difference, but the current flow of money was bleeding the land and then not letting the wounds heal.

The previous three decades of campaigning on financial issues were beginning to show some signs of response by the British public at large. At an important meeting held at Caxton Hall, Westminster by the British Committee of Congress and the London Indian Society on 30th July 1901, a motion was carried to protest against a proposed tax on India to maintain a garrison of British troops in South Africa. Lord Welby of the Royal Commission spoke in support of the motion. This was indicative of the growing feeling amongst the government and others that the handling of the Indian economy by the British rulers had been endured for long enough. At this meeting another resolution demanded that the British Exchequer should contribute to the cost of its army in India.

In 1901, Dadabhai joined the National Democratic League, which wanted to help smaller parties. From this and Dadabhai's contributions to a fund set up for the Labour leader, Keir Hardie, it can be seen that he gradually came to hold a more socialist viewpoint. If he had been born ten years later he may well have stood as a Labour Member of Parliament.

It is ironic that at the same time as some leaders showed support for the Indians, the actions of the rulers in India were becoming more regressive. That may well have been due in part to the increased stridency of the Indians and such a response was indicative of the greater feelings of agitation held by those in authority. It showed a general uncertainty on whether a more conciliatory or a tougher policy was their best approach. The dichotomy over which general strategy was the best one represented a watershed in the British rule over India that occurred in the first years of the century. The Indians also were approaching the same dichotomy, but for them it was not a question of trying to hold on to something that was slipping away, but rather which new way should they elect to take as a growing movement, which was soon to have a massive national support.

On 4th September 1903, on his 78th birthday, it was decided in Britain and India to hold a celebration on this day each year to be known as "Dadabhai Day", and this continued until the end of his life. The first such event was held at the People's Free Reading Room Library in Bombay.

One of the leading Indians of the time, the Judge Mahader Govind Ranade, had unveiled a life size picture of Dadabhai on 24th November 1900 in the hall of the Framji Cowasji Institute in Bombay, but regrettably this distinguished gentleman was to die prematurely, soon after this event. His widow indicated by her reply to Dadabhai's condolences that her husband had held his influence in high regard, perhaps in the matter of a disciple to his teacher. Ranade's work as a

155

compatriot has also been held in high regard by subsequent generations, and the feelings expressed in this letter were a worthy testament.

In his later years, Dadabhai probably spent as much time writing as speaking, though vast reams had already come from his pen and it is hard to say when his workload diminished.

He constantly wrote to the press and to many institutions and individuals in his drive to promote the Indians and India. These articles were published in many journals including the *India*, the *Contemporary Review*, the *Daily News*, the *Manchester Guardian*, the *Weekly News and Chronicle*, and the *Pearsons Magazine*. In 1905 he was still against the use of force, and feared that agitation was giving way to nihilism and hence unrestrained aggression. However just prior to that reaffirmation of his stance, the then Secretary of State for India Lord George Hamilton ,was doing all he could to remove Indians from the higher services, which only added to the anger. Dadabhai knew that all he could do was to point out that evolution was still better than revolution. He could see no positive end to an open fight and his articles reflected his mind on the way for reform.

He wrote replies to critics and to friends. He wrote to the Bishop of New York, the Right Reverend Henry Godman Potter in 1900, to correct his statements that India only prospered under British rule. Dadabhai wanted to publish their correspondence, but the Bishop would not agree to it. He wrote to the Dewan of Mysore in 1900, when that ancient state seemed to be on the verge of losing its fairly autonomous status, and have its policy dictates decided by Europeans rather than by Indians. His purpose was to encourage them to maintain their defence of their position. His aim in another series of letters was also to encourage but this time it was an industrialist who received his sentiments. The industrialist was another Parsee by the name of J N Tata, who was trying to begin an indigenous Indian industry, by raising Indian capital and was not going to use loans from Britain. The exercise succeeded and in 1907 the Tata Iron and Steel Works was established. The company has flourished since those days and is now a major combine in the Indian economy.

He wrote on the financial drain of India, adding to all he had written upon in the previous decades. He wrote on affairs of state, on more personal disputes, and on overstaffing in the administration, especially the military administration. The military also felt his attention focus on them because of the continued British policy of making India pay for their active incursions, even though that was primarily for British interests and "not exclusively Indian."

One particular piece of correspondence about Dadabhai, written by Lord George Hamilton to Lord Curzon, has already been referred to, and it arose from a correspondence between the two of them that carried on for several years from 1900. The Secretary of State was often challenged by Dadabhai on the grounds that changes were being introduced which spelt a backwards movement in the equality of access to the Administration and seemed to be a break with earlier Royal proclamations. One of his letters sent in October 1900 pointed out that "new generations have received the blessings of education and they now realize the present un-British violation of all pledges.... you will see that there is panic that the authorities were tending towards stopping even in England the competition of Indians for the Civil Service and that the subtle encroachments on the various other services are but a prelude to that disaster". Lord Hamilton was blunt in his earlier replies and these were tinged with some rancour. Later on, Dadabhai found he was not even going to get replies to his letters and the small amount of correspondence that remains from this time is an indication of a general refusal by those particular British authorities to enter into dialogue with him. However, the message of King Edward VII in 1906 helped reduce the burden of the Administration and Dadabhai picked up on this in a positive manner.

He was invited to attend an international meeting of the Socialists in Amsterdam on 14th - 20th August 1904. It created a stir in India, not least among the Indians for such a public figure to be ready to rub shoulders with Socialists. In reply, Dadabhai pointed out that the people of India should realize that support for their cause would often be more solid when it came from the working classes, and that they should be mindful not to expect too much from the well-off. He went to the meeting and addressed the audience on the needs of India and to familiarize them on what British rule meant in practice, as well as answering their questions on colonial policy. After a well-delivered speech which had not been expected of an Indian, Dadabhai was given a rousing ovation ending with a resolution. This response left him moved, as it came from the exploited and down-trodden of Europe, and was obviously their heartfelt expression for all of Indian's millions.

As the style and content of his speech, which was translated, was seen to be delivered in a way the other delegates had not expected from an Indian, they realized their expectations would have to be reviewed. They accepted that their need was to have their eyes and ears opened still further. One way for this to be achieved was for the report of that meeting and his resolution to be sent out to be read worldwide, and not least in Great Britain. So both the context of his speech and the call for Socialist connections to Indian's cause, was transmitted far and wide.

This was a red rag to the Anglo-Indian community. There was no large Labour party at that time, but as George Lansbury MP wrote in

1929, if Dadabhai had been of a later generation, he would have been a member, and a paramount one, of such a party. At the Socialist Congress in Stuttgart, the leading Indian agitators based in Europe, S R Rana and Madame Cama (or Bhikaji Rustom Cama who was the daughter-in-law of another well-known reformer, K R Cama), spoke again on behalf of the "dumb millions of Hindustan." Madame Cama had helped design and now unfurled for the first time, the Indian National flag at that Congress, to symbolize what their hope was now based upon. Two of Dadabhai's granddaughters, Perrin and Gosi, also got involved with the "revolutionaries" based in Paris, and when they returned to Britain, were prevented from holding any office.

Despite his incessant campaigning for India, Dadabhai had other issues away from India which he still wanted to see resolved. He had kept working for a British state pension scheme ever since he had stood for Parliament. He presented the arguments for it at a conference of Democrats and Radicals in 1905 as the Vice-President of the National Democratic League. On a connected subject, he had already produced a booklet entitled "The Rights of Labour." In this he published schemes for Industrial Commissioners courts to be set up and operated for the recognition and protection of Labour as a property. In many ways, he was amongst the growing number of public figures who were proposing parts of what we now call the Welfare State in Britain.

But although these Socialist programmes were what Dadabhai was getting more involved in and perhaps he was using the current language of the movement, it was with regard to India that Dadabhai's tone had become more radical and assaulting over the years. Though he did not lose faith in a British rule being established over an un-British rule, and held that faith when many younger followers could no longer believe that was achievable, he was more agitated and stern in the way he demanded reform.

Whilst he continued to pursue his ends by constitutional means, he certainly found that his own patience had grown thin. Yet when the Indian Congress asked Dadabhai to attend the 1904 Congress, he instead requested Sir Henry Cotton to accept the Presidency with William Wedderburn also going to attend. Dadabhai could not have gone, but made this request in any case, to point out that the Indian people should not lose all hope over the British conscience and that the endeavours made by Britons had not ceased, even though the rule of their country was getting more oppressive.

Despite some longer breaks because of his illness, he continued his efforts in Britain during these twilight years and was still touring and giving addresses at places like North Lambeth, Clapham Park, St. Albans and at Kennington in the London Area.

CHAPTER FOURTEEN

A SPLIT THAT
BOUGHT UNITY

As well as the inauguration of Australia in 1901 and its effects on Dadabhai's thinking, another event now took place which concentrated the mind of Dadabhai and many of his countrymen onto the self rule road.

Early in 1904, Lord Curzon, the Viceroy, delivered a speech that cast a slur on India's character and religion, at the Calcutta Union. New life had begun to stir and bring vitality into Indian's sinews and his speech was perhaps the best shot in the arm for the movement that now began to look distinctively nationalistic in its character. The Viceroy's pronouncements struck the whole country, and it rose to add its very considerable voice to that of the few stalwarts who had previously represented the majority.

Many who had never taken a part in politics voiced their opinion on this for the first time, including the 'tories' of India. Their complaints focused more on the manner of the Viceroy and raised questions about him and his style of Administration. Dadabhai found his small clique of colleagues increased many fold, although he really had nothing to do with demands for the Viceroy to be recalled. In one generation, the people who were calling for the Viceroy to be sent back home had changed from British to Indian and there was in consequence a complete turn around from the situation in the days of the Viceroys like Lord Ripon.

It was Lord Curzon's division of the province of Bengal which was arranged in 1904/5 and completed on 16th October 1905, which led to more and more protest in the ensuing years. Bengal was knit by its history, people and religion, and could not be split into two separate entities with their own capitals without splitting a single people. At a large meeting held in London at which Dadabhai presided, he pointed out how the principles of Mountstuart Elphinstone of over seventy years before had fallen down, because of the methods used by men such as Sir Henry Fowler in 1894, and then of Lord George Hamilton, Secretary of State, and now Lord Curzon who "out-Herods them all." These rulers' actions were making a mockery of the so-called benefits behind British actions. He pointed out how other prominent British statesmen and politicians warned their countrymen that the system of overbearing rule and zealous persecution of requests for justice was counter-productive and was really a stultified approach that made Britain unable to act creatively.

Dadabhai did try to remind this greatly enlarged grouping of active people to remember that they should remain fixed on the root of the issue and ask for a change in the whole system of Administration, not just one man. The clear demand for self-government came soon afterwards, and this had been the new demand that Dadabhai had begun to see as the only answer after the inauguration of Australia.

So at the London Indian Society meeting of 1st June 1904, Dadabhai pointed out that self-government under the British rule was now the way to stop the present rotting system. On 8th July 1904, he again asked British listeners to accept their role, by first asking them to assess what was the real relationship between Britain and India. Was it a master and slave relationship, and if so would they see that what India now wanted was self determination under a British paramountcy? America had just been going through a similar heart search on its role in the Philippines. He began to put a permanent paragraph in friendly papers to help raise awareness, and promote this new attitude.

A new determination was being forged within Indians who wanted to see self-government. Dadabhai said he might not live to see that day, but the initiative was with the Indians now - although the oppressed, they had begun to point the way forward. In some ways it had become a self-generating process and unquenched by outside pressures.

In Bengal a mass movement arose which in a sense heralded in the new methods which came to be identified with men such as Gandhi. A campaign of Swadeshi (literally 'of our country') was organized between 1903 - 1908 to get people to purchase the locally made goods and to boycott all foreign imports. It came about because of the British Government's aim to split Bengal and 'dethrone Calcutta.' As Lord Curzon put it, to stop Calcutta being "the centre from which the Congress party is manipulated throughout Bengal, and indeed the whole of India." The Bengalis had always been strong supporters for Congress and many of them were actively involved in the politics of dissent.

The mass of the population were not so aware of this political aim, which was the real purpose behind partition. As it was Congress had not enjoyed mass support because it had never operated as a popularist platform and such a movement was alien to its normal manner of operation. What the Congress had not done was now being done because people were reacting against the outright arrogance shown by the British Administration in making such a move, and because it was their homeland that was being split. The Bengalis led the way, through men like Tilak[1], but the rest of India's massive population also arose at this time with ordinary people taking to the streets.

The formal declaration for partition was made on 19th July 1905 and the Swadeshi movement was launched on 7th August 1905 at a meeting held at the Calcutta Town Hall. That meeting passed a famous boycott resolution, which hit the Manchester cloth and Liverpool salt trade. The boycott was economically effective and British cloth prices fell in some districts by five to fifteen times their original value.

The people of Bengal and India responded in numbers never seen before and nationalists of a different calibre were to lead it during those few years. The Congress of 1905 supported it, but would not go so far as the more militant nationalists such as Tilak and Bipin Chandra Pal, who sought to extend it to become more of an open and aggressive struggle. The general tempo had caught on, but the militant and moderate factions were now openly disputing with each other on how to activate the new consciousness of the Indian people.

Both sides at least had changed in their ultimate aims, which became one of Swaraj (self government) and grew out of the obvious success of Swadeshi. Dadabhai was to play a part in this during the next year, but at that time he was still referring to the faults of the British Administration's handling of the Bengal Partition Plan.

Dadabhai again criticised Lord Curzon's method of rule that year, because it was at times ill considered and because he defended the upset he caused in a rather peevish way, which rather than allowing for any progress, had actually dealt the severest blow to British rule. Worst of all, in the case of Bengal Lord Curzon was justifying his unfair and dictatorial actions by the tarnishing of the very same people who were to be most hurt by them. Dadabhai did also make the point that this same Lord Curzon had worked on improving the administrative load and, in an earlier period, had stopped any brutal treatment of Indians by Britons and had received criticism for his actions from his British colleagues. He reiterated what he had said before, that both Lord Curzon and Lord George Hamilton were quite capable. He did this to try and get across that it did not work to anyone's benefit if all that could be put forward was the denouncement of people, but that he would denounce their words and works and asked others to make their protest in a similar way. He still kept working with any supportive party and met other members of the administration during this time. Gosi his granddaughter remembers meeting Sir George Birdwood with her grandfather at that time.

Differences in approach were apparent, but like other Indians,

1. Tilak was not a Bengali, he was a Marathi

161

Dadabhai wrote and spoke to urge and encourage the Bengalis to keep up with their agitation on the 5th January 1906, to show that their backbone was true and by this show their character even if Bengal remained split in two. The Swadeshi Movement and the related activity of the time carried on for another two years, and then in 1908 it lost the initial momentum and was withdrawn until a later date, when other calls for country wide boycotts were again made to the people.

Parallel to his work in India Dadabhai became engaged in the needs of Indians over a similar timescale, but in another continent. The first indentured labourers from Calcutta and Madras reached South Africa on 16th November 1860. They were followed by Indian traders and free servants who were called "passenger Indians" and who came to Natal, the Transvaal, the Orange Free State and Cape Colony. The white colonists wanted no equals in their midst and the cry of "away with the Asiatics" became common. Repatriation or permanent debt were suggested as remedies, but the British Government refused to allow either policy. Indentured labourers were paid for the work they did and were bonded to sugar plantations. In 1870 indenturing was temporarily halted, although the labourers still had to carry permits and when they refused to work, were pressured to return to India. The other Indians wanted to be less antagonistic to the whites because of their status.

Major political changes were to occur which prevented further stonewalling of the ideas aimed at suppressing or removing the "coolies", as Natal achieved internal government in 1893. The Transvaal, as a self governing Republic, could already spurn ideas of equal treatment so that all Indians already living there had to register if they traded and were also required to pay a twenty-five pound fee. Nor was any Indian allowed to own land, which left them in a kind of flotsam and jetsam limbo, with no real hope of progress for their future. These regulations were made lighter at a later date and became three pounds and land could be held in certain designated areas on "urgent sanitary grounds", although no real sanitation problems ever occurred amongst the Indian population, and no hygiene remedies were ever provided by the State. In the Orange Free State no Indian could hold fixed property or carry on mercantile business, but they could be graciously given positions as a labourer. In Cape Colony, their children could not attend public schools, and by 1892 they lost their civic rights and privileges. To finalize some of these policies, an Act needed to be passed to make them constitutional, although their effects were being felt well before such a bill was presented.

An organization, the Coloured Agitation Committee, chaired by Mr H O Ally of Ali Brothers and Company, sent cables to Gladstone in 1892 and to Dadabhai to ask them to prevent the Act of the South

African State, by stopping Royal Assent. Dadabhai took up the matter with the Colonial Secretary, who was Lord Ripon in that October. Dadabhai also received a long list of grievances from the Natal-based Hayee Mohamed Dada and Company who were in communication with the Indian political agency.

They got Charles Bradlaugh MP to put questions up in the House. But his untimely death in that year hurt everyone and closed up this channel of access. C A V Conybeare was the next MP to be approached and he began his task by visiting South Africa. Letters coming from the Transvaal and the Orange Free State also showed more restrictions were to be imposed and Lord Ripon was informed. His position to influence matters was rather tenuous, as they were independent territories, and although the Queen and many in government desired equality of treatment for all British subjects, getting it done was neither a straightforward nor easily enforceable matter. Lord Ripon sent copies of all his correspondence in 1893 to Dadabhai, so that he could follow the dealings between the Imperial government and the territorial governments.

In April 1893 Mohandas Karamchand Gandhi arrived at Durban in South Africa and, after experiencing the insults and assaults of the white community, he began the work that has become history and was to carry him through to the next century. His early impressions of Dadabhai had already been formed in India and Britain, and he found a need to strengthen the link whilst in the Cape of No Hope. In 1894 Dadabhai heard that the government of Natal was going to disenfranchise Indians. He said it must be resisted and Gandhi agreed not to leave the country as had been his plan. Indeed he set up the Natal Indian Congress.[1] Between 1894 and 1906 Gandhi led what could be termed the moderate period of resistance. After 1906 his style changed to an open disobedience and challenge to the authorities, which Gandhi named 'Satyagraha'. He kept in regular contact with his mentors, Dadabhai and William Wedderburn, paying out some considerable extra postage for the communication. He commented on his "search for truth" in South Africa and on his lack of experience. He pointed out that the real reason for the disenfranchising of the Indians was for the Natal Government to make free Indians wish to leave, as that would be the only way they could loose their rights as free citizens. He asked Dadabhai to help as a father with his children. A petition was sent to Lord Ripon and widespread support was raised for the campaign.

It was in January 1895 that Gandhi heard that the Bill had been disallowed and asked Dadabhai to corroborate his good news. On 29th

1. This actually took place because on the eve of his departure from South Africa, local Indians asked him as the only lawyer present to help them stave off the bill. His real campaigning began then, when he was twenty-five and he was to stay on for twenty years.

August that year the Colonial Secretary Joseph Chamberlain heard the deputation of the British Committee of the Indian National Congress which consisted of Dadabhai, Allan Hume and W C Bonnerjee, on the grievances of British Indians in Africa. He countered their fears about the various bills being set up, by stating they were for 'sanitary reasons', which was rather a septic way of giving the truth. There were medically qualified people who had already stated that the Indians were if anything above average in their personal cleanliness. Mr Chamberlain said he would try to remove the threatening bills of the Cape Colony, Natal and the Transvaal. On October 7th the Volksraad of the South African Republic declared the term 'British Subjects' only covered 'White persons.' Dadabhai had covered this point with Chamberlain in the correspondence that he had sent him in 1895 after the deputation. Eventually in 1897 the Government sent a letter stating that Mr Chamberlain was not going to take serious action against Natal but to ask it to re-consider its aim.

By then Gandhi was telling people in India of the situation and a memorial was sent to Lord Hamilton, Secretary of State for India. This did not deter the South African authorities and one Mansukhal Nazar was sent to England to get more help and support. Dadabhai aided him by arranging contacts at the India Office and the Colonial Office. The weekly correspondence between Gandhi and Dadabhai of this time also included a request from the former to the latter for a photo, although Gandhi must have seen Dadabhai speak whilst he was in London. Actually this was not just a personal request, but one made by Gandhi as Honorary Secretary following a resolution, so that Dadabhai's likeness could be seen by the beleaguered community in South Africa. The weekly correspondence was kept up both during and after the Boer War (1899-1902). During that period Gandhi had been living in Natal and so had raised an Indian Ambulance Corps of 1000 men, for which he was awarded a medal. This pro-British action was a sincere one and in consequence did not always help his standing with his community because the situation worsened when British Rule was reimposed. But when Chamberlain visited the colonies, the Indian community asked Gandhi to represent them. Although no help came to the Indian residents, despite his repeated requests for civil rights, he raised his standing in the community through his efforts.

In 1903, Dadabhai pointed out to Lord Hamilton that the lack of action by the British authorities to readjust the imbalances was tantamount to saying that the soon to be formed self-governing colonies could use the bad example of the Government as a way to justify how they acted. It gave them the feeling that their actions would be overlooked if they followed suit. Justice was not upheld in the courts of that land, as everyone realized and the Indians had so low a status that murder could be committed without anyone being charged. Gandhi kept up his campaigning, but also formed a stretcher bearer corps for service with the native troops in 1906, during the suppression of a Zulu uprising which with his other activities, kept him tied to the country for several more years.

Dadabhai had written to Gandhi a short while before to come and make his case heard in Britain. In July 1906, Gandhi wrote back that the Transvaal was preparing to register Indians for a third time and that the Imperial Government did not really know what the State Government was planning. Mr Duncan, the Colonial Secretary, was named as the person who kept Mr Lyttleton and Lord Milner in the dark on the real effects of such legislation.

Dadabhai passed on such information to Chamberlain's successor, Lord Elgin. However, this Lord later approved of the pending Act. The draft Asiatic Law Amendment Ordinance wanted every man, woman and child over eight to be registered and finger-printed. This led to passive resistance by the entire community, which bore the thumb print of Gandhi wherever it took place. Gandhi had by now built up and refined his philosophy on 'Satyagraha' which basically sought change through nonviolent disobedience to the authorities. In effect Gandhi formulated the unwritten but very successful political and moral policy of the Indians who fought for India's Independence, during his years in South Africa. He and H O Ally then went to Britain to meet Dadabhai and the British Committee of the Congress.

Dadabhai welcomed the resistance action as opposed to further petitions being made to the Authorities. He advised on further constitutional means to aid the ends of the Indians and got real support from Sir Bhownaggree in Parliament and from Sir Lepel Griffin. The latter headed a delegation of Dadabhai, Gandhi and others to Lords Elgin and Morley. Although listened to sympathetically, only verbal reassurances were given.

The Asiatic Registration Act was due to come in on the 1st July 1908 and Gandhi had little time to organize the resistance that followed. He warned that racial segregation would spread once it had started. Dadabhai addressed the Annual Congress meeting in Calcutta about the dire situation, to get India fully informed. The Act came in but the resistance carried on. In 1909 although invalided with recurring illness, Dadabhai was again approached by the Transvaal Indians as the "father of the Indian Nation that is to be" for his help when they sent him a petition with 19005 signatures made out against the Act. He was still referring to the lack of appropriate counteraction by the British Government in 1913.

The Satyagraha movement eventually led to the capitulation of the law in 1914 through the Indian Relief Act of that year. Gandhi moved to Britain and helped raise a Field Ambulance Corps, but ill health forced him to return to India soon afterwards, to begin a larger struggle in due time.

One good result of the South African problem was that it seemed to unite all Asians together, no matter whether their differences were based on a national or religious or political slant. Dadabhai often had an ally in Bhownaggree and when for instance they questioned the India office about the high level of suicides among the indentured labourers, both men worked in co-operation. Bhownaggree carried on with his battles against South Africa's apartheid system up until the time of his death in November 1933. It seems amazing that the corruption of human dignity could last for so long and span the lives of so many diverse people. Many of those living then will never know the changes that have now being brought about in these latter years, but it should not be forgotten that as apartheid comes to an end, their endeavours were as important as the present generation's battles.

CHAPTER FIFTEEN

ANOTHER CONSTITUENCY

D adabhai's busy life had only postponed his thoughts for a new political career, and the search for a constituency had been kept up since his time at Central Finsbury. At one time South Hackney's Progressive Association had unanimously voted for him to be their candidate. Dadabhai said that provided the vote could be supported by evidence that a Liberal candidate could expect success, he would accept the position. But this proved harder to find and in the end nothing came of their hopes.

Other constituencies were tried, through the offices of the National Reform Union. When the election of 1900 was announced, Dadabhai had been in bed with bronchitis. His friends felt that the four years with the Royal Commission had overtaxed him. After that election and when he was only slightly better, Dadabhai wrote to Mr J Sieger, whose help at Finsbury had been a great boost. In reply he received an invitation from the Liberal and Radical Association in North Lambeth. Their political Council went on to vote for him and so did the local National League branch and a conference of members of Local Industrial, Trade Union and Temperance Leagues as well. As he had found in his previous selection, voting for a candidate was not a straightforward matter and there was a problem which arose because of a split in the Membership of Association.

Some members favoured a Mr W Wightman, a local resident with a good civic record. Dadabhai lost at a contest on 10th September by nine votes to ten. Nevertheless, he was asked to address the Executive again on Foreign and Home policy. On 1st October, he spoke to the members and, on the 26th November, was voted in as their choice once again, by sixty-six votes to fifty-nine.

The Secretary of the Association said that the votes needed to be agreed at a subsequent meeting by a two thirds majority and notified at a public meeting held after that one. But on 7th January 1902, Dadabhai was told that allegations were being made against him, namely that he was accused of giving money to certain people in the party. Dadabhai admitted to passing money on to friends for election purposes, but none had enrolled for him at the votes that had been taken. The Executive delayed calling a meeting to rectify this, until 13th October 1902, which was nine months later! In exasperation, Dadabhai wrote to say he was standing as their candidate and would they note this and agree to support him. John Maddy, the Secretary of the Association resigned and, with other supporters, started the 'North Lambeth Labour and Progressive Association', with Dadabhai as the President. Pandemonium arose at the Annual Meeting of the Liberal and Radical Association, some claiming he was forcing things and putting up references of 'Naoroji Cheques.' Others said the Association was politically dead. Mr Wightman then wrote to the press that he would stand to oppose Dadabhai. The next year on 16th February he said if Dadabhai withdrew so would he, so that a United party with another candidate could stand with a better chance. Dadabhai also received a letter from his long time friend Caine, saying no candidate had ever won in his position. However, Dadabhai brushed aside the olive branch and said he would continue to seek election as the representative of the party.

The Executive of the Association then decided to recommend another candidate, Sir Robert Peel. But on 24th March 1903 the President referred a request to the two parties, the pro-Naoroji and the pro-Wightman. He wanted them to bury the hatchet, but both sides were now determined to carry on fighting from their corners and the appeals got no response from either side. It may also have been in a few people's minds that as the Association had been the cause of the struggle in the first place, having picked and voted for both candidates, to then ask them to give way to a third man was an affront.

Dadabhai then received a letter from the Secretary on 10th April 1903 saying would he agree to refer the matter to Herbert Gladstone, the Liberal Whip, "for the purpose of arbitration by three gentlemen appointed by him, one of whom should be a Labour member." Dadabhai refused. By then an election seemed imminent, which compared to the machinations within the party, must have seemed to be a small affair. At a special meeting on April 23rd, the Executive voted by fifteen votes to three for Wightman. Dadabhai was unperturbed and began a door to door canvas of the streets of North Lambeth, with Arthur Allgood as his election agent, for the Lambeth District Trades and Labour Council. He was now nearing his eightieth birthday and yet he managed to cover all 6000 voters in the constituency.

At a conference held on 27th April, the principle members asked Dadabhai if he would stand under the Labour representation Committee's banner. Dadabhai readily agreed and toiled throughout the campaign, holding meetings and canvassing the voters in the constituency. Wightman tried to disparage him by referring to improper money deals and other improprieties. Two of Dadabhai's friends rushed to support him, namely Birdwood and Wedderburn, by writing to the press, so that a public retort could be made to the accusations. But in private Wedderburn saw the general situation as negative for Dadabhai, and felt he could not win the seat. He tried to get Dadabhai to retire.

W Wightman died before the election, but the two sides remained apart even though Dadabhai could then have become the only candidate, especially as Mr Homer, the Conservative candidate, was involved in financial problems. The Lambeth Association was asked by the London Liberal Federation to accept Dadabhai. The Chairman of the London Federation came to the Association, but found that body set against Dadabhai. The central body felt it must bow to the opposition and appointed Horatio Myer, a bedstead manufacturer with a record of civic service, as candidate.

The feelings of Dadabhai's group ran higher than ever at this turn of events. Dadabhai's supporters felt the actions of the Federation had been too weak willed. The Association started to re-attack Dadabhai in the press, making it personal in certain cases. Dadabhai put the matter with his solicitor, who in the 'Morning Post' of 6th January 1906 said, "(he) had suffered during the past three years from a large amount of slander and misrepresentation, without any tangible charge which could be investigated." He issued writs against the perpetrators, hoping to try and deter them rather than for the purpose of seeking a prosecution in the Courts.

To add confusion to this embroiled melee, the names of the two sides were sometimes mistaken by outside supporters. So allies in India who were for Dadabhai got the names the wrong way round, and they actually supported Dadabhai's opponents for a while. Some unexpected support came from Victor Rogas, who had worked for Mr Wightman, but now came to the aid of Dadabhai, and in particular spent much of his time answering the comments that were being made of Dadabhai, such as the observation that he was too old for the election. Admittedly, Dadabhai was an old man, but given the amount of political campaigning he undertook, plus the country wide campaigns he was conducting on India's needs, he was an exception to the rule, working at least as hard as younger men. Unfortunately, at the General Election, which the Liberals won in the national vote, the local votes went two-thousand-one-hundred- and sixty-two for H Myer, one-thousand-nine-hundred and four for Major Gestrell the Conservative candidate, and seven-hundred and thirty-three for Dadabhai.

Dadabhai lost with some generosity of feeling and pointed out that he was not yet ready for a return to India.

CHAPTER SIXTEEN

CONGRESS:
THE NEW AGE

The twenty-second Congress was to be a stock-taking event. It was also something of the coming of age as this was to be held in the twenty-first full year. It was the time to ask, had India achieved progress from the efforts of the past, and if not did the 'mendicant policy' of the Elders stand barren? Young India wanted more rapidity of change and a proper constitution for the Congress, and a vitalizing of the entire country. The older members paid scant attention, which was to their cost as these calls were not due to a desire for wrestling authority from the Elders or a passing feeling or fad. It was a change in the basic principles and perceptions held by the Indian people under the British rule.

The new drive was for autonomy, not self-government under Britain. The British and Anglo-Indian press had often shown a lack of concern for the reasons behind the growing political unrest, although conversely their scare mongering had played more than its part in stirring feelings up. This was a country that was beginning to move as a nation and the young had found that they had a temper and the will to see this movement gather its pace. The older guard had not challenged British supremacy, the young group wanted to, though the majority did not wish to do it by force but by boycott. The twenty-second Congress was the test bed for both sides to see if the new wine could fit in the old wineskins.

The conflict posed a dilemma for the organizers of that Congress about who should be a President. Someone was needed who was not seen to be too pro the one side or the other, nor too weak for anyone's taste, but was strong enough to be accepted by all sides at the Congress. The Elders were probably going to find that they were to be swamped by the Bengali delegates, who with the extremists favoured having Bal Gangadhar Tilak as their leader. Once Dadabhai had been approached by Surendranath Banerjea to be President, Tilak wrote soon afterwards to distance himself from the opposition to such a move, which was primarily opposed by the Bengali extremists. In fact, Tilak was their first choice, but he wanted to reserve a contest of strength until Congress and so he still kept a close contact with them on many other matters.

A meeting of the 'Calcutta Congress Reception Committee' was hurriedly formed, which gave short notice to all the members living in East Bengal. Despite some opposition, the meeting on the 11th November confirmed Dadabhai as the next president. This move paid off because as the respected and genuine Grand Old Man, Dadabhai was different. The Elders already knew Dadabhai and the Bengalis also knew him as someone who was not set solidly in his ways and he could therefore be seen by all sides as being above the power broking, without being out of touch with the issues that confronted them all. No one really wanted a split, except for perhaps a few extreme individuals and some pro-Tilakites.

Those same Tilakites saw they were outwitted and pointed out that because there was not real constitution, this type of appointment by choice was still allowed to happen. One of the reforms put up at the Congress that year was for a proper Constitution to be implemented. They accepted the choice of Dadabhai as President nonetheless as he was not just a moderate, and was known to be outspoken and to attack with his words in a very directed way if a problem was apparent.

During Lord Curzon's Viceroyalty it had been noted that Dadabhai did not mince his words, but he had made his challenges through the Institutions and the generally accepted modus operandi of public life. This was still the preferred form of attack and the way that most moderates wanted to keep to for the future. Dadabhai for his part wanted to keep the constitutional apparatus, but was looking for a reform to bring in Home rule.

He felt the British had never been tyrants and had kept plunderers at bay and given some uniformity to the country. What they had also shown they could do was to find ways of plundering India that were legitimate, which was far cleverer. It was not unlawful or brutal, but also showed how cold and remorseless was their intent. To use his own analogy, he felt that other invaders would bash a man on the head and then rob him. Whereas the British would firmly restrain such a person, but not injure him and then anaesthetize him and proceed to remove not just his possessions but with surgical precision cleanly cut him up as well, until nothing was left.

Dadabhai set off for Indian on 29th November 1905 on a P and O steamship after having a farewell breakfast, at which Wedderburn and Samuel Smith and others attended. They used the occasion to hold a series of addresses given in his honour. A law student (later Justice) B J Wadia gave an etymological epigram of Dadabhai's name, which has been recorded for posterity. He said the name Dada (Father) showed the position accorded to Dadabhai by all Indian by universal consent.

171

Then Bhai (Brother) showed his empathy for those who suffer and live under suffering. He was the first of India's sons working for the Nowruz (New Day) of Indian's Liberty and emancipation. Given the character and work of Dadabhai, such an eulogy was not trite pandering to the man.

Dadabhai arrived in India on 14th December to a very warm homecoming at Apollo Bunder docks in Bombay. He was taken by car to the Malabar Hills suburb, and the procession had to halt fifty times to let him be garlanded, with some garlands containing pearls intertwined with the flowers. The same enthusiasm and reception occurred when he came to Calcutta. The Calcutta Congress was to be the largest political event ever witnessed in India. The welcome address by Dr Ghose advocated Swadeshi and boycott and reminded everyone of the wounds made by the Bengal partition. Dadabhai's address was on Swaraj (self government) which was the first time a call for Swaraj had come from the Congress platform. He began his speech by quoting the Prime Minister, Sir Henry Campbell-Bannerman, "Good Government could never be a substitute for government by the people themselves." He told Congress that, "work consists of two main parts; - First and foremost is the question of the Policy and Principles of the system of Government under which India ought to be governed in the future.

Second is to watch the operation of the administration as it now exists ... till the present system of government is radically altered .... He said the questions of when and in what way were less pertinent. By comparison he pointed out how the British had not waited for ever for their Parliament, but had had to go through many years of evolution to attain the end result. He implored his audience with the words, "we have not petitioned or agitated enough at all in our demands. In very important matters we must petition Parliament with hundreds and thousands of petitions", and "Agitate, agitate over the whole length and breadth of India, if we really mean to get justice from John Bull."

But on the question of method, Dadabhai said that despite the obvious setbacks that had hit the supporters for Indian's freedoms, the mood should not swing towards using violent action. He did however pick up on the difference of opinion created by the generation gap in Congress between the younger radicals and the more wary older Congress-men, when he said, "The duty now lies upon the shoulders of the rising generation, whom I see with pleasure to be enthusiastic even giving a little poking to us, elders, for not going forward rapidly enough! I am so pleased, I regard it as a best result of all the political work during the past fifty years that we have decided upon a goal, we have decided upon one particular aim."

He would continue to seek change through representation and could say that through all the disappointments of broken promises or of blocks on the way, he had not stopped to consider a change in his style. To 'Persevere' was his reason for not despairing, and then the reason for his still being hopeful was the prospect of 'revival.' Revival in the minds and hearts of leading Statesmen was what he felt was happening, which would lead to honest efforts being made for a real start on the road to self-government. He was not therefore rebelling against British rule and still after fifty years of knowing its weakness, would put his hope in British ways overcoming un-British rule. His speech moved on to address the partition of Bengal, which was a fresh hurt to Indians and a bad blunder of the British. He gave no prescription on how that wrong could be redressed, but ended by calling for unity amongst all those present at Congress, if they were to see anything achieved.

His speech was conciliatory; it had tried to being in Swaraj under British paramountcy, and yet reaffirmed his sense of British fair play. This treading of an old way was not what the activists wanted. However mention of Swaraj brought angry condemnation from the Anglo-Indians, including a few who said India was to be ruled through the sword. At Congress, the refusal to make the boycott India wide was enough to force some of the more radical members to leave, although a motion of sorts was carried. However, to some with wiser heads, like Tilak, who could be disappointed by the tone of the address, the important thing was that unity had prevailed. They recognized that was the better way to dispel all the Anglo-Indian critics worst pronouncements and hopefully maintain the future of Congress and give Indians a hope. He wrote in January 1907 that, "His (Dadabhai) concluding speech was much better (than his Presidential address) and his placing Swarajya as a goal before the Congress in distinct terms was some advance on old ideas."

Dadabhai returned to London on 8th February having been able to see the Congress come through its metamorphosis of direction. Unfortunately, the coming together that was achieved at the Congress would not be maintained and a permanent split set in two years later. Still for Dadabhai it had been a worthwhile reason to travel to India and to top it all he was apparently in good health as an interview on his eighty-first birthday in September 1906 implied. But he soon suffered a bronchial attack, pains in his back and due to hydrocele problems, could not even take his regular walking exercise. This condition remained very hard to combat and his granddaughters, Gosi and Nergis, came up to London to nurse him. Not until 26th April 1907 was he again felt to be well enough to get around and meet callers. People advised that he should now return to India for his health. Dadabhai had just begun a new venture to put forward his proposals for self-government. He agreed to keep his efforts limited and to go by the summer, which then became autumn and then he was not well enough for a send off in the September, so he was put up in a nursing home in South Norwood.

On October 11th, Dadabhai was ready to go and the weather seemed good. He went by motorcar to Tilbury and transferred to the S S Moldavia under the care of a Dr Treasurywalla and a nurse. His grandson Jal Naoroji, delivered his farewell address for him before the departure. William Wedderburn offered to take his grand children into his care now that Dadabhai was leaving.[1] The London Indian Society was there for the send off. They wanted him to remain President for a while. Dadabhai was dubious, even of being the Honorary President in absentia. He agreed but told his successor, Mr Parikh, that if the mood for violent action which he had felt arising in India, was to catch on in Britain, he wanted his name removed from the Society and this was especially so if any actual violence ever took place.

1. An amusing story related by William Wedderburn to the grandchildren, (who were all adults by then), has been passed down. At a very formal dinner where the European guests were served by Indian waiters, one elderly lady with a hearing trumpet beckoned for some more food. The waiter stepped forward to serve her, but their communication was poor because of hearing and language difficulties and relied upon gestures. Eventually she pointed vigorously at her hearing trumpet which she was holding against her ear upon which the rather dense waiter, who was holding a serving dish of peas, served them into the trumpet!

CHAPTER SEVENTEEN

PERSEVERANCE

Hence Dadabhai left Britain for the last time in his eighty-third year. He arrived in Aden on November 8th and then steamed into Bombay. His health again deteriorated so he was taken straight to his home at Versova in the middle of November. Meherbanoo, his granddaughter, and Manekbhai, his daughter, looked after him. The Governor of Bombay, Sir George (later Lord) Clark, was the first to greet him at his home. By the middle of January, he was back and in good health, corresponding, meeting people and getting around. 'Dadabhai day' was given a bigger boost that year. His workload was impressive, especially as he was supposed to be semi-retired.

His corresponded with all his grandchildren, their tutors, his daughters and other family members, on a weekly basis. His granddaughter Gosi, wrote on his eighty-sixth birthday to say she had met Mr Gandhi and that he was very much Dadabhai's disciple. Dadabhai wrote back that he was very glad she had met "Mr Gandhi, a very good man" who had been "fighting a great patriotic battle". In fact Gosi and her younger sister Perin had met him in 1906 through Lord Ental's efforts as he was sympathetic to the Indian's needs in South Africa. One Peteti day ,(a Celebration day in the Parsee calender), Jamshedji Tata gave a party on a boat on the Thames, at which Gandhi attended dressed in a morning coat, stripped trousers and a diamond pin stuck onto his ready made up tie. She was attracted by his eyes but also teased him, by saying, "babu you have forgotten what you were dressed in (before), and you have not even done up your tie". He asked them to go to South Africa and join with him saying he had trained up ten thousand people in civil disobedience, who would someday fight for Indians and their freedom. She replied that she would not work for freedom from outside South Africa. She recalled that later on when she met him at a reception in Peddar Road, Bombay, at the flat of Mr and Mrs Jehangir Petit he was dressed in his more normal dhoti. Sometime later he described to her why he chose to wear the Khadi, (homespun cotton). He told her that he had met some village women and had noticed that one of them had a particularly soiled sari on. He asked her why she had not washed it and was surprised that she broke into tears. She told him that four of them lived together and had no money for their own clothes. So they had to share one sari and when one of them

175

went out the other three could not go out for modesty's sake. But also because they had to keep swapping the sari around there was rarely enough time to wash it. Being struck by the grief and shame that was caused by this poverty, he had chosen to wear Indian produced clothing. By doing that he was wearing the normally poorer quality material that was all the poor could afford and was also making a stand against the monopoly on price and choice which stemmed from the virtually enforced importing of British cotton into India. Gosi said it was Gandhi rather than her grandfather who influenced her to take part in the campaigns for India's freedom. She was arrested in the 1930s, having taken part in several events. She said that her younger sister Perin was the first woman to be arrested in connection to those events. She also felt that the rigours of the campaigns and the poor to miserable conditions endured in prison by three of her sisters, Khorshed, Perin and Nargiz contributed to them dying earlier than expected and that she was fortunate to live to her eighties.

Those Parsee women were a counterpoise to some Parsees who were more establishment orientated and indeed even to some in their own families. Gosi related that whilst many of them had sympathy for Indian aspirations in line with Dadabhai, they also used to sing gujerati songs in support of Queen Victoria and knew all the Royal family's names and could be pro monarchy. Even recently Parsees like the late Freddie Mercury of the pop group Queen, whilst seeming to live lifestyles very different to that of a pro-establishment person, have a strong sense of respect and loyalty to the Royalty. In India Dadabhai probably received more requests for help than at any other time. Not just advice on public affairs or requests for money, but husbands and wives in domestic disputes, pleas by prisoners on death row or in prison. The request came from European and Indian alike, and from those in mixed relationships. Some he could refer to the India Office or the House of Commons, with others he gave direct help, including the sending of money. He also received congratulations from India, China, Japan, Africa and Britain. He was maintaining a regular correspondence with many of the institutions and notable individuals in India.

He was beginning new correspondence on the pertinent issues of the time. Being in Versova, he was if anything all the more unable to keep away from current affairs and would not accept his role as being retired. The change and hardening of India attitudes to British rule, appeared to happen just when the British attitude was changing for the better. Lords Morley and Minto were putting reforms on the anvil, just as anarchic activities were getting worse.

This caused Dadabhai to have many concerns and he could not just let such matters ride along. However, he did not enter the public arena any more and confined his endeavours to private correspondence and meetings. His health was never as good as it had been and he remained active but in a state of semi-retirement which meant his routine was not as intense as it had once been. John Morley, who was the Secretary of State, and Lord Minto who was the new Viceroy, were putting together a list of reforms that Dadabhai had often campaigned for, and this was one time when he had to take as active a part as possible. On the one hand he wrote to them, and on the other he exerted whatever influence he could on the younger Indians.

By 1907/8, a definite split had appeared in the Congress membership between moderates and radicals. The younger men were using violence and it was anticipated that the Authorities would react harshly to such actions. This expectation was held both by those loyal to the State and by those who had campaigned against it but in the time honoured fashion. The government was becoming harsher in treating outbursts of lawlessness.

Dadabhai deprecated violence, but unlike other older leaders, did not denounce the younger sections. He wanted to see them take the lead from the older generation, but not by the use of violence. On the Dadabhai day of the next year, he made know his upset and anger after an Indian student, Madan lal Dhingra, assassinated Sir William Curzon Wyllie, the political Assistant District Commissioner, on 1st July 1908, and a doctor named Kaikhusro Lalcaca, who went to Wyllie as he lay wounded, was also shot and killed.

The Authorities had often suspected that a hostel for students called 'India House' at 65 Cromwell Avenue, Highgate in London, had been a centre of sedition. Dadabhai had been present at its opening by H M Hyndman on July 1st 1905 and now that the Authorities could connect a known assassin like Dhingra to the group based there, they inevitably closed the place down. Dhingra himself was hanged on 17th August 1909 at Pentonville Prison.

These happenings, by occurring at the same time as the Minto-Morley reforms or the Indian Councils Act of 1909, meant Dadabhai maintained his burst of renewed activity. Wedderburn remarked that many of the points in their minority report of the previous century were now being put forward as legislation. Dadabhai wrote personally to Lords Morley and Minto, to encourage them to continue and express his views that they were acting in a way that justified his faith in the British character, "after many cruel disappointments bordering on despair."

These reforms expanded the Imperial Legislative Council to sixty members and gave Indians more seats on both it and the Governor's Executive Councils. They allowed the terms of reference of the Viceroy's

177

Council and of the Secretary of State's Council to be widened, so that the members could look at more matters than the annual budget and could ask questions.

Dadabhai did however, make clear that the partition of Bengal had to be resolved and simultaneous examinations introduced in a comprehensive fashion. He was glad to receive the news of the appointment of an Indian to the Viceroy's Council in a letter addressed to him in April. At this time a separate or communal representation for Muslims was also introduced, following the formation of the Muslim League of 1906. It was in this year that Jinnah acted as personal secretary to Dadabhai.

His next letter to the Viceroy, sent in 1909, went right through the history of British rule from 1764 to 1903, and touched on all major issues. It was not so much a letter as a chapter and verse document, and this correspondence ran to eighty typed sheets. On April 23rd 1910, he compiled a full synopsis on the financial aspects of India's plight, and three months later drafted a similar paper on trade. It was a shortened version and update of his "Poverty and Un-British rule in India", written by a man who was now in his eighty-fifth year.

Dadabhai was bereaved when Gulbai died in May that year after more than sixty years of marriage. Though her life had never been centred on the same pursuits as his, and hence they had not shared in public matters, they had accepted their marital roles throughout. Not enough is known of the support she gave because she never entered the paths that Dadabhai kept in the more public arena and so far less is recorded. However from what can be gleaned from family reminiscences, the children had known that both parents were available to them, Gulbai all the more so because of Dadabhai's absences. There is no doubt though that their marriage was also unable to flourish because he was away so much and Gulbai must have felt alone at times and unsupported. Dadabhai's letters for instance seem to be mainly sent to his children and not his wife, (even if someone had to read them to her), and he does not appear to have given the same understanding and support to his wife that he gave to women in general. This is one area therefore where it appears to be right to surmise that Dadabhai was poor or negligent and in conclusion to infer where a real fault in his character existed. It can only really be guessed what in consequence this state of affairs did for Gulbai, but it must have weakened or wearied her own will to get on with life. It must also be presumed that she gave a lot for her children, particularly at the times when their father was not physically present as all of them grew up to make their own mark in life.

Messages of condolence were sent to Dadabhai from all over the world, including one from Sir George Clark, who had just suffered the bereavement of his own daughter. He and Dadabhai maintained a friendly contact with each other up until Sir George's departure in 1913, though Dadabhai did not let that deter him from refuting Sir George's pronouncements that progress in India was something that was happening but required patience. Sir George had sent Dadabhai a birthday congratulations on his eighty-sixth birthday in 1911.

He wrote on the progress that had been made in 1909 by the Congress and the Administration, to congratulate them for getting through a critical phase. He kept on looking at all available information sent from Britain, the US or India to support any contemporary arguments or moves, even if he himself was too old to actively take part. Surendranath Banerjea said once that "Dadabhai is living in a sea of Blue books." Dadabhai had written to him in October over plans to hold the next Congress in London.

The policy initiated in 1909 had to be worked on and made to work. No-one really saw the reforms as an end in themselves but as a means to an end. The Legislative Councils had if anything to become more vocal to make this happen. Then King George V announced he would come again to India and Dadabhai expressed the hope that his former good words could find some new dawns at this juncture.

Dadabhai was depressed when an assassination attempt was made on Lord Hardinge who was bringing about a change towards autonomy in provincial affairs since becoming Viceroy in 1910. He oversaw the reuniting of the two Bengals into a governor's province, and the removal of the capital from Calcutta to Delhi at the Great Delhi Durbar of 1911 at which King George V was present. In the same year, the appointment of a Royal Commission on the services in India gave him fresh hope, especially for simultaneous exams. In his birthday manifesto, he also touched on the need to see Britain involve itself in South Africa, to stop the tyrannies that were perpetuated there, after many years of a 'hands off' policy.

Dadabhai kept up his intercessions in the next year, when he wrote to Lords Crew and Hardinge on the Public Services Commission, which was looking into the Administration of India. He saw Lord Willingdon and Sir George Clark at Versova amongst many others, and continued to use his position as an elder statesman to meet people of all backgrounds; and many were now asking to come and meet him. He still maintained a sharp eye on what was said and done, and criticized Lord Hardinge that year on a speech he gave on India's financial position, which did not 'go well' despite his Lordship's observations that as the imports and exports of India grew, so the country was moving onwards and upwards at a rapid rate.

179

In 1912, Dadabhai said that reading between the lines of the Royal statements made during the State visit he felt that, "their Majesties" were giving thought to seek out methods for a new evolution or British-Indian relations. For his birthday message on 4th September that year he called for support for Indians in South Africa against the injustices they still suffered and asked why the Imperial government did nothing to help them make the Authorities take note of their grievances.

With the advent of the Great War in 1914, Dadabhai said that India must fight in that war for the British Empire. This is not an easy decision for any patriot to make, when they are in contention with the rulers of their country and the depth of feeling behind such a decision is perhaps not always appreciated, especially in the uproar of such times.

Dadabhai was clear in what he felt was the right course of action and wrote, "Fighting as the British people are at present in a righteous cause to the good and glory of human dignity and civilization, and moreover being the beneficial instrument of our own progress and amelioration, our duty is clear - to do, everyone, out best to support the British fight with our life and property." Certainly Lord Willingdon was very pleased as was Lord Hardinge, and both of them wrote to him to express their pleasure throughout the War. The support that came from India was splendid and worthy of the Nation. This genuine loyalty made Dadabhai write to W H Owen that he hoped it would be an act that was remembered in the years after the conflict.

Fifty thousand Indians died for the King of another country in that conflict, and many earned medals for their bravery. As had been stated earlier, one of Dadabhai's grandchildren, Kershap, fought in the war and after being wounded was later to be one of the first Indians promoted to officer rank in a non-Indian Regiment. Along with the other Asian troops he was separated from the European wounded and hospitalized at the Royal Pavilion in Brighton. Letters between him and Dadabhai could not bring home the graphic horror of that war. Certainly they were not tinged with the despair of some of the other letters sent home by the Indian troops. On top of the correspondence with his grandson, Dadabhai probably had visits from family members of the men fighting in the fields of France. Despite what the censors took out from the personal mail, there was enough information coming back to show that things were not as they seemed. The Indian who fought in the trenches also began to see the Europeans more as equals, because they were able to display the same fighting skills as them. But nonetheless racial boundaries were clearly kept to throughout the War.

Maybe Dadabhai knew more about the system and could more readily take in what was said, and had already accepted the feeling that the British were not as invulnerable as was believed. After the War many in India were re-thinking how to evaluate the British along the same lines and Dadabhai's correspondence anticipated this change.

When a friend, Dr John Pollen, wrote to him on his ninetieth birthday asking for contribution to the East Indian Association's fiftieth anniversary, Dadabhai had to disappoint him. Although it has been noted how much Dadabhai was ready to give to other causes, it was not true that he only gave and hence lacked the ability to say no to a request. In this case, he felt he only had an unfavourable opinion of the Association, because it had not done much in the intervening years.

For his ninety-first birthday a deputation of Hindu, Muslim and Parsee women went to honour him. Both a Mrs Sarojini Naidu, a well known poetess from Hyderabad and a Mrs Jamnabhai Sukhai of the Gujerati Streemandal gave addresses on him. Dadabhai in return touched on the recent memorial set up by William Wedderburn and others made to Austen Chamberlain for his help in getting education provided for women and girls in India.

But on his next Birthday, Mrs Annie Besant (1847-1933), who was a notable campaigner of the time, wanted to secure Dadabhai's support for the Home Rule League, which she hoped to set up. She had arrived in India in 1893 to work for the Theosophical Society having become a follower of Madame Blatavsky and her Theosophy sect. This was the same sect and leader who had influenced Allan Hume in the early 1880s. Although he had quarrelled with Madame Blavatsky in 1883 he continued to believe in the mystery gurus or mahatmas and they had some motivating effect to him for many years. Annie Besant had in fact actively promoted Theosophy through her own organisation in 1907 and by 1914 had expanded the interests of that group to include Home Rule. In 1914 both she and B G Tilak had sought to get Congress to welcome in the radicals but had been prevented through Pherozeshah Mehta and the Bombay moderates. However he was not around in 1915 and so Congress changed its decision that year. She wanted to set up Home Rule leagues but agreed to wait until September 1916 to give Congress the time to organize those groups. Therefore her league would make Home Rule of India its only objective and wanted to push Congress along a similar one-track approach.

When Dadabhai said he would be its President, it caused a sensation. Why was he becoming involved in the hurly-burly of politics for a group that seemed to overlap with Congress to such an extent that it may overlay that body in time? Annie Besant was well known for her methods from other campaigns she had waged, and these were not always appreciated. She would probably rely on extremist support before long. She had also asked S Subramania Aiyar and W Wedderburn to represent the older leadership in her league, by having Aiyar in India, Wedderburn in Britain and Dadabhai placed in the overall leadership position.

She visited Dadabhai with her Lieutenant, Mr B P Wadia. Dadabhai recognized that she had been with him in 1892 and asked that on accepting the position he would not be expected to give any addresses or produce any written material. He also stated that the League must not be turned against Congress or seek to remove it from its position in India.

Even Wedderburn wrote to stop Dadabhai and said in his letter he could not accept the role in an organization which had too different a set of tactics to Congress and yet claimed the same aims. It had for instance, striven to get concerted agitation organized whilst the War was in full play. However, Dadabhai would not relent. Wacha wrote a little later to state that Dadabhai was really supporting those who would eventually wreck Congress.

Because Mrs Besant realized that she must ply her course more slowly than Tilak her League was not to be started until later in 1916 and after full discussions were held with Congress.[1] Therefore it was September 1916 which became the start date for the League to commence its operations. At the Congress of December 1916 at Lucknow both Home Rule League leaders were invited to attend by the moderate President Ambikar Mazumdar and that led to the Congress League Pact being made, which was also known as the Lucknow Pact. Quite what Dadabhai's opinion on these events is not known, but they were significant because from then on Congress and Home Rule became far more synonymous.

1916 was the quietest year in Dadabhai's life. He and Pherozeshah Mehta were awarded the Bombay University Honorary Degree of Doctor of Law, which was a real honour for Indians and was only the fifth such presentation. Unfortunately Mehta had died the year before the ceremony. The Vice-Chancellor at the Convocation paid tribute to Dadabhai's character, his many years of service and on his political career. His words at the ceremony included a passage that, "the honour and success of Dadabhai's career were due in large measure to the high qualities of personal life and character which were so conspicuous in every part of it. Men of all shades of political opinion were quick to discern his transparent honesty, simplicity of purpose, and unselfish patriotism."

1. Tilak had not been a party to the agreement to wait until September 1916 and so had set up his own Home Rule League in April 1916. Annie Besant's followers therefore set up Home Rule groups at that time, which became the Home Rule Leagues in September 1916. There were therefore two organizations with the same name, who mutually agreed to work in different areas of the country to prevent any clashes. Their overall aim was the same, but quite a few of Mrs Besant's branches were connected to the Theosophical Societies, which meant they were less focused in their activities.

Dadabhai took a drive in a car with Manekbhai and Dadina, her husband, which became a pageant on their way to Peddar Road in Bombay. At around that time he gave his personal library to the Bombay Presidency Association, including Hansards from over a hundred years.

With provincial autonomy put on the table by Lord Hardinge and discussions on self-government combined with proposals for reform being considered by both the Viceroy and the Secretary of State, there was an air of expectancy that real change was coming to fruition. This became a reality in a Declaration of August 20th 1917, guaranteeing the increased association of Indians in very branch of the Administration and the development of self-governing institutions, to build them up to the realization of their own responsible government.

Before this happened Dadabhai had to be removed from his house at Versova because of his frail health, to Palitana House, Cumballa Hill, Bombay, the residence of Maneck Captain. He used to listen to his family reading from the newspapers and from his correspondence throughout this last period. It was noted that the death of Sir George Birdwood caused him to be upset when he heard of it. He was very weak and in consequence was often confined to his bed. His death came shortly after the move on June 30th. It meant he never heard the Declaration made just a few weeks later. He died peacefully amongst all his family, except for two granddaughters who were in Kashmir.

His body was consigned to the Tower of Silence, in accordance with the Zoroastrian religion. Fifteen thousand people went to his funeral and many prominent people spoke of his life and endeavours Sir Narayenraa Chandavarkar gave the final tribute.

"If we take stock of his life and his example, may I not say with perfect justice and truth that in his career, in all he did, in all he suffered, and in all he taught, he was the prophet Zoroaster's religion personified. Because he was the man more than anybody else of pure thought, of pure speech and of pure deeds ... The sun that rose just ninety-three years ago, over India is set. But I say it is set to rise again in the form of regenerated India, for Dadabhai lived and worked for us with a devotion which must remain for all of us, an inspiring example".

EPILOGUE

As it usual at the death of a national leader, there were the favourable tributes for Dadabhai in the papers. William Wedderburn, wrote for the *India* of 6th July 1917 that, 'The last time I saw Mr Dadabhai was in 1910 when on my way to Allahabad. I visited him in his retreat at Versova. It was a real pleasure to find him well and cheerful, spending the evening of his days in his peaceful home by the Indian sea, under the spreading palm trees, surrounded by loving relatives and friends.

Now he has gone to his well earned rest: and all India mourns the man who ever bravely held aloft the standard of high ideals, who never doubted that in the end there would be true union of East and West, based on justice and freedom."

In the same edition, an editorial gave its readers a feeling for Dadabhai's unique contribution to both Britain's and India's histories, when it said, "It fell to the lot of Mr Naoroji to act as a pioneer in many directions. He was the first Indian to be appointed to a professorship at a grammar college; and he came to England as a member of the first Indian Mercantile firm to be established in this country. He was also the first to fight the battle of the Indian for admission to the Indian Civil Service by open competition; as later on, he was the first Indian to be elected to the House of Commons; and the first to be placed upon a Royal Commission .... Alone among his countrymen he was three times elected to the Chair of the Indian National Congress ..... By Indians themselves he is affectionately known as the Grand Old Man.

His pre-eminence among them was undisputed, and his popularity was immense. It is over twenty years ago since Sir Pherozeshah Mehta voiced the universal opinion by describing him as the only man Indians recognize as having the right to make a representative claim for all India."

These articles distil three particular qualities that are of importance to understanding the nature of Dadabhai and the reasons why he remains unique. He was someone who had firm principles in his character, he was a pioneer and he could hold people together. He was not, as Telang remarked in 1887, "the only remedy, the whole remedy and nothing but the remedy." The cure for Indian's ills lay with the people, but he did provide the prescription. He was also akin to a tonic as he campaigned in the name of India and was able to accomplish real achievements. These were something that gave hope and placed expectation within the grasp of many people. Doubtless others could

184

have brought about some flourishing Indian Movement which would have still led to renationalization in this century. But in his day Dadabhai's presence was trail blazing a way that others just did not believe was possible. At times his pioneering activity acted as an advance guard cutting a path for others to follow in.

His persistence and perseverance paid off for him, as the major changes he sought and fought for could not be conveniently dropped while he was around to challenge or to suggest alternative methods. Indians were eventually allowed to gain experience in running their country as more and more were admitted to senior positions in the Indian Civil Service. The economic drain was not resolved but history books now acknowledge his arguments that Britain was utilizing the wealth of India for its own purposes. His works on the subject are still referred to as second to none by the United Nations and by authors in India.

Of course his legacy in Britain was to have become the first Asian member of Parliament. Because it happened so long ago, it is possible that we have missed the point of this event. Britain then ruled an Empire where colour did matter. Many conceptions of the present time were nutured at that time, because in those days the white races did rule directly over most of the earth with the attendant concept of white supremacy. Yet right in the middle of that time there arose a man who was to hold a high office in the heart of the Imperial administration, and who was voted in by a white electorate. His achievements gave all non-white people a great boost of self confidence. It also showed that his presence would be supported by a significant number of white voters and also showed to those who were opposed to his kind on racial grounds that their influence, whilst not without effect was not supreme.

In a broader sense he was an underdog who beat the bully without tainting his own character. In this case the bully was not so much a person, but rather the evil influences that we can all unconsciously follow especially when unlimited power is available. People had to react to Dadabhai's presence. The humanity in him transcended the inhumanity of the system. That is a rare fit at any time, and if he was around today, we would still find that what he did in terms of encouraging other people would mark him out. In his day almost everyone seemed to feel that Dadabhai belonged to them and he could in turn make them seek common goals and work together, even with their differences unchanged.

He is part of Britain's history in another way, as he became the first Indian 'ambassador' to this country. In Britain everyone has heard of Gandhi and of his great accomplishments in the twentieth century, which were really carried through in India alone. It is strange that in a way the

Grand Old Man of the Nineteenth Century is such an unknown in Britain despite the fact that he is the person responsible for a number of historical happenings in the Country, not only as an MP but as the most significant representative or plenipotentiary from India, the star in the Crown, to Britain. For almost a quarter of a century he was the person who Britain could look to for the Indian viewpoint, and he made India's needs known to the British people.

He has a Gandhian stature in himself and yet he only reserves a third class place in the history of events. Perhaps the lack of dramatic gestures contributes to this. Unfortunately, unlike other major characters on the stage of Indo-British relationships there is no-one alive today who can remember him. But he does not deserve to be forgotten. A nation is fortunate to find a leader of vision who still remains a true man of his people. Both Britain and India should remember with gratitude the patient and reassuring way he brought two peoples together and made mutual understanding so much easier.

APPENDICES

Appendix 1a

THE GOVERNMENT OF INDIA

During the period of Imperial rule, India was divided by the Administration into the 'British territory' and the 'Native States.' Three-fifths of the land and four-fifths of the population lived in the former, and the remainder belonged to the latter grouping.

The Native States kept their own hereditary rulers who controlled the internal affairs of their land and were expected to allow a political agent to attend their Courts. By this means any untoward or improper actions were kept in check, but a fair degree of independence could be maintained. All in all, there were over 500 such states at any one time, with the larger ones e.g. Hyderabad and Rajputana, being mini nations, and the smallest ones being the size of a large city.

The British territories were originally split into three Presidencies, namely Bengal, Madras and Bombay. Madras and Bombay survived as smaller Administrations under their own Governor. The Bengal Presidency was easily the largest, and it had to be subdivided into divisions, with each division under a lieutenant-Governor or Chief Commissioner. (Burma was part of the Indian 'Empire' in those days).

NATIVE STATES (in 1891)

	Area in Square Miles	Population
Rajputana	130,268	12,016,102
Hyderabad	82,698	11,537,040
Central India	77,808	10,318,812
Mysore	27,936	4,943,604
Cashmere	80,900	2,543,952
Baroda	8,226	2,415,396
In Bombay	69,045	8,059,298
In Punjab	38,299	4,263,280
In Madras	9,609	3,700,622
In Bengal	35,834	3,296,379
In Central Provinces	29,435	2,160,511
In North West Provinces	5,109	792,491
TOTALS:	595,167	66,047,487

PRESIDENCY

Province	Style of Government	Area in Sq Miles	Population in 1881
BENGAL			
Bengal, Behar and Oriss	Lieutenant-Governor	151,534	71,346,987
North West Provinces and Oudh	Lieutenant-Governor	107,503	46,905,087
Punjab and Delhi	Lieutenant-Governor	110,667	20,880,847
Delhi Central Provinces	Chief Commissioner	86,501	10,784,294
Assam	Chief Commissioner	49,004	5,476,833
Burma	Chief Commissioner	171.430	7,605,560

188

MADRAS			
Madras	Governor	141,189	35,620,440
BOMBAY			
Bombay and Sind	Governor	125,144	18,901,123
	TOTAL	942,981	217,537,169

The British territories alone counted for roughly one seventh of the population of the world at that time, and the land area of the whole of the Indian Empire equalled that of Western Europe.

Given that the totals for the Native States were: 595,167 66,047,487

This leaves four-fifths of the population who were under direct British rule

By comparison the totals for the British Isles were: 88,226 37,888,153

Appendix 1b

The Government of India was represented in the British Parliament by the Secretary of State for India, who was a member of the Cabinet. He had a parliamentary Under-Secretary and a Council of ten to fifteen members under him.

The Executive Government was under the Viceroy and Governor-General, who had an Executive Committee which virtually acted as if it were the Cabinet of India. The legislation of the 'Empire' as it was termed, was carried through by a Legislative Council, comprising of members of the Executive and other senior appointees. The Viceroy and Governor-General, and all these other positions, were held for up to five years by each individual. Traditionally, the Viceroy and Governor-General was left to his own affairs, and the Secretary of State did not personally intervene or even visit India.

The Administration was handled by the predominantly European staffed Indian Civil Service. Its higher administrative appointments were secured through an Act of Parliament in Britain and parcelled out to Europeans, and only the lower positions held in local offices would accept local Europeans, 'Eurasians' and some natives.

The Army was a heavy burden on the land. It usually stood at around 200,000+ Native and European soldiers. Europeans held the Senior posts but there were some Native commissioned officers. There was also a smaller Navy to support as well, and both these services were financed from the taxes imposed on the country.

THE PROCLAMATION OF 1858

The Queen's Proclamation of 1858 stated that, "We hold ourselves bound to the natives of our Indian territory by the same obligations of duty which bind us to all our other subjects; and those obligations, by the blessing of Almighty God, we shall faithfully and conscientiously fulfil.

And it is our further will that, so far as may be, our subjects, of whatever race or creed, be freely and impartially admitted to offices in our service, the duties of which they may be qualified by their education, ability and integrity duly to discharge.

In their prosperity shall be our strength, in their contentment our security, and in their gratitude our best reward. And may the God of all power grant to us and to those in authority under us, strength to carry out these our wishes for the good of our People."

THE VICEROYS OF INDIA WITH DATES OF APPOINTMENT

12th January 1869	The Earl of Mayo
9th February 1872	Mr John Strachey
2nd April 1872	Lord Napier of Merchistown
3rd May 1872	Lord Northbrook
12th April 1876	Lord Lytton
8th June 1880	Marquis of Ripon
13th December 1884	The Earl of Dufferin
10th December 1888	Marquis of Landsdowne
27th January 1894	Earl of Elgin and Kincardine
6th January 1899	Baron Curzon of Kedleston
30th April 1904	Baron Amsthill
13th December 1904	Baron Curzon of Kedleston
18th November 1905	Earl of Minto
28th November 1910	Baron Hardinge of Penshurst
4th April 1916	Baron Chelmsford

THE SECRETARIES OF STATE FOR INDIA WITH DATES OF THEIR APPOINTMENT

21st February 1874	Marquis of Salisbury
2nd April 1878	Viscount Cranbrook
28th April 1880	Marquis of Kimberly
24th June 1885	Lord Randolph Churchill
6th February 1886	The Earl of Kimberly
3rd August 1886	Sir Richard Assheton Cross
18th August 1892	The Earl of Kimberly
10th March 1894	Mr H H Fowler
4th July 1895	Lord George Hamilton
9th October 1903	Mr St John Brodrick
11th December 1905	Mr John Morley
7th November 1910	The Earl of Crewe
7th March 1911	Viscount Morley of Blackdown
25th May 1911	The Earl of Crewe
27th May 1915	Mr Austin Chamberlain
20th July 1917	Mr E S Montagu

Appendix 2

The following appendix is a list of the Parliamentary debates held during the Liberal administration of 1892 - 95 to which Dadabhai Naoroji was connected.

Date of Debate	Topic	Hansard Vol.	Page No.
9th August 1892	Queen's Speech	VI & V11	260
1st February 1893	Lincoln's Inn Field (transfer bill)	VIII	176
16th February 1893	Indian Council's amendment	VIII	902
16th February 1893	Indian currency	VIII	1566
28th February 1893	International Monetary Conference	IX	653-57
2nd March 1893	*Civil Service (East Indian) Bill	IX	764
3rd March 1893	Professor at Sanskrit College	IX	958
16th March 1893	Indian Rupee	X	217
28th March 1893	*Civil and Military Services (East India)	X	1384-91
30th March 1893	British representative at Hyderabad	X	1494
13th April 1893	*India Civil Service Examination	XI	202
27th April 1893	*Indian Finance	XI	1293
27th April 1893	*Indian Return	XI	1303
5th May 1893	Condition of India	XII	193
9th May 1893	Progress of India	XII	451
2nd June 1893	*Civil Service of India (exam) resolution	XIII	111-17
23rd June 1893	Public Works Expenditure	XIII	1763
30th June 1893	Indian Opium Revenue	XIV	632
3rd July 1893	Pensions - Indian Civil Service	XIV	658
8th August 1893	Indian Currency question	XV	1610-14
21st August 1893	Hyderabad Plot	XVI	636
31st August 1893	Hindu-Muslim riots	XVI	1567
3rd September 1893	*Indian Expenditure	XVI	1871
4th September 1893	Survey North Tirhoot	XVI	1872
7th September 1893	*Indian Budget	XVII	477
8th September 1893	Civil Service and Revenue Departments	XVII	714
9th September 1893	Legislative Council	XVII	751
11th September 1893	Bombay and Madras Armies Bill	XVII	931-932
15th September 1893	*Indian Budget	XVII	1291
20th September 1893	*East Indian Revenue Accounts	XVII	1759-98
11th March 1894	Land Values (Taxation by Local Authorities) Bill	XXII	456

13th March 1894	Queen's Speech	XXII	220
20th April 1894	*Officers Pay	XXII	970
25th May 1894	Parliamentary Election Expenses	XXIV	1355
29th May 1894	London County Council Powers Bill	XXIV	1508,9 and 1516
6th July 1894	Baladhun Murder Case	XXVI	1084
17th July 1894	Colonel Mitchell Vs War Office	XXVII	158 and 533
9th August 1894	British Indians in Madagascar	XXVIII	447
14th August 1894	*East Indian Revenue Accounts	XXViii	1053-72
23rd August 1894	Parliamentary Expenditure	XXIX	349
12th February 1895	Queen's Speech	XXX	567-79 and 584-601
20th February 1895	Council of India	XXX	1259
21st February 1895	Indian Cotton Duties	XXX	1359-61
28th February 1895	Indian Administrative Offices	XXXI	42
14th March 1895	Army Supply (Indian Contribution)	XXXI	1105
28th March 1895	*British India (returns)	XXXII	321
4th April 1895	*British India (returns)	XXXII	908
8th April 1895	Post Office and Electric Lights	XXXII	1144
9th April 1895	Speaker's retirement	XXXII	1299
2nd May 1895	Indian School Teachers	XXXIII	278
2nd May 1895	Locomotive Acts and Street Cars	XXXIII	290
20th May 1895	Post Office Employees and Politics	XXXIII	1591

* Subjects of interest to the Royal Commission's deliberations.

SOME PUBLIC ACTS IN 1894

Industrial and Provident Societies, Trustee Act (1893) Amendment, Public Works' Loans, Merchandise Marks' Prosecutions, Commissioners of Works, Wild Birds' Protection, Outdoor Relief Friendly Societies, Prevention of Cruelty to Children (Amending Clauses), Registration of Electors' Acceleration, Industrial Schools' Act Amendments, Charitable Trusts, Prize Courts, Regulation of Quarries, Building Societies Amendments Act, Coal Mines' Check Weighers, London Equalization of Rates, Railway and Canal Traffic, Housing of the Working Classes, Merchant Shipping.
The above are only some of the Acts passed.

Appendix 3

The official entry on the Bills in which Dadabhai Naoroji was the prime mover.

LINCOLN'S INN FIELDS TRANSFER BILL
On Motion of Mr Naoroji, Bill to transfer the trusteeship of Lincoln's Inn Fields, and the powers, estates and duties connected therewith to the London County Council, ordered to be brought in by Mr Naoroji, Mr Benn and Mr James Rowlands. 1893 - 94: IV: 201 Bill 82

CIVIL SERVICES (EAST INDIA) BILL
On Motion of Mr Naoroji, Bill to provide for simultaneous holding in India and the United Kingdom of the first examinations for appointments to the Civil Services of India, ordered to be brought in by Mr Naoroji, Mr Schwann and Mr Birkmyre. 1893-94: I: 755 Bill 243

LAND VALUES (TAXATION BY LOCAL AUTHORITIES) BILL
On Motion of Mr Naoroji, Bill to provide for the taxation of Land Values by Local Authorities, ordered to be brought in by Mr Naoroji, Mr Lough, Mr James Stewart and Mr James Rowlands. 1894: IV: 709 Bill 55

Appendix 4

The following are a list of the Parliamentary Debates which were of interest to Dadabhai Naoroji, listed by General theme and Subject areas. The initials stand for: USSI = Under-Secretary of State for India; SSI = Secretary of State for India; SSW = Secretary of State for War; USSFA = Under-Secretary of State for Foreign Affairs; PG = Postmaster General.

Theme: "CONDITION OF INDIA"

Date	Subject	Reply	Hansard Vol.	Page No.
1893				
28 May 1893	East Indian (Civil and Military Services Resolution	USSI	X	1386-90
27 April 1893	Indian Finance	USSI	XI	1293
27 April 1893	Indian Return	USSI	XI	1303
5 May 1893	Condition of India	USSI	XII	193-94
9 May 1893	Material and Moral Progress of India	USSI	XII	451
23 June 1893	Public Works Expenditure	USSI	XIII	102
3 July 1893	Pensions - Indian Civil Service	USSI	XIV	658
4 September 1893	Indian Expenditure	USSI	XVI	1871
7 September 1893	Indian Budget		XVII	477
8 September 1893	Civil Service and Revenue Department		XVII	714
15 September 1893	Indian Budget Chancellor of the Exchequer		XVII	1291
20 September 1893	East Indian Revenue Accounts		XVII	1759-72
1894				
13 March 1894	Queen's Speech		XXII	220
20 April 1894	Officers' Pay		XXII	970
14 August 1894	East India Revenue Accounts		XXVI	1053-71
1895				
12 February 1895	Queen's Speech		XXX	568-80
21 February 1895	Indian Cotton Duty		XXX	1359-60
14 March 1895	Army Supply (Indian Contribution)		XXXI	1105
28 March 1895	British Indian (Returns)	USSFA	XXXII	321
4 April 1895	British Indian (Returns)	USSI	XXXII	908

Theme: ROYAL COMMISSION

Date	Subject	Reply	Hansard Vol.	Page No.
1893				
29 May 1893	East Indian (Civil) and Military Services		X	1390-91

30 June 1893	Indian Opium Revenue		XIV	633
8 August 1893	Indian Currency Question		XV	1613
20 September 1893	East Indian Revenue Accounts		XVII	1760

1894

| 14 August 1894 | East Indian Revenue Accounts | | XXVIII | 1071-72 |

Theme: INDIAN CIVIL SERVICE

1893

28 February 1893	International Monetary Conference		IX	656
2 March 1893	Civil Service (East India) Bill		IX	764
13 April 1893	Indian Civil Services Examination	USSI	XI	202
2 June 1893	Civil Service of Indian (Examination) Resolution		XIII	111-17
23 June 1893	Expenditure, Public Works in India	SSI	XIII	1768
3 July 1893	Pensions for Indian Civil Service	USSI	XIV	658
30 September 1893	East India Revenue Accounts		XVII	1762

1894

| 14 April 1894 | East India Revenue Accounts | | XXVIII | 1061, 1065, 1067, 1069-70 |

Theme: INDIAN COUNCILS

1893

9 February 1893	Indian Councils Amendment	USSI	VIII	902
8 September 1893	Madras and Bombay Armies Bill		XVII	751
11 September 1893	Madras and Bombay Armies Bill		XVII	930-1, 932

1895

| 20 February 1895 | Council of India | SSI | XXX | 1259 |

Theme: INDIAN CURRENCY

1893

16 February 1893	Indian Currency	USSI	VIII	1566
28 February 1893	Indian Monetary Conference		IX	653-57
16 March 1893	Indian Rupee	USSI	X	217
8 August 1893	Indian Currency		XV	1610-14

Theme: INDIAN PETITIONS

1893

3 March 1893	Professor at Sanskrit College	USSI	IX	958
30 March 1893	British Representative at Hyderabad	USSI	X	1494
21 August 1893	Hyderabad Plot	USSI	XVI	636
31 August 1893	Hindu-Mussulman Riots	USSI	XVI	1567
4 September 1893	Survey North Tirhoot	USSI	XVI	1872

1894

6 July 1894	Baladhun Murder Case	SSI	XXVI	1084
17 July 1894	Colonel Mitchell v. War Office	SSW	XXVII	158
17 July 1894	Colonel Mitchell v. War Office		XXVII	553
9 August 1894	British Indians in Madagascar	USSFA	XXVIII	1054

1895

2 May 1895	Indian School Teachers	SSI	XXXIII	278

Theme: ENGLISH TOPICS (mainly local Constituency interests)

1893

1 February 1893	Lincoln's Inn Fields (Transfer) Bill		VIII	176

1894

11 March 1894	Land Values (Taxation by Local Authorities) Bill		XXII	456
25 March 1894	Parliamentary Election Expenses		XXIV	1355
29 March 1894	London County Council Powers		XXIV	1509,1569

1895

8 April 1895	Post Office and Electric Lights	PG	XXII	1144
9 April 1895	Speaker's Retirement		XXXII	1306
2 May 1895	Locomotives Acts and Street Cars		XXXIII	290
20 May 1895	Post Office Employees and Politics	PG	XXXIII	1591

Appendix 5

Membership of Indian Parliamentary Committee - May 1894 (-as given by 'India'
May, 1894, p.139)

Ainsworth, D
Ambrose, Dr R
Baker, J
Barrow, R B
Bayley, F H
Bayley, T H
Beith, G
Benson, G R
Birkmyre, W
Burnie, R J D
Byles, W P
Caine, W C*
Cameron, Sir C Bart
Channing, F A
Clark, Dr G B
Clough, W A
Cobb, H P
Coldwells, F M
Colderridge, Hon B
Condor, T J
Conybeare, C A V
Cremer, W R
Curran, T B
Dalziel, J H
Diamond, C
Dilke, Sir C W Bart
Dodd, C
Ellis, J E*
Esmondes, Sir T C Bart
Eventh, R L
Farquhaurson, R
Field, W
Flynn, J C
Fry, F C
Furniss, C
Gilhooly, J
Grove, T N A
Hardie, J Keir
Harrington, T
Hoard, H
Holden, A
Holland, W H
Hopwood, C H
Hunter, W A
Huntington, C P
Husband, J

Illingworth, A
Jones, D B
Kearley, H E
Keay, S
Kennedy, P J
Kitoon, Sir J Bart
Lawson, Sir W Bart
Leigh, J
Leng, Sir J Bart
Lewis, J H
Logan, J W
Lough, T
Lultrel, H C F
MacDonald, J A M
MacGregor, Dr D
MacNeil, G J S
Maguire, J R
Mains, J
Mansfield, M P
McCarthan, M
McCarthy, J
McHugh, E
McLaren, W S B*
Moorson, J H
Morton, A C
Naoroji, Dadabhai*
Norton, Captain C W
Nussey, T W
O'Brien, J F X
O'Connor, J
Owen, T
Palmer, G W
Paul, H W
Pease, H F
Picton, J A
Pinkerton, J
Priestly, B
Provard, AD
Randell, D
Reid, R T
Richardson, J
Roberts, J H (Secretary)*
Roche, J
Rowlands, J
Samuelson, Sir B
Saunders, W

Schwann, C E*
Sheehan, J D
Sheeling, D
Smith, H
Smith, S*
Snape, T
Spicer, T
Spicer, A
Stewart, H
Storey, S
Stuart, J
Sutherland, A
Thomas, A
Tuite, J
Waddy, S D
Wallace, J S
Walton, J L
Wason, E
Webb, A
Wedderburn, Sir W Bart
(Chairman)*
Whitbread, Sir J Bart
Williams, W
Wilson, C H
Wilson, J (Durham)
Wilson, J H
Woods, S
Wright, C
Young, S

The names marked (*) are
the founding members of
the Committee.

Appendix 6

A Further Listing of Functions Attended by Dadabhai, held within his Parliamentary Constituency.

This list gives only an indication of the range and frequency of the events Dadabhai attended and is by no means exhaustive. It is meant to reflect the range and amount of work done by Dadabhai outside Parliament in the service of the people of the Central Finsbury constituency. The list is gleaned from the 'Weekly News and Chronicle' newspaper of that time.

Date of Report	Function
30 July 1892	Central Finsbury Radical Club - Dadabhai lectured on "Duty of Today"
15 October 1892	St. John Square Chapel – evening entertainment Dadabhai presided.
12 November 1892	Annual Dinner and presentation of prizes Dadabhai attended.
19 November 1892	Veron Lodge – 21st Anniversary Dadabhai gave address.
26 November 1892	Court "Robert Bruce" of Foresters Dadabhai gave speech.
24 December 1892	St. Paul's – Band of Hope – Flower Show Dadabhai presented prizes.
24 December 1892	City Road Congregational Church Dadabhai lectured on "Want of India."
4 February 1893	Goldsmiths and Jewellers Trade Union Dadabhai presided.
18 March 1893	Clerkenwell United Rate Payers Society Dadabhai attended.
25 March 1893	Central Finsbury Radical Association – Ward Meeting – thanks for election.
1 April 1893	Central Finsbury Radical Association – Ward Meeting Dadabhai attended.
29 April 1893	Stone and Zinc Preparers' Association Dadabhai unfurled banner.
9 September 1893	Temperance Movement – opening new association Dadabhai attended.
30 September 1893	Central Finsbury – Radical Association Dadabhai addressed.
7 October 1893	"Marquess of Northampton" Lodge Dadabhai unfurled banner.
6 January 1894	St. John Lodge – Special Message to Dadabhai MP (in his absence)
24 February 1894	St. John's Harries – Annual Dinner Dadabhai attended.
3 March 1894	St. John's Ambulance – Talk Dadabhai presided.
10 March 1894	London Society of Jewellers and Goldsmiths Dadabhai presided.
24 March 1894	Central Finsbury Liberal and Radical Association – AGM Dadabhai attended.
14 April 1894	Ratepayers Association – Dinner

Dadabhai attended.

25 April 1894	King's Cross Good Temple Mission – welcome to Mr Dadabhai.
12 May 1894	Central Finsbury Radical Association – Ward Meeting Dadabhai attended.
16 June 1894	Clerkenwell Vestry Hall – laying of foundation Dadabhai addressed
17 November 1894	Finsbury Radical Club – Concert Dadabhai attended.
9 February 1895	East Finsbury Liberal Association – Ball Dadabhai attended.
23 February 1895	Jewellers and Goldsmiths Association – Festival Dadabhai attended.
30 March 1895	Central Finsbury Radical Association Dadabhai gave words of eulogy.
10 April 1895	Rate Payers Association. Dadabhai attended.
21 May 1895	Radical Meeting – Ward 2 Dadabhai given hearty welcome.
25 May 1895	Central Finsbury Liberal Association – Fifth ward meeting. Dadabhai highly successful.
15 June 1895	Opening of Clerkenwell Town Hall Dadabhai addressed
6 July 1895	Temperance Association – Meeting Dadabhai presided.

Appendix 7

D NAOROJI — Address to his fellow Electors Central Finsbury Parliamentary Election

Gentlemen and Fellow Electors,

In my address to you at the last Parliamentary Election in July, 1892, when you did me the honour of electing me as your Representative in the House of Commons, I promised that -

'Should you do me the honour to return me, I will devote all my time to Parliamentary duties, and your local wants and interests shall have my especial attention.'

Both of these promises I have faithfully fulfilled to the very letter, as will be seen by the following record:

In 1892 there was only one division in Parliament, and I voted in it.

In 1893 to 4 the Session was divided into two parts. In the first part there were 310 divisions, and I voted in 304 of them.

During the second part of the Session I visited India, carrying with me your generous and kind message given through the Council of the Central Finsbury United Liberal and Radical Association. This journey necessitated a short absence.

In 1894 there were 246 divisions, and of these I voted in 231.

In 1895 there were 139 divisions, and of these I voted in 118.

It was only when my attendance was required at some function in Clerkenwell, or when engaged in advancing the Liberal cause in some other way, that I was absent from any division.

But as even in my few personal absences from the Division Lobby I was always paired, not a single vote was ever lost by the constituency.

In my Committee work also, I have been as closely attentive.

With regard to my second promise – the local wants and interests of Clerkenwell have always had my prompt, earnest, and careful attention.

I have thus fulfilled my pledges, and for which, I gratefully acknowledge, you several times generously expressed your entire satisfaction. I cannot, therefore, but hope that you will return me again with a large majority.

Within the limits of this address, it would be impossible to do adequate justice to the great and good work accomplished by the Liberal and Radical party during the last three years, but I may be permitted to point out, that despite all the continuous obstructive opposition of its opponents, the Government has to their credit, as having passed 73 Public Acts and 229 Local and Private Acts in 1893 to 4: 68 Public Acts and 216 Local and Private Acts were passed in 1894, while up to 21st June in 1895, 17 Public Acts passed, and 16 Bills passed in the House of Commons; and 8 Local and Private Acts have been passed and 39 Bills passed in the House of Commons.

In 1892 the Liberal Party was returned with a majority to carry out the Reforms included in what is known as the Newcastle Program, and the way this party has fulfilled its mandate has been described by the Right Hon. Joseph Chamberlain in the following words:

'I do not think that in the history of our legislation for the last 20 years, you can find any Parliament in which more has been done as to the importance of the Bills which have been passed.' (18th July, 1894).

The next day 'The Times' said in its leaders: ' Few Governments have passed a greater body of important legislation in a single Session.'

The Home Rule Bill, the Budget of 1894, the Parish Councils' Act, the Employers'

Liability Bill, the Factory and Workshops' Bill (expected to pass), may well evoke such testimony, and will remain monuments of beneficial Liberal Statesmanship.

We are generally apt to fix our attention on the great Acts, but we have also to remember much useful legislation which affects our everyday life and comfort. I append a list of some of the Acts passed, from which it will be seen that the tendency and spirit of all this legislation has been the promotion of the welfare of the masses of the people, and of labour particularly, which is the backbone or foundation of all National wealth and greatness.

Over and above actual legislation, much reform has been effected departmentally and by resolutions.

Though thus, a good deal of beneficent, progressive, and important legislation has been done, much of the great Newcastle Programme still remains to be carried.

It follows that all Liberal and Radical Electors should exercise their sovereign power, and send back the Liberal Party to carry through successfully the great work which was entrusted to them in 1892.

I shall state a few of the items of progressive and important work which is still before us.

For the Irish Home Rule, the Liberal party are bound by every duty of honour, and even by self-interest. It will be one of those glorious land-marks of civilization in British history with which it is replete during the present century. The Welsh Disestablishment; Home Rule for London in all its various important requirements; the restriction of the Veto of the House of Lords, if not is Abolition; Taxation of Land Values for National and Municipal Purposes (a Bill for the latter purpose has been twice introduced to me); Division of Rates between Owners and Occupiers; Payment of Members; Perfect and easy Registration of Electors by Responsible Public Registration Officers; One Man One Vote; Residential Adult Suffrage; Eight Hours; Direct Popular Veto of the Liquor Traffic, and many other important Liberal Measures.

It is the Liberal Party who has mainly done, or forced the Conservatives to do, progressive legislation; and it is from the Liberal or Progressive Party alone that we can expect such legislation in the future.

INDIA

Lastly, I address a few words about India. The Electors of Central Finsbury have inaugurated a great and brilliant chapter in the already great history of the British people, by holding out their generous and kind hand of common fellowship to their Indian fellow-subjects, and I trust the Electors will renew that noble and generous act in the present election by returning me again.

When I visited Indian in 1893 to 4 the people of India, of all classes and creeds, gave me a reception the like of which has not been, it is said, witnessed in living memory, in its vast extent, spontaneity and enthusiasm, with an expression of gratitude, deep and sincere, towards the Electors of Central Finsbury – a name which is a household word throughout India.

I content myself with appending the expressions of sentiments that have taken place both in Central Finsbury and in India towards each other. The sentiments of gratitude to the Electors in all parts of Indian which I visited, were similar to and relected in the resolution of the Indian National Congress.

During the three years I have been your Representative in the House of Commons, I have experienced at your hands uniform courtesy and kindness, and I take this opportunity of making my sincere acknowledgements for the same.

Trusting that you will continue your generous confidence in me, and return me again as your Member to the House of Commons,

I have the honour to be, Yours faithfully,

D NAOROJI

8, Percival Street, Clerkenwell, EC
and
National Liberal Club, Whitehall, S.W. 5th July, 1895

Appendix referred to in my foregoing Address. – DN

A Message from India

Being a Resolution passed at the Meeting of the Great Indian National Congress at Nagpur, December 30th, 1891:

'That this Congress hereby puts formally on record its high estimate and deep appreciation of the great services which Mr Dadabhai Naoroji has rendered, during more than a quarter of a century, to the cause of India, that it expressed its unshaken confidence in him, and its earnest hope that he may prove successful at the coming elections in his candidature for Central Finsbury; and at the same time tenders, on behalf of the vast population it represents, India's most cordial acknowledgements to all in England, whether in Central Finsbury or elsewhere, who have aided or may aid him to win a seat in the House of Commons.'

India's Thanks in 1892

Eighth Indian National Congress, held at Allahabad on 28th, 29th, and 30th December, 1892:
Resolved, that this Congress most respectfully and cordially tenders, on behalf of the vast population it represents, India's most heartfelt thanks to the electors of Central Finsbury for electing Mr D Naoroji their Member in the House of Commons. And it again puts on record its high estimate and deep appreciation of the services which that gentleman has rendered to this country, reiterates its unshaken confidence in him, and looks upon him as India's representative in the House of Commons.

The Central Finsbury United Liberal and Radical Association, send a Greeting to the forthcoming Indian National Congress, 1893.

The Central Finsbury United Liberal and Radical Association, in view of Mr Naoroji's visit to India at the end of November next, have passed the following Resolution:
'1. That the General Council of the Central Finsbury United Liberal and Radical Association desire to record their high appreciation of the admirable and most exemplary manner in which Mr Dadabhai Naoroji has performed his duties as representative of this constituency in the House of Commons, and learning that he is, in the course of a few months, to visit Indian to preside over the Ninth Session of the Indian National Congress. request him to communicate to that body an expression of their full sympathy alike with all the efforts of that Congress for the welfare of

India, and with the Resolution which has been recently passed by the House of Commons (in the adoption of which Mr Dadabhai Naoroji has been so largely instrumental) in favour of holding Simultaneous Examinations in India and in Britain of candidates for all the Indian Civil Services; and further express the earnest hope that full effect will, as speedily as possible, be given by the Government to this measure of justice which has been already too long delayed.

'2. That a copy of this resolution be forwarded to Mr Dadabhai Naoroji.

'(Signed) Joseph Walton,

'Chairman of Meeting.'

India's Thanks

Resolved, – That this Congress tender its best thanks to the Electors of Central Finsbury, both for their kindly sympathy in its objects, and for having so generously accorded to it the valuable services of their honoured member Mr Naoroji, who is destined, the Congress hopes, long to represent both Central Finsbury and India in the British House of Parliament.

Some Acts relating to the United Kingdom passed in 1893

Trade Union Provident Funds, Police Disabilities Removal, Municipal Corporations, Weights and Measures, Public Works Loan Railway Regulation, Friendly Societies, Prevention of use of Barbed Wire in Road Fences, Conveyance of Mails, Industrial and Provident Societies, Public Works Loans, Education of Deaf and Blind Children, Public Health Act (London, 1891) Amendment, Elementary Education School Attendances, Status Law Revision, Metropolis Management (Plumstead and Hackney), Company's Winding up, Married Women's Property, Shop Hours Regulation, Hospital Isolation, Savings Banks, Parish Councils Acts, Day Industrial Schools (Scotland), Local Authorities' Loans (Scotland), Reformatory Schools (Scotland), Burgh Police (Scotland), Improvement of Land (Scotland), Burghs Gas Supply (Scotland), Cholera Hospitals (Ireland), Congested District Boards (Ireland), Law of Distress and Small Debts (Ireland), Irish Education, County Surveyors (Ireland), and Light Railways (Ireland).

BIBLIOGRAPHY

Books

Allen, Charles and Shurada Dwivedi. *Lives of Indian Princes*, Century Publishing, 1984

Bannerjea, D N. *India's Nation Builders*, 1919, p.115-129

Bannerjea, D N. "Dadabhai Naoroji: Speeches and Writings 1915", *The Trumpet Voice of India*, Sons of India Limited, 1918

Boyce, Mary. *Zoroastrians: Their Religious Beliefs and Practices*, Routledge and Kegan Paul, 1979

Chambers Encyclopedia, Volume 6, 1895

Chandra, Bipan. *India's Struggle for Independence*, Penguin Books, 1988 "Dadabhai Naoroji" in *Builders of Modern India*, p. 196

Dobbin, Christine. *Urban Leadership in Western India: Politics and Communities in Bombay City 1840-1885*, Oxford University Press, 1972

Ganguli, B N. "Dadabhai Naoroji and the Drain Theory", *Dadabhai Naoroji Memorial Lectures*, 1964

Gibson, Michael. *Gandhi and Nehru*, Wayland Publishers Limited, 1981

Gifford, Zerbanoo. *The Golden Thread: Asian Experiences of Post Raj Britain*, Pandora Press, 1990

Gopalkrishnam, P K. *Development of Economic Ideas in India: 1880-1950*, 1959

Hinnells, John R. *The Parsees: A Biographical Survey 1*, University of Manchester, 1980

Hinnells, John R. *Zoroastrianism and the Parsis*, Ward Lock Educational, 1981

Johnson, Dr Gordon. *Provincial Politics and Indian Nationalism: Bombay and the Indian National Congress 1880-1915*, Cambridge University Press, 1973

Kelkar, N C. "*Dadabhai Naoroji: Life Sketches and Appreciation, The Grand Old Man of India*", 1910

Kulke, Eckehard. *The Parsees of India; A Minority as Agents of Social Change*, Weltform Verlag, Munich, 1974

Masani, R P. *Dadabhai Naoroji: The Grand Old Man of India*, George Allen and Unwin Limited, 1939

Masani, R P. *Naoroji* (abridged version), 1960

Morris, James. *Pax Britannica: The Climax of an Empire and Heavens Command: An Imperial Progress*, Faber and Faber, 1968

Naoroji, D. *Poverty and Un-British rule in India*, Swan Sonnenschein and Co., 1901

Naoroji, D. *Poverty of India*, Vincent Brooks, Day and Son, 1878

Natesan, G A. *Famous Parsis*, Mittal Publications, New Dehli, 1990

Nigosan, S A. *The Zoroastrian Faith: Tradition and Modern Research*, McGill-Queens University Press, 1993

Noss, John R. *Man's Religions*, MacMillan, 1974

Parekh, Chunilal Lallubhai ed. *Essays, Speeches, Addresses and Writings of Dadabhai*, Caxton Printing Works, 1887

Pelling, Henry. *Social Geography of British Electorers 1895-1910*, MacMillan, 1967

Pinto-Dushinsky, M. *Political Thought of Lord Salisbury*, 1854 onwards

Rawal, Munni. *Dadabhai Naoroji: A Prophet of Indian Nationalism 1855-1900*, Amol Publications, New Dehli, 1989

Salvadori, Cynthia. *Through Open Doors: A View of Asian Cultures in Kenya*, Kenway Publications, Nairobi, 1989

Seal, Anil. *The Emergence of Indian Nationalism: Competition and Collaboration in the Later Nineteenth Century*, Cambridge University Press, 1968

Spear, Percival. *The History of India 2*, Penguin Books, 1975

Squires, Mike. *Saklatvala: A Political Biography*, Lawrence and Wiseheart, 1990

The Fifth Commandment, Miranda Press, 1991

The Men Who Ruled India, Volume 1, "The Guardians", Johnathan Cape, 1953

The Men Who Ruled India, Volume 2, "The Founders", Johnathan Cape, 1954

Vadgama, Kusoom. *Indians in Britain*, Robert Royce Limited, 1984

Van Thal, Herbert ed. *The Prime Ministers*, Volume 2, Allen and Unwin, 1974

Visram, Rozina. "Ayahs, Lascars and Princes", *Indians in Britain 1700-1947*, Pluto Press, 1986

Wacha, D E. R P Patwardhan ed. Dadabhai Naoroji correspondence, vol 2, Part 1 correspondence with D E Wacha 1884-1895, Part 2 correspondence 1895-1917, 1977

Articles

A *Biographical Sketch*, "Indian Worthies" by Dadabhai Naoroji, Volume 1, 1906

A *History of the Black Prescence in London*, "Indians in Parliament", Greater London Council, Ethnic Minorities Unit, 1985

Asian Herald, "History Lesson: Britain's Indian MPs" by Hilary Clarke, 7th May 1987

Book of Tracts, "Revolution at Baroda 1874-1875" by Dinshah Ardeshir Taleyarkhan, British Library, Bombay 1875

Dadabhai Naoroji by S F Captain, 4th September 1825 - 30th June 1917

The Daily News and Leader, "The G O M of India" by S N Ratcliffe, 3rd July 1917

The Dictionary of National Biography edited by L G Wickham Legg, 1931-1940

Dragon's Teeth, "Dadabhai Naoroji: Britain's First Black MP" by Rozina Visram and Audrey Dewjee, p9-121, no.17, 1984

Eight Major Religions in Britain, "The Teachings of Zoroaster" Entry on Dadabhai Naoroji (1825-1917), High Commission for India

Freiburg, "A Biography of an Indian Mutiny" by Eckehard Kulke, 1968

Hindustan Review, "Dadabhai Naoroji: A Character Sketch", Volume 22, p307-14, 1910

The Illustrated Islington History Journal, "Immigrants into Islington" by Angela Fussell, p6-7, August 1990

Indian National Congress, 1885-1985, Centenary Celebration by Kusoom Vadgama, October 1985

Indians in Britain by Rozina Visram, p46, B T Batsford Limited, 1987

Journal of Social Psychology, "The Parsee Ethic: Ambition and Dominance Among the Jews of India" by J J Ray, 1983

Journal of the K R Cama Institute, "The Parsis and the Emergence of the Indian National Congress" by Candida Monk, p115-245, no.52, Bombay, 1985

Journal of the K R Cama Institute, "The Parliamentary Life of Dadabhai Naoroji (1885-1895)" by David Mellor, p1-113, no.52, Bombay, 1985

Journal of the K R Cama Institute, "Parsis and the British", Government fellowship lectures by Professor John Hinnells, p1-92,volume 46, Bombay, 1978

New Equals, "The Passion of a Black MP in Britain" by Peter Street, no.24, Summer 1986

New Society, "Parsis: The Jews of India" by Neil Berry, 22nd January 1988

The Parliamentary Lives of Dadabhai Naoroji and Mancherjee Bhownaggree by C J Monk, a Masters Phil. thesis, University of Manchester, September 1985

The Parsee Religion by Dadabhai Naoroji, University of London, 18th March 1861

Parsees in Britain: The Experience of a Religious Minority Group by G M Towler-Mehta, New Community, Vol. 10, No.2, CRE, Winter 1982

The Rights of Labour by Dadabhai Naoroji from The Westminster Review, July 1890, Fred W Evans, London, 1904

Spanning East and West, "Zoroaster, the Greeks and the Romans" by John R Hinnells, units 26, 27 and 28 of The Open University, 1978

The Sunday Times, Letter on Britain's first black MPs by Kusoom Vadgama, 21st March 1982

The Voice, "The Old Campaigners" Parliamentary sketch by Joel Kibozo, 19th April 1988

Who Was Who, p767, House of Commons Library, 1916-1928

Who Was Who; Volume 3, 1929-40, Second edition

Who's Who of British Members of Parliament; p264, Volume 2, 1886-1918, House of Commons Library

Other Items

Admission of educated natives to the Indian Civil Service, 1868

Commentary on Lord Salisbury's speech on the candidature of Dadabhai Naoroji for Holborn, 1889

Clerkenwell Almanack and Business Directory, 1895

Condition of India correspondence with the Secretary of State for India, 1881

Contemporary biographies; Volume 1, Biographical Press Agency, 1905

Dadabhai Naoroji: a Study, 1907

Dadabhai Naoroji's election address to the electors, 1895

Dadabhai Naoroji's memorial. Its conception and completion, Bombay's public tributes, 1927

Dictonary of Labour biography, volume 6, p.233, 1982

European and Asiatic races. Observations on paper read by John Crawford, 1886

"Fair Play" in *Speeches and Writings 1893*, an open letter (to Queen Victoria), 1918

Indian Exchanges and bimettalism

Letters from Dadabhai Naoroji from the National Liberal Club to William Digby, 1892

Letters of William Digby and press cuttings
for period 28th June 1889-30th
September 1892
Letter from Dadabhai Naoroji to George
Hadfield, Manchester, 26th July 1898
Lord Salisbury's blackman. Extracts from
articles in British papers Mr Dadabhai
Naoroji and Mr Schnadhorst, 1892
Newspaper cuttings on Central Finsbury
Liberal and Radical Club, 1892
On the duties of local Indian Associations in
connection with the London Associations,
1868
The first Indian member of the Imperial
Parliament, being a collection of the main
incidents relating to the election of Mr
Dadabhai Naoroji to Parliament, 1892
The Hon Dadabhai Naoroji. Extracts from
newspapers relating to Dadabhai's
intention to stand as a candidate, 1886
The Indian Civil Service, 1917
The late Dadabhai Naoroji on Swaraj,
Presidential address, 1917
The local historian (Islington), volume 19,
no.1, February 1989
"The Wants and Means of India" by
Dadabhai Naoroji, 1870
Hansards, 1892-1895 inclusive
BBC2, *East* programme, 24th September
1992
BBC Radio, interview with Gosi Captain
(nee Naoroji), January 1972

Newspapers

City and East London Observer, 1934
Clerkenwell - press cuttings, 1892-1895
Bethnal Green News, 1933
Eastern Argus, Hackney, 1895
Evening Standard, 1933
Statesman, no.691
The Graphic, 1886
The Strand Magazine, 1892
The Times, 17th January 1936

Index

207